Preachers, Poets, and the

Early English Lyric

Preachers,
Poets,
and the Early
English
Lyric

Siegfried Wenzel

Princeton University Press

Princeton, New Jersey

Library of Congress Cataloging in Publication Data will
be found on the last printed page of this book

ISBN 0-691-06670-1

Publication of this book has been aided by the Whitney
Darrow Fund of Princeton University Press

This book has been composed in Linotron Times Roman

Clothbound editions of Princeton University Press books
are printed on acid-free paper, and binding materials
are chosen for strength and durability

Printed in the United States of America by Princeton
University Press, Princeton, New Jersey

PR 317
. P 73
W 46
1986

For Elizabeth and Liesbeth

Contents

Acknowledgments

In collecting material on the relation between preaching and the Middle English lyric I have enjoyed the hospitality of many major repositories of medieval manuscripts: the Bodleian Library and the library of Merton College, Oxford; the British Library and the library of Lambeth Palace; Cambridge University Library and the library of Jesus College, Cambridge; Trinity College Library in Dublin; the National Library of Scotland; the cathedral libraries at Durham, Lincoln, and Worcester; and the Vatican Library. To the respective librarians and their staffs and to the corporate owners of the manuscripts that I have been permitted to examine and quote from, in some cases with the additional help of a microfilm copy, go my sincere thanks. I further acknowledge with gratitude receiving various pieces of information from Susan Cavanaugh, Ian Doyle, Joseph Goering, and Sister Maura O'Carroll. Finally, I thank the two readers of Princeton University Press for a number of suggestions which, I hope, have made this book more readable. And I am grateful to Oxford University Press and to Dr. Edward Wilson for their permission to reproduce a number of poems.

This book is the result of sweeping in a rather dim and little visited corner of the history of English literature. In this process, some objects which former scholars prized as precious coins have upon closer inspection turned out to be plain buttons, and what were thought to be intricate designs on them have proven to be merely the holes through which they once were fastened to a coat. In clarifying this much, it has been regrettably inevitable to raise some unpleasant dust, which however I hope will not cloud the issue.

The following chapters were conceived and largely written in Rome. The historical and cultural air of that wonderful and living museum of Western civilization proved far more stimulating than I had dared to hope, and I am deeply grateful to the John Simon Guggenheim Memorial Foundation for making the yearlong stay possible.

Acknowledgments

The latter experience was shared, and the ups and downs of life—scholarly and otherwise—were cheerfully borne by my wife and our youngest daughter. To them the outcome is affectionately dedicated.

Abbreviations

AH	Dreves, Guido Maria, and C. Blume, eds. *Analecta hymnica* (Leipzig, 1886-1922). Quoted by volume and item number.
Dobson	Dobson, Eric J., and Frank L1. Harrison. *Medieval English Songs* (New York, 1979).
EEC	Greene, Richard Leighton, ed. *The Early English Carols*, second edition (Oxford, 1977). Quoted by item number.
EETS, es	Early English Text Society, Extra Series
EL	Brown, Carleton, ed. *English Lyrics of the XIIIth Century* (Oxford, 1932). Quoted by item number.
Erb	Erb, Peter C. "Vernacular Material for Preaching in MS Cambridge University Library Ii.III.8," *MS* 33 (1971), 63-84. Quoted by page.
GR	Oesterley, Hermann, ed. *Gesta Romanorum* (Berlin, 1872; reprinted Hildesheim, 1963). Quoted by item number.
HP	Robbins, Rossell Hope, ed. *Historical Poems of the XIVth and XVth Centuries* (New York, 1959). Quoted by item number.
IMEV	Brown, Carleton, and Rossell Hope Robbins. *The Index of Middle English Verse* (New York, 1943); and Robbins, Rossell Hope, and John L. Cutler, *Supplement to the Index of Middle English Verse* (Lexington, Ky., 1965). Quoted by index number.
Pfander	Pfander, Homer G. *The Popular Sermon of the Medieval Friar in England* (New York, 1937).
PL	J.-P. Migne (ed.), *Patrologiae cursus completus . . . Series Latina*. 221 volumes (Paris, 1844-64).
RL XIV	Brown, Carleton, ed. *Religious Lyrics of the XIVth Century*. Second edition, revised by G. V. Smithers (Oxford, 1952). Quoted by item number.
RL XV	Brown, Carleton, ed. *Religious Lyrics of the XVth Century* (Oxford, 1939). Quoted by item number.

Abbreviations

SL	Robbins, Rossell Hope, ed. *Secular Lyrics of the XIVth and XVth Centuries*, second edition (Oxford, 1955). Quoted by item number.
Stemmler	Stemmler, Theo. "More English Texts from MS Cambridge University Library Ii.III.8," *Anglia* 93 (1975), 1-16. Quoted by item number.
Tubach	Tubach, Frederic C. *Index Exemplorum: A Handbook of Medieval Religious Tales.* FF Communications 204 (Helsinki, 1969). Quoted by item number.
"Unrecorded"	Wenzel, Siegfried. "Unrecorded Middle-English Verses," *Anglia* 92 (1974), 55-78. Quoted by item number.
Verses	Wenzel, Siegfried. *Verses in Sermons. "Fasciculus morum" and Its Middle English Poems* (Cambridge, Mass., 1978).
Walther, *In*	Walther, Hans. *Initia carminum ac versuum medii aevi posterioris latinorum* (Göttingen, 1959). Quoted by item number.
Walther, *Prov*	Walther, Hans. *Proverbia sententiaeque latinitatis medii aevi*, 6 vols. (Göttingen, 1963-67). Quoted by item number.
Woolf	Woolf, Rosemary. *The English Religious Lyric in the Middle Ages* (Oxford, 1968).

Editorial Principles

In quoting Latin and Middle English texts directly from the manuscripts, I have silently expanded abbreviations and introduced modern capitalization and punctuation. In Latin texts, u/v and i/j have been normalized to modern practice. The name "Jesus" has been normalized to *Iesus* in both languages. In poems taken from printed sources I have similarly normalized capitalization and punctuation to modern usage. Translations of medieval and modern sources are my own unless otherwise noted.

Preachers, Poets, and the

Early English Lyric

1

Preachers

and

Poets

Despite the massive study of preaching in medieval England by G. R. Owst—whose second book was subtitled *A Neglected Chapter in the History of English Letters and of the English People*—it is fair to say that the relations of Middle English literature to contemporary preaching are far from exhaustively studied and known. Owst's own interests were limited to showing that such large features of late medieval "letters" as realism, social satire and criticism, and the use of allegory were fully paralleled in contemporary sermons, rather than pointing to specific verbal material or structural elements which Chaucer, Langland, Gower, or the Corpus Christi plays had borrowed or imitated from sermons. This neglect of close investigation holds even more true of lyric poetry, and as a result the connection of English poems with sermons often goes undetected and even unsuspected. A good case in point is the poem entitled "How Christ Shall Come." During the last generation, it has held the attention of half a dozen critics who have attempted to elucidate and appraise its aesthetic achievement without realizing that the lines are nothing but the rhymed divisions of a Latin sermon and that several of these critical attempts looked at only one half of the English text.[1]

Besides demonstrating that it always pays to examine a medieval poem's context, the embarrassing critical miscarriage of this case also elicits some deeper and more disturbing questions. If experienced readers have been struck by a certain lyrical power and emotion contained in these verses, where then does the line run that would distinguish versified prose which had a precise structural function in a sermon, from genuine lyric poetry? And further, since the images utilized in these stanzas as well as their meaning and their composition are completely conven-

[1] A full account of the criticism devoted to this "poem" together with the complete text of the sermon can be found in Wenzel, "Poets, Preachers, and the Plight of Literary Critics," *Speculum* 60 (1985), 343-63.

tional, what precisely does a critic evaluate in judging the accomplishment and beauty of a poem whose verbal texture is not particularly noteworthy—as was indeed acknowledged by the critics who dealt with these verses? Whatever answers he may propose to such nagging questions, the critic of medieval English literature must at least face up to the historical fact that the early English lyric was closely related to preaching. It is this fact that the following chapters will explore further.

The best known facet of this relation is that a large number of early English lyrics—most of them religious, but some also secular—have been preserved in manuscripts that were unquestionably connected with preaching. One of the foremost students of the Middle English lyric has stated that the four large groups of manuscripts: friar miscellanies, sermons and sermon notebooks, mystical and devotional works, and closet hymns, "are almost the sole source for our knowledge of Middle English verse to the end of the fourteenth century";[2] and even if one excludes "mystical and devotional works" as not directly related to preaching, and reduces the so-called "friar miscellanies" by several items whose association with preaching cannot be maintained, the debt of the early English lyric to preaching is still very impressive. With respect to their relationship to preaching, the manuscripts that have thus preserved the early English lyrics can be classified as follows:

(1) *Sermon collections.* Manuscripts which contain primarily a series of complete sermons. The series may be a regular cycle, running for instance from the first Sunday of Advent to the last Sunday after Trinity, or it may be a more or less haphazard gathering of sermons following no recognizable order. The sermons may differ in length, structure, completeness, and even language; come from one or a variety of authors; and be written in a single or several different hands. English verses here will normally appear within a definite sermon context and have a clearly discernible function in a sermon, even if they should have been added in the margins after the main text had been written.[3]

(2) *Preaching tools.* Works written for the purpose of aiding preachers in composing their sermons. These are of many different kinds and forms, some of which will be mentioned at the beginning of chapter 4. In contrast to sermon collections, which were of course also intended to aid preachers as models and source books, preaching tools do not nor-

---

[2] Rossell Hope Robbins, *SL*, p. xxi.
[3] For an example, see ch. 3, p. 85.

mally provide full and finished sermons but only their raw material or rules of general guidance. A good example is *Fasciculus morum*, a Franciscan work which offers preaching material discursively and arranged in the order of the seven deadly sins and their opposite virtues.[4] Bromyard's *Summa praedicantium* furnishes similar material but organizes it instead in a large number of separate articles arranged in alphabetical order.[5] John of Grimestone's commonplace book, which will be examined more closely in chapter 4, is very similar to Bromyard's *Summa* in presenting an alphabetical series of topics, but the material in the individual articles is here more haphazardly gathered without the logical and schematic arrangement and the more discursive treatment one finds in Bromyard. To this type also belongs the *Speculum Christiani*, which was even translated in its entirety into English.[6] All these texts contain English verses. Depending on the nature of the preaching tool, the verses will have more or less context; but they normally lack any indication to what precise service they were put in an actual sermon.[7]

(3) *Preacher's notebooks.* Manuscripts that contain a variety of preaching materials, usually copied down without any particular order. These notebooks may contain *exempla*, extracts from the Fathers, short paragraphs on theological or moral topics (such as, transubstantiation or abstinence), sermon outlines, and even entire sermons; but these different materials appear together in a rather helter-skelter way, and it is this lack of both homogeneity and orderly arrangement that distinguishes notebooks from preaching tools.[8] Good examples of preacher's notebooks with many English verses are British Library, MS. Harley 7322, and several manuscripts compiled by the fifteenth-century priest and recluse John Dygoun.[9] Such notebooks are not always easy to distinguish

---

[4] See *Verses*, pp. 9-13, 41-59.

[5] Preserved in several manuscripts (e.g., British Library, MS. Royal 7.E.iv) and early prints (Basel, 1484; Nürnberg, 1485; etc.).

[6] Recent investigation has suggested that this work and others served as tools not so much in formal preaching as in other forms of religious instruction, such as teaching the catechism: Vincent Gillespie, "*Doctrina* and *Predicacio*: The Design and Function of Some Pastoral Manuals," *LSE*, n.s., 11 (1980), 36-50.

[7] Robbins's category of "closet hymns" (*SL*, p. xxi) might be included in my group of preaching tools, though the use of these poems needs further investigation.

[8] These notebooks often differ further from sermon collections characteristically in their size, handwriting, and layout. Typical early examples are: Bodleian Library, MS. Hatton 107; or Oxford, New College MS. 88.

[9] See below, ch. 7, n. 60.

from sermon collections proper, even upon close examination of the respective codex. In some cases a preacher copied an entire series of sermons into what he intended to be his notebook. In others, a scribe added some stray paragraphs on the incompletely filled pages of a sermon collection. And in yet other cases a sermon collection was later bound together with different materials, resulting in a composite manuscript that comprises "booklets" belonging to different types of our classification. This complex situation calls for detailed study of each individual manuscript, its physical makeup as well as its contents—a field of investigation that still awaits much patient work. Nonetheless, it is usually not difficult to tell whether the environment of an English poem, the particular section of a manuscript where it occurs, is that of a sermon collection or of a notebook.

(4) *Miscellanies*. Collections of various texts including poems, but the latter do not appear in a specific context of sermons or preaching material. In manuscripts I would include in this category, an English poem is sometimes accompanied by musical notation. Thus, Oxford, Corpus Christi College MS. 59, from Llanthony Priory, Gloucestershire, and written shortly after 1265,[10] is in general very much like the notebooks of the previous category, and some of its material may or may not have been used in preaching. But the three English poems it preserves (one a translation of the Lord's Prayer, the second a hymn with music) are not thematically or functionally related in the codex to a preaching context. Similarly, British Library, MS. Arundel 292, from the Benedictine cathedral priory of Norwich, contains material that very probably was used in preaching;[11] yet its nine English items in verse, of two different periods, appear without specific sermon (or for that matter, any other) context. The distinction I have drawn between categories three and four may strike some readers as a trifle pedantic, but it will serve as a necessary reminder that, for example, the poems in MS. Arundel 292, such as "The Blacksmiths," must not be automatically associated with preaching on the ground of the general nature of the manuscript in which they appear.

(5) *Poetic anthologies*. A collection of pieces primarily in verse, although some prose items may be included. The poems do not have any clear sermon context. This category comprises such famous manuscripts

[10] Carleton Brown, "A Thirteenth-Century MS. from Llanthony Priory," *Speculum* 3 (1928), 587-95; see also Dobson, pp. 166-72.

[11] It contains the famous sermon on *Bele Aliz matin leua*, ascribed to Stephen Langton (fols. 38-39).

as Bodleian Library, MS. Digby 86; Oxford, Jesus College MS. 29; British Library, MS. Cotton Caligula A.ix; MS. Harley 2253; and others. Together with narrative verse, such as Laȝamon's *Brut* or *The Owl and the Nightingale*, they all contain larger numbers of lyric poems, often in English, French, and Latin.

(6) *Non-preaching books*. This category comprises books whose subject matter is homogeneous and is not directly related to preaching, but is not a collection of poetry. They may include one or two English poems. To this type belong, for example, liturgical books that carry isolated poems on their flyleaves,[12] or the copy of *Ancrene Wisse* that preserves an English song at its end,[13] or chronicles whose text contains one or more verses including some that are also found in sermons.[14] I would also include here cases like *Nou goth sonne vnder wod*, which appears in a summa of Christian doctrine with guidance for meditation. The poem may have later been quoted in sermons, but its original context is that of a non-preaching book.[15]

Regarding the preservation of early English lyrics in books made and used by preachers, a special problem attaches to a group of seven manuscripts which have been labeled "friar miscellanies." These "Golden Treasuries or Oxford Books of Verse of the thirteenth century," as they have been called,[16] are of primary interest to the student of medieval lyrics and narrative poetry, not only because of the large number of the English poems they contain but also because of their outstanding poetic quality . Their assignment to one of the mendicant orders rests either on the association that the respective codices may have held with a religious order—an association that is frequently very tenuous—or else on the fact that they *share* certain poems with manuscripts whose connection with a mendicant order is more definite. The prime case in the latter respect is MS. Harley 2253,[17] but its association with friars can no longer be seri-

---

[12] *IMEV* 4223, in Bodleian Library, MS. Rawlinson G.18, fols. 105v-106, also preserved in a miscellany and a poetic anthology.

[13] *IMEV* 631, in British Library, MS. Cotton Nero A.xiv, fol. 120v.

[14] A good example is *IMEV* 1811, the poem of Cambyses' warning, found in Higden's *Polychronicon* (see *Verses*, pp. 88-89).

[15] *IMEV* 2320, an integral part of Saint Edmund Rich's *Speculum Ecclesiae* in its Anglo-Norman, Latin, and English versions. See Edmund of Abingdon, *Speculum religiosorum and Speculum Ecclesiae*, ed. Helen P. Forshaw, Auctores Britannici Medii Aevi 3 (London, 1973), p. 93.

[16] Robbins, *SL*, pp. xvii-xviii.

[17] In "The Authors of the Middle English Religious Lyrics," *JEGP* 39 (1940), 236, n. 33, R. H. Robbins argued as follows: "MS. Harley 2253 has 24 English lyrics: seven [later

ously maintained.[18] With regard to their possible connection with preaching materials, of the manuscripts once included among "friar miscellanies" I would consider Cambridge, Trinity College MS. 323 a preacher's notebook (class 3); Bodleian Library, MS. Digby 2, and British Library, MS. Harley 913, miscellanies (class 4); and MS. Digby 86, Oxford, Jesus College MS. 29 (part II), British Library, MS. Cotton Caligula A.ix (part II), and MS. Harley 2253, poetic anthologies (class 5).[19]

But the connection of Middle English lyrics with preaching goes far beyond their preservation in manuscripts that were made by and for preachers. A good many of these poems were actually used in sermons. This, too, is not a new insight. Yet the fact that such poems had a precise function in sermons beyond being merely decorative, and the precise nature of this function, is evidently not fully understood and appreciated by literary critics, as the case of "How Christ Shall Come" has shown us. How such lack of awareness can seriously mislead literary critics as well as historians of literature and of medieval society may be illustrated with the history of another text. The following three stanzas are found in one of the sermons that were apparently preached in the 1430s by Friar William Melton and collected by his Franciscan confrere Nicholas Philip:

> For þou art comen of good blood,
> Or for art a riche man of good,
> For þou art well loued of moo,
> And for þou art a ȝong man alsoo.

revised to six: *Anglia* 82 (1964), 511] occur in the Franciscan or Dominican MS. Bodleian 1687 [= Digby 86] . . . ; one is in the Franciscan MS. Bodleian 1603 [= Digby 2] . . . ; one in the Franciscan MS. Harley 913 . . . ; one in the Dominican MS. 323 at Trinity College Cambridge. . . . Nearly half the English religious lyrics of MS. Harley 2253, therefore, occur in earlier *friar* books." But notice that one lyric in Harley 2253, *IMEV* 1461, is counted twice, since it appears in both Digby 86 and Trinity 323. The resulting total of eight poems shared with the mentioned manuscripts therefore forms not "nearly half" but exactly one third of the religious lyrics in Harley 2253. Further, Digby 86 (with its six shared items) has been shown to have been composed by or for a layman. And lastly, the poem supposedly shared with Harley 913 (*Erþe toc of erþe*, *IMEV* 3939) deals with the same topic but is a completely different treatment. For the results of recent investigations into the association of these manuscripts, see Karl Reichl, *Religiöse Dichtung im englischen Hochmittelalter* (Munich, 1973), pp. 6-82 and 94-95.

[18] See Reichl, *Religiöse Dichtung*, p. 94, n. 39.

[19] Carter Revard, "*Gilote et Johane*: an Interlude in B. L. MS. Harley 2253," *SP* 79 (1982), 122-46, shares my view by calling the manuscript "*miroir*" and "anthology" (pp. 127, 138). Professor Revard's important investigations into the date and composition of the manuscript await publication.

Þin fader was a bond man,
Þin moder curtesye noun can,
Euery beste þat leuyth now
Is of more fredam þan þow.

3if þou art pore, þan art þou fre,
3if þou be riche, þan woo is þe.
For but þou spendyte well ere þou goo,
Þin song for euer is well-ay-woe.[20]

The poem's first modern editor called this "a three-stanza song of a non-religious nature." In a footnote he added that its second stanza "might be a separate poem inserted. Its sentiment suggests that it belongs to the popular song of freedom of medieval England," which however he could not "identify."[21] The poem then entered the major collection of historical poems under the title "A Song of Freedom" with its second stanza called "a genuine fragment of a worker's song,"[22] and this new label has since assured it a place among the lost poetry of medieval England.[23] Finally, a recent study of fifteenth-century political poetry tells us that the second stanza "is clearly meant to be an expression of discontent at the bondman's condition of villeinage," though the writer then adds that, judged by the third stanza, this particular bondman was apparently not terribly resentful but "accept[ed] his condition."[24]

A fresh look at the manuscript brings a number of surprises. First, contrary to speculation that has suggested a date of 1434,[25] the sermon is clearly signed "1431." Next, the three edited stanzas are only part of a total of five. And finally, their Latin context and their function in the sermon make it very improbable that they voice social protest or preserve a popular song. The sermon in question is on the text *Qui custos est domini sui gloriabitur* ("He that is the keeper of his master shall be glorified,"

---

[20] *IMEV* 849; *HP* 22. Here reproduced from Bodleian Library, MS. Lat. theol. d. 1, fol. 174.

[21] Pfander, p. 49 and n. 9.

[22] *HP*, p. 278.

[23] R. M. Wilson, *The Lost Literature of Medieval England*, second edition (London, 1970), p. 197.

[24] V. J. Scattergood, *Politics and Poetry in the Fifteenth Century* (London, 1971; New York, 1972), p. 358. The poem appears similarly in the section "The Literature of Protest" in R. B. Dobson, *The Peasants' Revolt of 1381* (London, 1970), pp. 384-85.

[25] Robbins, *HP*, pp. xxv and 62. The correct date appears at the end of the sermon, fol. 175.

Proverbs 27.18). Its introduction speaks of the king of England or France entrusting the custody of a beloved city to his officer, and applies this image to God entrusting the care of our souls to each one of us. This leads to the following division:

He has enjoined on each one of us, under pain of imprisonment, to keep this city in peace and quiet. Therefore, in order to keep this city, we must do four things which are commonly done to men of this world in their honor, namely:

Loke his wonnyng be clene a-dy3te;	dwelling; prepared
Loke his mete be made a-ry3te;	
Loke [he] hafe good cumpanye:	
And loke he hafe good mynstralcye.[26]	

All four parts are then developed in the sermon at some length, and all contain some English verses. The second principal part, "see to it that his food be prepared right," stipulates that Christ takes delight in four *sewys delicatis* ("delicate savory dishes"), which are, together with their moral meanings, the following:

Rys—by the first I understand our rising from sin;
Maumene—by the second, contrition of sin;
Blancmanger—by the third I consider the contemplation of things
above;
And a sarsine—by the fourth, the contemplation of things below.[27]

The preacher's verbal wit, already manifest in this subdivision with its (understood) English pun on "the rice of rising from sin," appears again when he develops the second dish, *maumene*. This word normally des-

---

[26] "Et quod custodiamus istam civitatem in pace et quiete cuilibet nostrum iniunxit sub pena carceris. Et ideo ad custodiendum istam civitatem oportet quatuor facere que comuniter mundialibus viris fieri sole[n]t pro honore, et sunt hec: Loke his wonnyng . . ." Bodlein Library, MS. Lat. theol. d. 1, fol. 173.

[27] "Et ideo si vis Christum bene pascere, tales sewes oportet te sibi preparare. Fac sibi ista quatuor: Rys—per primum intelligo resurreccionem a peccato; / Maumene—per secundum contricionem de peccato; / Blanmanger—per tercium considero contemplacionem supernorum; / And a sarsine—per quartum contemplacionem inferorum." Fol. 174. The dishes are, respectively, rice, chopped chicken, and chopped chicken or fish boiled with rice (for the latter two, see *Middle English Dictionary*). *Sarsine* likewise contains almonds, rice, and chicken; see Thomas Austin (ed.), *Two Fifteenth-Century Cookery-Books*, EETS 91 (London, 1888; repr. 1964), pp. 19, 30, 113. It is said, in the sermon, to look repulsive but taste good.

ignates a dish of chopped or teased chicken with spices and other ingredients, but the preacher tells us that its etymology means *yuelelad*, and consequently the dish can be moralized as a man's "ill-led" life which must be prepared for Christ's coming by contrition. In reply to the question how a man may have grief for sin, the preacher argues as follows: If man had never sinned, he would have cause for joy as long as he lives. Now, in this life, man can rejoice in four things: noble descent, wealth, love and friendship, and youth and strength. But experience shows that none of these four is a true cause for joy, for reasons that are explained in due order. Therefore, there is no real joy in this world but only grief, whose ultimate cause is original sin. This syllogistic development of the moral meaning of *maumene* is expressed in English quatrains. The first of these, "For þou art comen of good blood," summarizes the four possible causes of worldly joy. The first cause, noble descent, is then shown to be fallacious for the reasons adduced in stanza 2, "Þin fader was a bond man." These reasons, summarized in the English lines, are explained in the surrounding Latin commentary:

> But surely, none of these is matter for joy but rather for grief if you examine them carefully. For if you rejoice in noble blood, you are a fool, because your lineage from which you come is this:
>
> Þin fader was a bond man . . .
>
> For your first father, Adam, was bound (*obligatus*) to God and further to death, which is the greatest degree of servitude. Similarly, your mother is earth. When you come to her, you will have only worms, who will eat whoever he was and however vile he may be. "Every beast is more free" because it has to die only once, but you will die often unless you have done well. Therefore, even if you are descended from noble blood, you have no cause for joy.[28]

In the same fashion, being "a riche man of good" is shown to be no matter for rejoicing either, for reasons adduced in the third of the quoted

---

[28] "Sed pro certo nullum istorum est materia gaudii sed pocius doloris, si bene conspiceretur. Nam si gaudes de nobili sanguine, fatuus es, quia talis est tua progenies unde venisti: 'Þin fader . . .' Quia pater tuus primus Adam Deo obligatus fuit, sed eciam morti, et que maxima servitus est. Similiter mater tua est terra. Cum enim ad ipsam perveneris hoc solum habebis vermes, ut comedent quecumque fuerit illa et quam vilis sit. Eueri beste is more fre quia ipsa semel debet mori, tu autem nisi bene feceris frequenter. Igitur de nobili licet sanguine sis exortus, nullam habes materiam gaudii." Fol. 174. The English quatrain was mistakenly copied after *gaudii* but is marked for insertion at the place as edited.

stanzas ("ʒif þou art pore"). And the remaining two potential causes for joy, namely being "well loued" and being "a ʒong man," are equally refuted by two further stanzas that have not been published by Pfander and his followers:

> Werdys lowe lestyth but a qwyʒle:
> In werdly loue is alwey gyʒle;
> Leue may commen and lofe may goon
> But trost lofe is þer noon but oon.

[Latin commentary follows.]

> Deth bringith down lowe þat ben belde;   bold, strong
> Deth takyth ʒong as well as helde;
> Þe more stowt þou art and more gay,
> Per auenture þe nere þin endyng-day.[29]   nearer

After a brief commentary in Latin on the last stanza, the preacher concludes this section of his sermon's second principal part:

> If you reflect on these things, you will grieve for the sins you have committed; and if you do this, you will prepare the second dish for Christ, which is *maumene*, that is, if you reflect on how badly you have led your life here.[30]

And with this he turns to the third dish, *blancmanger*.

The so-called "Song of Freedom," therefore, is in fact a rhymed distinction on *materia gaudii* (st. 1) followed by four (not two, as printed by Pfander) sub-distinctions, each listing three reasons why the respective worldly value is untrue. In this way the sermon applies with a vengeance a major principle of scholastic sermon structure which will be examined in chapter 3. One may ask why these English quatrains, especially 2-5, were included at all since their content is also given in Latin prose. But this question applies to most English verses in prose sermons, and more will be said about this practice later on. One might also ask whether stanza 2 ("þin fader was") could not after all be a secular song or part thereof because, as chapters 6 and 7 will show, secular songs were indeed quoted and utilized by medieval preachers. But it should be

---

[29] Fol. 174v.

[30] "Ista si cogites, utique dolebis pro commissis, et si sic feceris, secundum ferculum Christo preparabis, quod est maumene, scilicet si cogitaveris quam male vitam tuam hic duxeris." Fol. 174v.

clear by now that the thought and sentiment behind the stanza's images—human bondage to sin, the failure of Mother Earth and her worms to distinguish between courtly folk and peasants, and the absence of moral responsibility in subhuman life forms—go back to the Bible, early Church Fathers, and Boethius. In addition, there is no hint in this sermon—in contrast to other cases—that stanza 2 derives from anywhere other than the preacher's invention, and as Pfander recognized, no other occurrence, least of all outside sermon literature, is known. And the last argument Pfander proposed for the "non-religious" background of this stanza, namely his impression of its peculiar "rhythmic swing," dwindles before the fact that all five stanzas have exactly the same form of four-stress lines rhyming *aabb*.

The putative "Song of Freedom" and the earlier "How Christ Shall Come" thus reveal that medieval preachers created English poems for specific structural purposes in their prose sermons. With this observation we reach the most significant facet of the connection between preaching and poetry: that the work of preachers formed, as it were, a generative center for the production of English lyrics. Again, the mere fact that preachers wrote poems for use in their sermons is well enough established. But how far this practice extended, how creative individual preachers were, what sources may have inspired them or furnished their material, what effects were aimed at and achieved, and even how, if at all, such creative work by preachers differed from that of "genuine" poets, are all questions that demand further exploration.

It may seem that my claim for the significant influence preaching had on the development of the early English lyric places this book in fundamental opposition to Rosemary Woolf's pointing to the *meditative* tradition and to specific meditative passages as the major inspiration for the medieval religious lyric in England.[31] To conceive of such an opposition would be quite wrong. Certainly, the *act* of preaching is radically different from the act of meditation: public address and exhortation as opposed to private and silent reflection. Yet the subject matter and ultimate purpose of both are entirely the same.[32] Moreover, many of the primary sources that tell us anything about meditation are in effect not recordings of actual meditations but exhortations and guides on what to reflect upon—exactly like sermons on such topics as Christ's Passion or death.

---

[31] Rosemary Woolf, *The English Religious Lyric in the Middle Ages* (Oxford, 1968).
[32] See my remarks in *Verses*, p. 126.

Chapter 1

I have elsewhere shown how a handbook for preachers urges the audience to meditate on such topics and furnishes precisely the conventional meditative commonplaces that became so fruitful in the development of the lyric.[33] In chapter 5 we shall see once more how preaching tools and actual sermons utilized the subject matter that had been collected in the great compendia on meditation, such as the *Meditationes de vita Christi* attributed to Bonaventure and the *Vita Christi* by Ludolf of Saxony. Sermons in fact share the same steps of reflection that are suggested in meditative treatises, that is, the progression from recounting or remembering a biblical scene to extracting moral and emotional lessons from it and on to the meditator's response in the form of a prayer.[34] Even the image of "chewing," which was applied to meditation in earlier centuries, reappears in late medieval preaching.[35] It will therefore not come as a surprise if we encounter what may be called a metrical recipe for meditation on Christ's Passion included in a preaching tool.[36]

It must be said, however, that the Middle English religious lyric poses some large questions which Woolf's study never fully addressed, let alone answered. One concerns the appearance and precise function of poems in sermons and their stylistic or tonal difference from "genuinely" meditative verses. Woolf often refers to sermons or preachers, but these terms are employed in an ideal, abstract way to establish a merely formal distinction. For instance, in discussing lyrics on the Passion, Woolf distinguishes the "setting . . . of sermon address," in which "the preacher exhorts his hearer to gaze at Christ," from that of first-person monologue, in which "the meditator in his imagination stands at the foot of the Cross," and further from Christ's direct appeal to man.[37] This triple distinction may be very helpful in analyzing the *Gestalt* of religious lyrics, but it does not at all coincide with their concrete use and function,

---

[33] *Verses*, pp. 126-32.

[34] Thus, the sequence of *articulus* (section of biblical narrative)—*documenta* ("teachings" or "lessons")—*actus conformacionis*—*oracio*, which appears throughout Ludolf of Saxony's *Vita Christi*, is utilized in many Passion sermons including *Amore langueo* (Cambridge, University Library MS. Kk.4.24, etc.) and *Dilexit nos* (Lambeth Palace Library MS. 352), which will be discussed in chapter 5.

[35] See Jean Leclercq, O.S.B., *The Love of Learning and the Desire for God*, trans. Catharine Misrahi (New York, 1961), pp. 78-79; and the course of Lenten sermons by Geiler von Kaisersberg, who offers a "honey cake" from which he breaks off a piece every day *ad masticandum*, see P. W. von Keppler, "Zur Passionspredigt des Mittelalters," *Historisches Jahrbuch* 3 (1882), 301-2.

[36] *IMEV* 441 in Grimestone, No. 4.   [37] Woolf, p. 35.

because lyrics of the second kind (for instance, *Wenne Hic soe on rode idon*) and of the third (for example, *Byholde, mon, what I dree*) are as much quoted in actual sermons as are lyrics of the first.[38] Woolf's study is simply not concerned with the *Sitz im Leben* of the Middle English religious lyric, with the concrete use to which supposedly "meditative" poems were put. It is precisely to this grey area of literary scholarship that I hope the following chapters will bring some light.

If I see no substantive difference between preaching and the meditative tradition in their impact on the genesis and production of religious lyrics, I would however sharply differentiate preaching from the tradition of medieval hymnology. Hymns and sequences sung within and eventually without the liturgy of the Church exerted a profound influence on the development of vernacular lyrics, religious and probably secular as well. It predated the impact that was to come from preaching and later, after roughly 1250, must have continued alongside the latter. Thus, many if not all of the earliest Middle English lyrics that have been preserved from the middle of the thirteenth century clearly stand in the tradition of medieval Latin hymns. After that, Latin hymns were Englished by preachers (such as William Herebert and James Ryman) and quite often recited or at least quoted in sermons. But I believe one must also claim a separate further development of the hymn tradition leading to longer poems of praise and meditation, such as Thomas of Hales's "Love-Ron," the poems by Richard Rolle and his school, or the lyrics of the Vernon MS. The continuity of this tradition and its influence on the vernacular lyric still need to be traced in detail. In the present study it can concern us only briefly and as a point of departure.

In some of the just mentioned poems, notably the "Love-Ron," public chanting of hymns as part of the communal worship has given way to private singing "mid swete stephne."[39] This transition is neatly illuminated by a miracle story reported in two medieval commentaries on the sequence *Ave, praeclara maris stella*. The sequence was originally composed for use in the Mass and occurs as such in many liturgical books. But in the following case it is reported as being used in private devotion:

> There was a young monk in the monastery of Saint Chrysantus, called Daniel, the master of students there. He used to say this sequence with

---

[38] The two poems are quoted by Woolf on pp. 33 and 38. For their use in sermons see ch. 7, p. 236, and *Verses*, pp. 166-67.

[39] *EL* 43, line 203.

15

great devotion every day on his knees in the crypt of the chapel in front of the altar of Blessed Mary. One day, as in singing it he came to the place: "Pray, Virgin, that we may become worthy of that bread of heaven," he saw the glorious one come from the altar and offer him bread that was whiter than snow. He was greatly comforted by this vision and continued to be even more devout in her worship.[40]

Such transition of a text from public worship to private devotion forms only a small part in the wide and deep change that occurred in Western European spirituality during the high Middle Ages and that had the most profound effects not only on manifestations of the religious life, including meditation and preaching, but equally on all sectors of artistic expression in word, painting, sculpture, and music. Springing from roots in the eleventh century, this change blossomed forth in the new spirituality of the twelfth, with such figures as Saint Bernard of Clairvaux and Ailred of Rievaulx and their followers and treatises on the spiritual life. From the early thirteenth century on, the new spirituality became popularized and spread among the masses outside the monastery, mainly through the activities of the mendicant orders, primarily the Franciscans. The story of this development, at least in its major trends and characteristics, has been often told, even on television, and I will spare my readers trotting over well-known territory again.[41] Suffice it to recall that in the area with which this book is especially concerned, the most important thrust of this change lay in its new and strong appeal to emotions and sentiment, an appeal that found its main stimulus in focusing attention on Christ's humanity and particularly on his Passion. The early English lyric fully reveals the impact of this new "affective piety," with its consequent changes from public liturgy to private devotion, from Christ in majesty to the suffering Son of Man, from rational and speculative meditation to an affective exploration of Christ's suffering and his human relation to his mother and her own feelings, from the fruits of redemption

[40] R.B.C. Huygens, "Deux commentaires sur la séquence *Ave, praeclara maris stella*," *Citeaux* 20 (1969), 124; see also pp. 166 and 116.

[41] A comprehensive history of this chapter in Western spirituality with attention to specific texts and their background remains to be written. A good beginning may be found in the monograph by Walter Baier, *Untersuchungen zu den Passionsbetrachtungen in der "Vita Christi" des Ludolf von Sachsen. Ein quellenkritischer Beitrag zu Leben und Werk Ludolfs und zur Geschichte der Passionstheologie*, 3 vols., Analecta Carthusiana 44 (Salzburg, 1977), esp. vol. 3.

to its price, even from the joy and hope of cosmic triumph to the more self-centered anxieties of a penitent sinner.

The story about Brother Daniel that I have quoted raises another question: did preachers actually *sing* their poems from the pulpit? Pfander thought so, and his view has since been much expanded. There is of course no question that members of religious orders chanted a good deal, during and probably also outside the official liturgy; nor is there any question that friars, especially Franciscans, were highly active in creating texts for singing, from hymns to *laude* and carols; and there is some evidence that itinerant preachers would attract attention by singing a song. But cases like that of "Brother Trumpet" reported by Friar Salimbene—of a non-religious preacher wandering through the countryside, blowing on his little brass horn and beginning and ending his preaching with an Italian *lauda* which he evidently sang[42]—cannot serve as evidence for singing within the formal sermon. The latter belief rests on the following passage found at the end of the sermon quoted several pages ago, a passage that was poorly transcribed and misinterpreted by Pfander:[43]

> Et sic secure Deo clames dicens sibi sic. Et cantes devote in corde:
>> Iesu þat woldist for mannys sake
>> Comen from heuen to oure wendyng,
>> Suffrest þin bonys to crake,
>> And bore þe corounne þat was pynnyng:
>> Vs from syn fre þou make
>> And bryng vs alle to good endyng.
>
> Istam melodiam si feceris ore mundo et corde puro, Deus sine dubio te exaudiet et tecum manebit et post vitam istam in gloria celesti te videbit ad sui honorem et tui gloriam. Ad quam nos perducat. Amen.

(And thus you should safely call to God, saying to him as follows; and you should devoutly sing in your heart: Iesu, þat . . . If you were to make this melody with clean lips [*literally*, a clean mouth] and pure

---

[42] Salimbene de Adam, *Cronica*, ed. Giuseppe Scalia, Scrittori d'Italia 232 (Bari, 1966), 1:100-101.

[43] Pfander, p. 48. Pfander's transcription errors have been doubled in David L. Jeffrey, *The Early English Lyric and Franciscan Spirituality* (Lincoln, 1975), p. 175. Here and throughout, Jeffrey's views on singing friars are based on too many faulty readings to deserve serious attention; see *Verses*, pp. 102-3.

heart, God will without doubt hear you and remain with you and see you after this life in his heavenly glory, to his honor and your glory. To which he may bring us. Amen.)[44]

The English verses had already been used in the preceding sermon, where however they are introduced with ''let us therefore *say (dicamus)* . . .'' But in the present sermon, so Pfander thought, they were *sung* because ''I do not know of any case in which *melodia* is used of verses which were spoken.'' This argument unfortunately does not pay sufficient attention to the context. Let us recall that this entire sermon is based on the common experience of receiving a guest, an image that is then allegorically applied to receiving God into our heart. In order to do so properly, we must attend to four things, as expressed in the sermon division quoted earlier, the last of which was to ''loke'' that he—our guest, i.e., God—''hafe good minstralcye.'' As the preacher comes to the fourth principal, he declares: ''In that [i.e., minstrelsy], men take bodily delight, and in such God takes spiritual delight. But you ask what melody you should make for him. I answer: take your heart as a musical instrument and tune it with good contrition and confession, and thus you should safely call . . .''[45] In other words, the *melodia*/minstrelsy mentioned before and after the ''song'' in question is part of the literal image of receiving a guest but applied and to be understood spiritually as the ''melody'' of prayer infused with repentance. The exhortation to ''sing devoutly in your *heart*'' shows beyond question that the following verses are intended as a prayer spoken with a pure heart and clean lips. It provides no evidence that they were sung.[46] To draw such an inference would be like saying that the same preacher's exhortation to ''prepare a dish of maumene for Christ'' sent his congregation to the kitchen.

The material with which I shall in the following chapters illustrate the precise contexts of Middle English preaching verses and their concrete functions comes primarily from macaronic sermons, whose basic language is Latin into which English lines and phrases are mixed in various

---

[44] Newly transcribed from Bodleian Library, MS. Lat. theol. d. 1, fol. 175.

[45] ''Quarto et ultimo dico quod si vis bene custodire virum istum, idest Iesum Christum, quem accepisti hodie, loke þou hafe minstralcye, et in hoc delectantur homines corporaliter et in huiusmodi spiritualiter Deus delectatur. Sed queris qualem melodiam sibi facere debeas. Respondeo: accipe cor tuum tamquam instrumentum musice et id cum bona contricione et confessione tempera, et sic secure Deo clames . . .'' Ibidem.

[46] A more reliable beginning for the discussion of the relations between preaching verses and singing has been made by Reichl, *Religiöse Dichtung*, pp. 92-93.

forms and to different extents.[47] This peculiar form of preserving English poems with extensive contexts reflects the fact that at least until about 1450 sermons were regularly written down in Latin, even when they were without question preached in the vernacular. We are less certain about the audience before which a particular sermon was preached. No direct inference can be drawn from the language in which a sermon has been written down, for the rule developed a century ago, that sermons addressed to the clergy were preached in Latin, while sermons before lay people were given in the vernacular,[48] cannot be reversed ("sermons extant in Latin were preached to the clergy," etc.). Formulas of address may give us some hint; but while sermons beginning with "Reverendi patres" point to a clerical audience, it does not follow that others with a plain "Karissimi" always address laymen. And the same uncertainty attaches to the intellectual level of our texts. One might think that references to Aristotle and Albumasar appealed to the learned, while peasants were entertained with homespun proverbs and gruesome anecdotes. But again, many surviving texts tend to have some of both in the same sermon. It is true that none of the texts here used deal with matters of speculative theology as if they were *quaestiones disputatae*, and in that regard they all are "popular" sermons, but do not tell us more about their audiences. It makes best sense to think of these sermons as texts either worked out before their delivery or (and I believe this applies much less often) written down by a *reportator* or the preacher himself after they were preached. In neither case must they be taken to represent the actual sermon as delivered. Though some of them may be shown to come very close to the form in which they must have been preached, it is safer, as a general rule, to treat them as literary texts written out to serve preachers for study or as guidelines which could be adapted in actual delivery to whatever audience a preacher had before him. That English verses found their way into the literary texts shows us again how important a place poems held in late medieval preaching, an importance that the label "scraps" misses altogether.

The following chapters are intended as a series of explorations of their common subject, the connection between preaching and the early Eng-

[47] I have offered a preliminary classification of macaronic sermons in a paper abstracted in the "Report of the Medieval Sermon Studies Symposium 1982," *Medieval Sermon Studies Newsletter*, ed. Gloria Cigman, Univ. of Warwick.

[48] Albert Lecoy de la Marche, *La Chaire française au moyen âge, spécialement au XIIIᵉ siècle, d'après les manuscrits contemporains*, second edition (Paris, 1886), p. 235.

lish lyric. They do not aim at providing a comprehensive, let alone definitive, account of the influence that preaching had on medieval English literature as a whole, though I hope that this book may contribute its share to such an account. The next chapter will explore the medieval hymn tradition, starting from an appraisal of the poetic features in what I have found to be one of the most remarkable achievements in that tradition, and then turning to ask what influence that tradition had on early English lyrics. Chapter 3 will demonstrate that formal sermon writing from about 1250 to the end of the Middle Ages cultivated certain artistic qualities and provided the occasion for making or utilizing vernacular poems. In the following two chapters, 4 and 5, I turn to the poetic work of one English preacher to discuss the sources and variety of his preaching verses, their function in actual sermons, and their literary merits. Chapters 6 and 7 will deal with two specific kinds of poems, complaint verses and secular love songs, in an attempt to explore the utilization of material from vernacular and oral sources and to see what sermon verses can tell us about such traditions and about popular songs that have not been recorded elsewhere. Finally, chapter 8 will examine some ways in which the style of preaching verses differs from that of genuine poets whose lyrics were definitely not written for use in preaching.

This book is, therefore, primarily a historical study. But it is also coincidentally concerned with critical evaluation. In a recent introduction to Middle English literature, John A. Burrow has drawn a succinct and helpful distinction between two fundamentally different components that make "literature" what it is and that lead to two quite different critical concerns and approaches: "eloquence" and "ficticity." The former is concerned with the way literary texts use language, while the latter has to do with the peculiar nature of literature as "a fictional, or non-affirmative, or non-pragmatic, or hypothetical mode of discourse."[49] What critical concern this book includes lies squarely in the area of "eloquence." The analysis of some medieval hymns and sequences in the next chapter will serve, not only as a historical background to preaching verses, but also as a practical demonstration of this concern.

---

[49] J. A. Burrow, *Medieval Writers and Their Work. Middle English Literature and its Background 1100-1500* (Oxford, 1982), pp. 12ff.

2

The

Medieval Hymn

Tradition

When preaching verses were first written down in sermon manuscripts, roughly in the third quarter of the thirteenth century, religious lyrics in Middle English had already been produced for at least a generation. These earlier poems had been translated and developed from Latin hymns and sequences, with which they formed a rich and diversified tradition. In order to examine the poetic achievements that characterize this tradition, I have selected a sequence attributed to the erudite paralytic monk Hermann of Reichenau (1013-1054).[1] Though it apparently did not directly influence the early English lyric and in fact seems not to have been popular in England,[2] this poem brilliantly demonstrates the great verbal artistry that the medieval Latin hymn was capable of attaining.

> 1. Ave, praeclara
> maris stella,
> in lucem gentium,
> Maria,
> divinitus orta.

[1] The attribution is controversial. For a rapid survey of opinions see Josef Szöverffy, *Die Annalen der lateinischen Hymnendichtung*, vol. I (Berlin, 1964), pp. 376-79. For Hermann's life and works, see Franz-Josef Schmale, "Hermann von Reichenau," in *Die deutsche Literatur des Mittelalters. Verfasserlexikon*, second edition, vol. III (Berlin and New York, 1981), cols. 1082-90.

[2] For one exception, see Dom Hesbert, *Le Tropaire-Prosaire de Dublin. Manuscrit Add. 710 de l'Université de Cambridge (vers 1360)*, Monumenta musicae sacrae IV (Rouen, 1966), p. 25, n. 56. The early manuscripts that preserve the sequence are all from Germany or German-speaking regions. Likewise, a number of German translations and adaptations were made from the twelfth century on: see Walther Lipphardt, *Verfasserlexikon*, I (1978), 568-70; and H. Brinkmann, "*Ave praeclara maris stella* in deutscher Wiedergabe. Zur Geschichte einer Rezension," in *Studien zur deutschen Literatur und Sprache des Mittelalters. Festschrift für Hugo Moser zum 65. Geburtstag*, ed. Werner Besch et al. (Berlin, 1974), pp. 8-30. *Ave praeclara* was also imitated in Latin hymns, as in "Salve, Maria, / Christi parens, / intacta / gladio / doloris / intus transfixa": Chevalier, *Repertorium hymnologicum*, No. 18008; printed in *AH* 8:54.

Chapter 2

2a. Euge, Dei porta,
    quae non aperta
    veritatis lumen,
    ipsum solem iustitiae,
    indutum carne
    ducis in orbem.

3a. Te, plenam fide
    virgam almae stirpis Iesse,
    nascituram
    priores
    desideraverant
    patres et prophetae.

4a. Tu agnum regem,
    terrae dominatorem,
    Moabitici
    de petra deserti
    ad montem filiae Sion
    transduxisti.

5a. Hinc gentium
    nos reliquiae
    tuae sub cultu memoriae,
    mirum in modum
    quem es enixa,
    propitiationis agnum,
    regnantem caelo
    aeternaliter,
    devocamus ad aram
    mactandum mysterialiter.

6a. Fac fontem dulcem,
    quem in deserto
    petra praemonstravit,
    degustare
    cum sincera fide
    renesque constringi
    lotos in mari,

2b. Virgo, decus mundi,
    regina caeli,
    praeelecta ut sol,
    pulchra lunaris ut fulgor,
    agnosce omnes
    te diligentes.

3b. Te, lignum vitae,
    sancto rorante pneumate
    parituram
    divini
    floris amygdalum
    signavit Gabriel.

4b. Tuque furentem
    Leviathan serpentem
    tortuosumque
    et vectem collidens
    damnoso crimine mundum
    exemisti.

5b. Hinc manna verum
    Israelitis
    veris, veri Abrahae filiis,
    admirantibus
    quondam Moysi
    quod typus figurabat, iam
       nunc
    abducto velo
    datur perspici;
    ora, virgo, nos illo
    pane caeli dignos effici.

6b. Fac igni sancto
    patrisque verbo,
    quod rubus ut flammam
    tu portasti,
    virgo mater facta,
    pecuali pelle
    discinctos pede

anguem aeneum in cruce
speculari.

mundis labiis cordeque
propinquare.

7a. Audi nos,
nam te filius
nihil negans honorat.

7b. Salva nos,
Iesu, pro quibus
mater virgo te orat.

8a. Da fontem boni visere,
da purae mentis oculos
in te defigere,

8b. Quo haustu sapientiae
saporem vitae valeat
mens intellegere,

9. Christianismi fidem
operibus redimire
beatoque fine
ex huius incolatu saeculi,
auctor, ad te transire.[3]

1. Hail, bright star of the sea, Mary, divinely risen as a light to the nations.
2a. Rejoice, God's portal, you who without being open yourself bring the light of truth, the very sun of justice, clothed in flesh, into our world.
2b. Virgin, splendor of the world, queen of heaven, most bright as the sun, beautiful as the light of the moon—hear all who love you.
3a. The ancient patriarchs and prophets had longed for you to be born, you who are full of faith, the rod from the bountiful root of Jesse.
3b. Gabriel greeted (*or* blessed) you, the tree of life, when you were to give birth to the almond of the divine flower under the breathing of the Holy Spirit.
4a. You have led the lamb, the king, the ruler of the earth from the rock of the desert of Moab to the mountain of the daughter of Sion.

[3] I have taken the text from G. M. Dreves, *AH* 50:241, with correction of *solem* (2a) and *flammam* (6b). *Ave praeclara* desperately needs a critical edition based on a full study of all the manuscripts. A recent but incomplete list of manuscripts is given by Hans Oesch, *Berno und Hermann von Reichenau als Musiktheoretiker* (Bern, 1961), pp. 143-44, to which the following manuscripts in the Vatican Library can be added: Rossianus 76 (formerly VIII.18), fols. 252v-254v (gradual from Aquileia, xiv or late xiii); Rossianus 181 (formerly VIII.120), fol. ccxix, r-v (missal from Paderborn, xiii); Palatinus lat. 500, fol. 91r-v (missal, 1314); and Vaticanus lat. 10773, fols. 178v-180 (Dominican gradual, Diessenhofen, xiv).

4b. You have saved the world from fateful injury by bruising the fierce Leviathan, the coiling serpent and the bar serpent.

5a. Therefore, we, the remnant of the nations, in worship of your memory call him down to our altar to be mysteriously slaughtered whom you brought forth to life in wondrous fashion, the lamb of reconciliation who reigns eternally in heaven.

5b. Therefore, the true manna, once prefigured to Moses, is now, after the veil has been taken away, given to the true Israelites, the children of the true Abraham, for their admiring beholding. Virgin, pray that we may become worthy of that bread of heaven.

6a. Make us taste with sincere faith that sweet fountain which the rock in the desert prefigured, [make us] gird our loins after being washed in the sea, and look upon the brazen serpent on the cross.

6b. Make us, O Virgin made mother, approach the holy fire and the Father's word, which you carried as the bush did the flame, [approach him] with our feet unbound of the animal hide and with clean lips and heart.

7a. Hear us, for your son honors you and denies you nothing.

7b. Save us, Jesus, for whom the Virgin-Mother prays to you.

8a. Grant us to long to behold the fountain of goodness, grant us to fix the eyes of our pure mind on you.

8b. So that our mind, when it has drunk its wisdom, may be able to perceive the taste of life.

9. [Grant us] to crown our Christian faith with works, and after a blessed ending pass on to you, Creator, from our dwelling in this world.

Sequences are liturgical compositions of varying length, consisting of verses (or versicles) that vary in form within the same sequence and are, at least in the early phase of their history, prose sentences—that is, devoid of rhyme or a repeated metrical pattern. The verses occur in parallel pairs—in our case, 2a-2b, 3a-3b, etc.—but the opening and closing verses (1 and 9) are single units. Accompanied by music of the same structure, sequences were created for antiphonal singing by the two halves of a choir or a religious community on designated feast days at a specific point during the Mass, namely the *Alleluia* which precedes the reading of the Gospel.[4] The sequence under discussion has been pre-

---

[4] My description of the early sequence should be read as the generalization of a nonspecialist. A more authoritative account can be found in Bruno Stäblein, "Sequenz (Ge-

served in a large number of missals, graduals, and other liturgical books dating from the twelfth to the fifteenth century.

As part of the liturgy, this sequence is essentially religious in substance and function: an act of worship in which man speaks to God. As such, it is also a public and official speech act: the prayer is spoken by a community, and its language is shared, understood, and sanctioned by the entire Church. In its overall structure the sequence follows precisely the movement of a formal prayer, from invocation to praise and on to a specific petition. Formal prayer structure can be illustrated with the collect for the Vigil of the Assumption:

(Invocation)	God,
(Praise)	who have deigned to choose the virginal chamber of Blessed Mary for your dwelling place,
(Petition)	grant, we pray, that she may make us who stand fortified in her protection celebrate her feast in joy.
(Doxology)	You who live and reign . . .[5]

It should be noted that the section I have called "praise" usually mentions a past or present act or event involving the person addressed which has some direct relevance to the occasion of the prayer, that is the feast on which it is used.

Like the quoted collect, the sequence *Ave praeclara* begins with an invocation of the Virgin (*Ave, praeclara . . . Maria . . .* , verse 1). Next, it praises her (*Euge,* 2a)[6] by highlighting her function in the history of salvation, which was to conceive and give birth to the Son of God and thereby to share in the redemption of mankind. The three pairs of verses that thus celebrate her do so in different ways. The first pair (2a-2b), continuing the form of verse 1, pronounces her titles: *Dei porta* in 2a, and *regina caeli* in 2b (together with *Virgo* and *decus mundi*). These titles mark the timeless and continuing dignity of Mary. But her dignity does

---

sang)," in *Die Musik in Geschichte und Gegenwart*, vol. 12 (Kassel, 1965), cols. 522-49; and in Richard L. Crocker and John Caldwell, "Sequence (i) ," in *The New Grove Dictionary of Music and Musicians*, ed. Stanley Sadie (London, 1980), 17:141-56.

[5] "Deus, qui virginalem aulam beate Marie in qua habitares eligere dignatus es, da quesumus ut sua nos defensione munitos iocundos faciat sue interesse festivitati. Qui vivis et regnas." *The Sarum Missal*, ed. J. Wickham Legg (Oxford, 1916), p. 307.

[6] Verse-pair 2 could be considered part of the invocation, with the "praise" beginning at 3. But in light of the poem's great craftsmanship, I see the transition from greeting to praise signaled in the shift from *Ave* to *Euge*.

not stand frozen; it is presented in flowing action, here expressed linguistically by present-tense verb forms that describe her continuing role as the human being through whom God's light comes into the world (*ducis*, 2a) and who intercedes for all who love her (*agnosce*, 2b). Verses 3a and 3b then turn to history, sacred history, in which Mary's coming was longingly expected by forefathers and prophets, and her motherhood prepared in the Annunciation. In both instances Mary's role was a passive one, here expressed by the accusative case *te* with which the two verses open. The following pair of verses, however, turns to her active part in salvation history, that of bringing Christ to the Church (4a) and, by crushing the serpent's head, saving the world (4b). The change from passive to active is beautifully signalled by the nominative case of the pronoun *tu*, again occupying initial position. The change is further marked by passing from a literal-historical predication (the fathers longed for her, Gabriel greeted her) to a metaphysical or rather figural one (she led the lamb, she bruised the serpent). By playing with such contrasts as timelessness and history, active and passive, literal-historical and figural, the three verse pairs which speak Mary's praise make use of a surprising richness and variation in their approach.

With verse 5a the sequence turns from celebration to petition. The stark, almost blunt *hinc* with which the verse pair opens makes it clear that it is Mary's exalted position in salvation history that establishes the reason for the following petitions and causes the speakers to approach her with confidence, humbly but without groveling. Instead of more polished formulas such as *concede quaesumus* or *quaesumus ut* . . . , which are common in collects, we here find a blunt *ora, fac, audi* (continued in *salva* and *da*). Verse 5a also marks a turning to the speakers. The first *nos* in the sequence appears at this point and is accompanied by a verb in the first-person plural form (*devocamus*). The petitions are, specifically, for being made worthy to receive Christ in the Eucharist (verses 5-6) and are, again, first expressed in a more literal form—if indeed calling the consecrated host *panis caeli* (5b) can be termed literal—and then in a figural mode, by reference to drinking the water that issued from the rock and looking upon the brazen serpent (Numbers 21.4-9), and to approaching the burning bush (Exodus 3.1-6). These specific Eucharistic petitions, addressed to Mary as man's intercessor (cf. 7a-7b), finally give way to a series of four or five petitions addressed directly to Christ[7]

---

[7] The text of verses 8-9 as printed by Dreves may not be the original form, for verse 8b is lacking in several early witnesses (see Dreves, p. 315), a fact recognized by the medieval commentaries mentioned below, n. 14.

which ask for the gift (*da*, 8a) of the final and direct vision and of eternal communion with God. The sequence has no explicit doxology that would name the persons of the Holy Trinity ("Who with the Father and the Holy Spirit live and reign . . .") such as is found in collects and hymns. But one can detect an allusive doxology in the naming of *Iesu* (7b), *auctor* (9), and *sapientiae* and *saporem vitae* (8b), which was already anticipated in the references to "the holy fire" and "the Father's word" in 6b. It would therefore seem that instead of tacking a separate doxology onto his sequence, Hermann has skillfully integrated the naming of the divine persons into his final biblical *figura* (6b) and the larger final prayer.

The overall structure of *Ave praeclara* thus follows in a general way the movement of formal liturgical prayers. In its particulars, however, the sequence is more specifically indebted to the ninth-century hymn *Ave maris stella*.[8] Like our sequence, the hymn addresses Mary as *maris stella, Dei mater, semper virgo,* and *caeli porta* in its opening stanza. The following five stanzas contain a series of petitions in short imperative forms (*funda, solve,* etc.).[9] These are introduced with a reference to the Annunciation (*Sumens illud Ave / Gabrielis ore*) in a way that suggests that this historical event in Mary's life is taken as the ontological reason for the Church's appeal for Mary's prayers, a thought that recurs at the very heart of the petitions and the entire hymn when Mary's motherhood (*Monstra te esse matrem*, st. 4) is connected with her intercessory power before her son (*sumat per te precem* . . .). The petitions themselves climax in a prayer for purity and for a safe journey to the vision of Christ and to eternal joy. In contrast to *Ave praeclara*, to which it has thus given its overall structure and thought as well as some verbal detail, the hymn then closes with a formal doxology (*Sit laus Deo Patri . . .* , st. 7).

Hermann's sequence *Ave praeclara* was assigned by its modern editor to the feast of the Assumption, since it is thus marked in some liturgical manuscripts and early prints. Yet the sequence contains no such customary references to the Assumption as the Virgin's uncorrupt body or her

---

[8] See Hennig Brinkmann, "Voraussetzungen und Struktur religiöser Lyrik im Mittelalter," *Mittellateinisches Jahrbuch* 3 (1966), 37-54. *Ave maris stella* has received a massively detailed commentary from Heinrich Lausberg, *Der Hymnus "Ave maris stella,"* Abhandlungen der Rheinisch-Westfälischen Akademie der Wissenschaften 61 (Opladen, 1976).

[9] The great model for such short imperatives may be the *Te Deum*: "Te ergo quaesumus, tuis famulis subveni . . . , fac . . . , fac . . . , rege . . . , extolle . . ."

rise to heaven and reception by rejoicing angels,[10] though this argument holds no great force since Hermann and his monastic community may or may not have explicitly believed in Mary's bodily assumption, and the precise nature of Mary's assumption, celebrated in the West on August 15 since the seventh century, was not defined until 1950.[11] More importantly, the early manuscripts assign the sequence to different feasts, especially the Purification, or do not assign it to a particular feast of the Virgin at all.[12] It would therefore seem that *Ave praeclara* may originally have been composed only as a general Marian sequence. Nonetheless, its later connection with the Assumption is very fitting. In commemorating a series of separate but connected events—namely, Mary's death (*dormitio, transitus*), her rising (whether bodily or only spiritually) into heaven, and her coronation as queen—the feast celebrated her ongoing role in the Church, which began with her being chosen as mother of Christ and continues in her intercession for the faithful on earth.[13] I suggest that it is not specifically Mary's Assumption but her continuing and timeless role that constitutes the central thought of this sequence. This conception informs its structure and movement in a variety of ways. Her invocation and titles at the beginning of the sequence span time from the moment of her divine motherhood (*Dei porta*) to the end of history, expressed in the allusions to Revelation 12.1 (*regina caeli* and the comparison to sun and moon, 2b); while references to her continuing interces-

---

[10] Such references appear in the contemporary standard sequences for the Assumption, *Congaudent angelorum chori* and *A rea virgo* (or *Area virgo*): Ulysse Chevalier, *Repertorium hymnologicum* (Louvain, 1892), Nos. 3783 and 16 (or 1320). Both can be found in Legg (ed.), *Sarum Missal*, pp. 534 and 479. *Ave praeclara* is Chevalier No. 2045.

[11] For a critical history of the doctrine of the Virgin's Assumption, see Martin Jugie, *La Mort et l'Assomption de la Sainte Vierge*, Studi e testi 114 (Vatican City, 1944).

[12] The earliest witness, an eleventh-century antiphonary from Saint Peter's, Salzburg, gives the sequence simply as "De s. Maria," unconnected to any specific feast. The Einsiedeln fragment assigns it to the Purification; the four Vatican manuscripts mentioned in note 3 assign it to no specific feast.

[13] The connection of Mary's death and assumption with her intercession appears in the Mass for the Vigil of the Assumption, in the *Liber sacramentorum* attributed (wrongly) to Gregory the Great: "Dei Genitricis oratio, quam idcirco de praesenti saeculo transtulisti ut pro peccatis nostris apud te fiducialiter intercedat" (PL 78:132-33). The same connection is depicted in several representations of the tenth century made in the Bodensee region: a picture of Mary rising above her empty bed in the position of Orans; and similarly an ivory plaque inscribed "Ascensio sancte Marie." See Wilhelm Vöge, *Eine deutsche Malerschule um die Wende des ersten Jahrtausends*, Westdeutsche Zeitschrift für Geschichte und Kunst, Ergänzungsheft 7 (Trier, 1891), pictures 315 and 317.

sion recur throughout the sequence climaxing in the final *te filius nihil negans honorat* (7a) and thereby making her honor the very *raison d'être* of this prayer. Further, the central verses of the poem (4-6), with their cluster of biblical images relating to the Exodus, to Moses and the Israelites' wandering through the desert,[14] do not so much restate the exegetical commonplace of the spiritual identity of Mary and the Church as develop the contrast between Mary who rules in heaven (as a state, not a place) and the Church who on earth is still undergoing a "desert experience" (again, as a state, not a place) which was foreshadowed in such Old Testament events as the desert of Moab (4a, cf. Isaiah 16.1ff.), the slaughter of the lamb (5a, cf. Leviticus 23.26-32), the manna (5b, cf. Exodus 16), the water from the rock and the brazen serpent (6a, cf. Exodus 17.1-7, Numbers 20.2-7, 21.4-9), and the burning bush (6b, cf. Exodus 3.1-6).[15] Finally, the entire sequence is infused with a movement toward the future, which again agrees beautifully with the life and role of Mary. Her own "progress" is explicitly indicated twice in the poem: first, as already mentioned, from her rising (*orta,* 1) as the star of the sea to her queenship in heaven, her function at the end of time as seen by Saint John, and her continuing intercession (2b); and secondly, from the longing expectation of her birth (3a) through the Annunciation (3b) to the lasting effect of her life in the process of redemption (4b) and, once more, her continuing intercession (5b-7b). But Mary's "progress," though unique, also anticipates that of all mankind, for the sequence's movement to the future applies likewise to the Church which, from looking back to Old Testament *figurae,* prays in anticipation of the immediate communion with Christ in the Eucharist (5b-6b) and, beyond that, longs for the full and everlasting vision (8a-8b) in the anticipated transition from this life to its Creator (9). This entire movement is summed up most beautifully in the last word of the sequence, *transire,* for *transitus* was

---

[14] These biblical images, and the entire sequence, were discussed by at least two medieval commentators; see R.B.C. Huygens, "Deux commentaires sur la séquence *Ave, praeclara maris stella,*" *Citeaux* 20 (1969), 108-69. They have also been repeatedly discussed by Hennig Brinkmann: "Voraussetzungen" (n. 8, above), and *Mittelalterliche Hermeneutik* (Tübingen, 1980), pp. 410-34.

[15] The connection between the Israelites' Exodus and Mary's Assumption is explicitly made in the Preface of the Mass for the Assumption in the "Gothic Missal" (679x835): "die prae caeteris honorando, quo fidelis Israhel egressus est de Aegypto, quo virgo dei genitrix de mundo migravit ad Christum." Leo Cunibert Mohlberg, O.S.B. (ed.), *Missale Gothicum.* Rerum ecclesiasticarum documenta. Series maior, Fontes, V (Rome, 1961), p. 29.

one of the several terms to designate the event and feast of Mary's Assumption in the earlier Middle Ages,[16] and the final phrase, *ex huius incolatu saeculi . . . transire,* echoes the language in which the Church prayed for its deceased members.[17]

Thus, the structure of this poem relies ultimately on a linear progression which is established by the successive parts of a formal prayer as well as by the pattern of salvation history. Its parts have been chosen and ordered with a particular reason, and it would certainly be wrong to think that its major images, as for instance the biblical *figurae* of verses 4-6, are simply juxtaposed as they might be in an episodic structure. Repeated readings of the sequence reveal more and more of a very sophisticated craftsmanship in the poet's selection of material and his linking it together, a craftsmanship that is not just theological but poetical in that it utilizes verbal resources—such as, punning, word repetition, and syntactic parallelism—to express theological notions. Verse-pair 4, for instance, praises Mary's active participation in salvation history and does so, as already pointed out, by speaking of her giving birth to Christ (which is presumably the meaning of 4a) and of her overcoming the power of Satan (4b). Both acts could have been expressed with the help of a number of different biblical *figurae.* Why did Hermann choose the particular ones of the lamb that was to be sent from the desert to the mountain of the daughter of Sion (4a) and of Leviathan (4b)? Undoubtedly, theological traditions had some influence. But in addition I suggest that the former image was chosen in anticipation of the Lamb of the Eucharist mentioned in 5a and because it simultaneously fits into the theme of ''desert experience'' which holds the various Old Testament images together. Moreover, *transduxisti* of 4a verbally links this verse to *ducis* of 2a. The parallel image of Leviathan in 4b may have been selected similarly for two reasons: Leviathan is an evil animal, contrasting with the good *agnus* of 4b, and he is the opponent in the apocalyptic vision of Saint John from which details in 2b have been taken. Thus, both parts of verse-pair 4 link back to their respective antecedents in verse-pair 2. The contrast between good and evil animals may have been carried even fur-

---

[16] Thus for example in the Mass for the Assumption in the ''Gothic Missal'' just cited, p. 30. See also Bellamy, ''Assomption,'' *Dictionnaire de théologie catholique,* vol. 1 (Paris, 1931), 2128; and Mario Righetti, *Storia liturgica,* second edition, vol. 2 (Milan, 1955), pp. 281-91.

[17] PL 78:467, a Carolingian prayer.

ther into verse-pair 6, where the brazen serpent, a figure of Christ, could be seen as contrasting with *pecualis pellis,* the animal skins used as footwear which Moses is commanded to take off before approaching Jahweh in the burning bush. Would it be too farfetched to detect a witty crossover, from the evil serpent of 4b to the good one of 6a, and conversely from the good lamb (4a) to the allegorically evil footwear made of sheepskin (6b), a crossover rendered even more piquant by the auditory similarity of *anguem* to *agnum*?

The sequence's linear progression and the linking of its parts are thus created by a variety of means. In addition to repeated words and images, the poem uses a progressive series of verb tenses, from pluperfect (*desideraverant,* 3a) to perfect (3b-4b) to present (5a-5b) and on to present imperative and infinitive with future meaning (6-9). And the major sections of the prayerlike structure are neatly linked together by a carryover of significant stylistic elements: the section of praise (2-4) continues the use of Mary's titles from the invocation (*maris stella,* 1, to *Dei porta,* etc., 2a), while the theme of "desert experience" so prominent in the petition (5-6) is already sounded at the end of Mary's praise (4a).

The same combination of continuity and forward flow exists not only in the poem's vertical structure (as one reads it) but also horizontally. The sequence form requires that the two halves of a verse pair be absolutely parallel. This parallelism can be seen at a glance from the printed text: the corresponding lines are always of equal length, and the two verses of each pair usually begin with the same word or at least the same grammatical form (7). The exception to the latter rule may again be quite deliberate, in that the difference in the opening words of the first verse pair (2a-2b) is mirrored by that of the last (7a-7b or 8a-8b).[18] In addition, as Hennig Brinkmann has shown, by using the same type of *cursus* the last lines of each verse pair run parallel rhythmically.[19] Verses 7a and 7b even rhyme with each other. Yet such verbal and rhythmic parallelism does not at all mean that the b-verses repeat or restate the lexical content of their corresponding a-verses. On the contrary, in this horizontal direction one finds the same forward movement as observed in the vertical direction. Thus, for instance, in pairs 2-4 the two halves show the progression in historical time or in salvation history (giving birth to Christ—

---

[18] For the textual uncertainty, see above, n. 7.

[19] Brinkmann, "Voraussetzungen," pp. 47-48.

destroying Satan) we noticed earlier. Verses 7a-7b express a different progression, from Mary to Christ. Such a combination of repetition and change occurs most startlingly in verse-pair 3. Here the third lines, *nascituram* and *parituram,* are almost identical on the surface: the same grammatical case, number, gender, and verb form (future participle) are used, creating two sound structures that are identical except for two consonant phonemes (*n:p* and *s:r*). And yet the difference in meaning could hardly be greater, as passive yields to active: to be born—to give birth.

The images and the verbal material with which Hermann has constructed his sequence are predominantly biblical and liturgical. Only in 8a does he allude to a different text, Boethius' *Consolation of Philosophy.*[20] Thus the verbal substance of this sequence is highly traditional, and it resonates with the meanings which these particular biblical images or events had acquired through centuries of an exegetical tradition reflected in both theology and the liturgy. So traditional and consequently well-known were these images with their acquired meanings that Hermann could utilize them in the most succinct, sparing fashion, without a word of commentary. The result is a verbal structure of extreme density. But this is more than the automatic result of using well-known material which did not require explanation; it is likewise the outcome of great verbal craftsmanship. I believe one cannot find a single word in the entire sequence that is used only to fill out a line or rhythmic pattern. Take for instance *quondam* in 5b: far from being mere padding, it emphasizes (with *iam nunc* in the next line) the sharp difference between spiritual past and present, between figure and reality, a distance whose bridging enhances Mary's role in salvation history (*transduxisti,* 4a).[21] Similarly, *illo* in the same verse stresses the distance between the speakers and "that bread from heaven," the manna, while at the same time it points to a specific event in history whose fulfillment is now about to occur. Such verbal concentration and economy is no easy accomplishment, and it was not consistently within the reach of every medieval Latin poet. Adam of St. Victor, for instance, another creator of masterful hymns and sequences, was not above producing lines that may strike us as padded:

[20] *De consolatione Philosophiae*, III, m. ix, 22-24 (CC 94:52). This allusion was recognized by the medieval commentators.

[21] Notice that *traductio*, as a rhetorical term, was used in biblical exegesis ("to interpret allegorically") and could be applied to God's Word as bringing a prophecy or prefiguration to its historical fulfillment. The latter notion is explicitly referred to in verse 5b. It is rather breathtaking that in *transduxisti* Hermann gives this function to Mary.

Caeli rorant, nubes pluunt,
Montes stillant, colles fluunt,
Radix Jesse germinat,

or

Qui nos gustu, nos odore,
Nos invitat specie.[22]

It could be argued that here and in general Adam was seeking to achieve very different poetic effects from those in *Ave praeclara*; but his lines certainly lack the admirable vigor and tight linguistic control of Hermann's sequence.

Other aspects of Hermann's verbal craftsmanship have already been noted in discussing the parallelism and verbal links and echoes with which the sequence is replete. There are, further, instances of wordplay, as in the paradox of *porta . . . non aperta* (2a) and in the emphatic repetition—technically a *traductio*—of *verum . . . , veris, veri* (5b). I should like to add one more suggestion. Verse 5a contains two words, *devocamus* and *mactandum* ("we call the Lamb down to our altar to be mysteriously slaughtered"), which are not found in Scripture but have a firm standing in "pagan" literature.[23] I wonder if Hermann chose them because they fit their subject so well: "we, the remnant of the nations *or* Gentiles." If so, then even the rather barbaric alliteration of *mactandum mysterialiter* might be deliberate and meaningful, a witty allusion to the poet's native tradition of alliterative poetry.[24]

This sophisticated verbal art including wordplay and "wit" shows likewise in the form of the verses. Since these do not have a regular metric pattern, such as one finds in Horace's odes or in an Ambrosian hymn, they are not strophes. In fact, the whole sequence is "prose," and each of its verses is one complete prose sentence, with its verb at or near the

---

[22] *AH* 54:99, verses 6 and 10.

[23] For instance, Jupiter is called down from heaven to the sacrifice (Pliny) or for help (Livy); see Lewis and Short, *A Latin Dictionary*, under *devocor* and *macto*. But notice that *mactari* was applied to Christ already by Gregory, *Homiliae XL in evangelia*, hom. 37.7 (PL 76:127), and by John de Fécamp, *Meditationes* 41 (PL 40:941).

[24] Hermann's native language was almost certainly German, and the monastery of Reichenau is famous for its place in the early history of German letters. In addition, the sequence *Ave praeclara* seems to have been preserved almost exclusively in manuscripts written at monasteries situated in the German language territory. For a suggestion of similar wordplay in *Ave maris stella*, see Lausberg, *Der Hymnus*, pp. 74 and 112-13.

end, where one would properly expect it in classical Latin. However, each verse or verse-pair has its own carefully made rhythm which is repeated in the halves of the pair but never from one verse to another. There is much play with the syntactic order within these sentences. In 3a-3b, for example, we find the order direct object—predicate—subject; but in 4a-4b, subject—direct object—predicate. And much use is made of artificial word order, as for instance in *pulchra lunaris ut fulgor* (2b), where the natural order *pulchra ut fulgor lunaris* would yield the same rhythmic pattern, at least in an accentual system, or in *priores desideraverant patres* (3a) and elsewhere. Yet it should be added that artificial word order is not obtrusive in this poem, is certainly not *recherché* or manneristic.

This combination of the familiar and the strange or unexpected on the various levels of vocabulary, syntax, rhythm, images, allusions, and overall structure constitutes a most fascinating aspect of Hermann's craftsmanship. It makes for a verbal composition that requires a good deal of meditation to discover its inner beauty, like a good prayer which not only addresses the Godhead but leads the attentive mind to him, or like a good poem.

Although *Ave praeclara* itself enjoyed little popularity in England,[25] the entire genre of medieval sequences and hymns, of which it is one of the most brilliant representatives, exerted a profound influence on the early Middle English lyric. In a general way, the conception of religious poetry as prayer, with its two major components of praise and petition, informs much lyric poetry throughout the Middle English period. A poem on the Five Joys of Mary, for example, uses the progression of invocation—praise—petition repeatedly to structure each of its five stanzas. In the opening stanza, on the Annunciation, the pattern thus fills lines 1, 2-10, and 11-12:

Seinte Marie, leuedi brist,		bright
Moder þov art of muchel mist,		
Quene in heuene of feire ble.		appearance
Gabriel to þe he liste	4	alighted
Þe he brovste al wid riste		when he brought
Þen holi gost to listen in þe.		
Godes word ful wel þov cnewe;		
Ful mildeliche þer-to þov bewe	8	bowed
Ant saidest so it mote be,—		

[25] See above, n. 2.

34

Þi þonc was studeuast ant trewe.   thought
For þe ioye þat to was newe,   then
Leuedi, þov haue merci of me.[26]   12

This pattern even seems to underlie the great secular love songs of medieval England[27] (and of the Continent as well), which almost inevitably contain, as their two basic ingredients, a praise of the beloved lady and a petition for her favors.[28] But more specifically, a number of Latin hymns and sequences were either directly translated or imitated in the earliest Middle English lyrics that have been preserved. What happened in this process of *translatio* will occupy our attention in the following pages.

The main characteristics of English lyrics that came into being under the inspiration of Latin hymns can perhaps be best approached through an analysis of *Gabriel fram evene-king*, which is so well known for its music and for its prominence in Chaucer's Miller's Tale. Its source is a pious Latin song, a *cantio*, apparently composed in the late thirteenth or very early fourteenth century and later incorporated into the liturgy of the Church.[29] *Angelus ad Virginem* consists of five stanzas:

1. Angelus ad virginem
      subintrans in conclave
   virginis formidinem
      demulcens inquit: "Ave,
      ave, regina virginum.   5
   Celi terreque dominum
      concipies,
      et paries
      intacta
   salutem hominum,   10
   tu porta celi facta,
   medela criminum."

---

[26] *EL* 18.

[27] For example: *Bytuene Mersh and Aueril* (*EL* 77) and *Ichot a burde in boure bryht* (*EL* 83).

[28] The third major feature in secular love poetry, the speaker's lament, usually with a description of his lovesickness, also has a close parallel in religious poetry; see below, pp. 55-56.

[29] John Stevens, "*Angelus ad Virginem*: The History of a Medieval Song," in *Medieval Studies for J.A.W. Bennett aetatis suae LXX*, ed. P. L. Heyworth (Oxford, 1981), pp. 297-328. The Latin and English texts as well as the music have also been critically examined and edited in Dobson, pp. 176-83, 261-68, and 303-5.

2. "Quomodo conciperem
que virum non cognovi?
Qualiter infringerem   15
quod firma mente vovi?"
"Spiritus Sancti gracia
perficiet hec omnia.
    Ne timeas,
      sed gaudeas,   20
    secura
quod castimonia
manebit in te pura,
Dei potentia."

3. Ad hec Virgo nobilis   25
respondens inquit ei:
"Ancilla sum humilis
omnipotentis Dei,
tibi, celesti nuncio,
tanti secreti conscio,   30
    consenciens
      et cupiens
    videre
factum quod audio.
Parata sum parere   35
Dei consilio."

4. Angelus disparuit
et statim puellaris
uterus intumuit
    vi partus salutaris,   40
quo circumdatur utero
novem mensium numero.
    Post exiit
    et iniit
    conflictum   45
affigens humero
crucem, qui dedit ictum
soli mortifero.

5. Eya, mater Domini,
que pacem reddidisti   50

angelis et homini,
    cum Christum genuisti.
Tuum exora filium,
ut se nobis propicium
    exibeat,   55
    et deleat
    peccata,
prestans auxilium
vita frui beata
post hoc exilium.   60
        Amen.[30]

1. The angel, entering stealthily into the Virgin's chamber, allayed her fear and said to her: "Hail, hail, queen of virgins. You will conceive the lord of heaven and earth, and without being defiled will give birth to the salvation of mankind, you who have become the door of heaven, the remedy for [all] sins."
2. "How should I conceive who do not know man? In what way should I break what I have vowed with firm intention?"—"The grace of the Holy Spirit will accomplish all this. Do not fear but rejoice, be assured that chastity will remain undefiled in you through the power of God."
3. In answer to this the noble Virgin said to him: "I am the humble handmaiden of Almighty God; I agree to your will, heavenly messenger, sharer of such a great mystery; and I wish to see happen what I hear. I am ready to obey God's plan."
4. The angel has disappeared, and at once the Virgin's womb began to swell with its salutary fruit. In her womb he lies enclosed for nine months. Then he came forth and entered the battle, laying the cross on his shoulder, which gave the blow to the only deathbringer.[31]
5. Rejoice, Mother of the Lord, who have brought back peace to angels and man when you bore Christ. Pray your son that he may show himself gracious to us and cancel our sins, giving us help to enjoy the blissful life after this exile. Amen.

The structure of *Angelus ad Virginem* is essentially narrative: a story is told, that of the Annunciation, which includes the dialogue between Gabriel and the Virgin and follows selectively the account of Luke 1.26-

---

[30] Text taken from *AH* 8:51.

[31] Or perhaps *hosti mortifero*, "the deadly enemy"; see Dobson, p. 182, on line 48.

38. But then stanza 4 reports the historical consequences of that event: Mary's pregnancy, Christ's birth and, in stark contrast, his Passion; and stanza 5 further points to its spiritual consequences for mankind: Mary has become the peace-bringer and is now petitioned to intercede before Christ so that we may gain his forgiveness and eternal life. In its broad lines the movement of *Angelus ad Virginem* is thus very reminiscent of *Ave praeclara*.[32] The song also shares the earlier sequence's tight verbal texture of great economy, and although its form is strophic, the verbal rhythms and end rhymes within its stanzas are delightfully light and varied. Following its biblical source, it places a noteworthy emphasis on Mary's perpetual virginity (lines 9, 15-16, 21-24) and, beyond that, stresses her role in salvation history, again with images and titles already familiar from *Ave praeclara* (lines 5, 11, 12, 50-52). But in contrast to the biblical account as well as the sequence, *Angelus ad Virginem* develops an atmosphere of great intimacy between Gabriel and the Virgin: the angel comes stealthily into her bedchamber (2); he tenderly allays her fear (*demulcens*, 3-4), even with a repeated greeting (4-5); and the two share a secret (29-30). There is something daring in this atmosphere of intimacy, expressed in verbal structures that are apparently not common formulas of medieval Mariolatry.[33] These expressions may indeed set a mind like hende Nicholas's—or for that matter, that of some modern directors of medieval Annunciation plays—on the wrong track.

The song was put into English at least twice, in different forms but both closely following the metrical shape of the music. We are here concerned with the earlier version made in the late thirteenth century:

    1. Gabriel, fram evene-king
       Sent to þe maide swete,
      Broute þire blisful tiding
      And faire he gan hire greten: 4
      "Heil be þu, ful of grace a-rith!
      For Godes sone, þis euene lith,
        For mannes louen
        Wile man bicomen,   8

---

[32] Perhaps one might even detect an allusive parallel to the references to Christ's Eucharistic sacrifice which are so prominent in *Ave praeclara*: compare the *propitiationis agnum* of the sequence with *propicium* here (st. 5), although the latter word is basically an adjective meaning "favorable, gracious."

[33] I would therefore give the author of *Angelus ad Virginem* more poetic credit than John Stevens allows him (pp. 298-99).

And taken
Fles of þe maiden brith,
Manken fre for to maken
Of senne and deules mith.''   12

2. Mildeliche im gan andsweren
    Þe milde maiden þanne:
  ''Wichewise sold Ichs beren
    Child with-huten manne?''   16
    Þangle seide, ''Ne dred te nout;
    Þurw þoligast sal ben iwrout
        Þis ilche þing,
        War-of tiding   20
        Ichs bringe.
    Al manken wrth ibout
    Þur þi swete chiltinge,
    And hut of pine ibrout.''   24

3. Wan þe maiden understud
    And þangles wordes herde,
  Mildeliche with milde mud
    To þangle hie andswerde: 28
    ''Hur Lordes þeumaiden iwis
    Ics am, þat her a-bouen is.
        Anenttis me,
        Fulfurthed be   32
        Þi sawe;
    Þat Ics, sithen his wil is,
    Maiden, withhuten lawe
    Of moder, haue þe blis.   36

4. Þangle wente a-wei mid þan,
    Al hut of hire sithte;
  Hire wombe arise gan
    Þurw þoligastes mithe.   40
    In hire was Crist biloken anon,
    Suth God, soth man ine fleas and bon,
        And of hir fleas
        Iboren was   44
        At time.

39

War-þurw us kam god won,
He bout us hut of pine
And let im for us slon.   48

5. Maiden, moder makeles,
   Of milche ful ibunden,
Bid for hus im þat þe ches
   At wam þu grace funde,   52
   Pat he forgiue hus senne and wrake,
   And clene of euri gelt us make,
      And eune blis,
      Wan hure time is   56
   To steruen,
Hus giue, for þine sake
Him so her for to seruen
Pat he us to him take.[34]   60

It will be seen at once that the English rendition has altogether lost the
daring, innovative features we noticed in the Latin song. These have
been replaced with pious platitudes at the level of the poem's content,
and with various padding devices on the level of its verbal structure. For
instance, in adapting the angel's greeting, the Latin song had changed
the biblical *Ave, Maria, gratia plena* significantly and in keeping with its
consistent emphasis; but the English simply reverts to the biblical text
(5). It does so similarly at the climax of Mary's acceptance: "Hur Lordes
þeumaiden, iwis, Ics am" (29-30; compare the biblical: *Ecce ancilla
Domini*) and thereby loses the wonderful wordplay of *parata sum parere*
(35). Moreover, the English poem is full of such pious commonplaces
as, "Manken fre for to maken / of senne and deules mith" (11-12) or
"And hut of pine ibrout" (24, repeated in 47) or "Suth God, soth man
ine fleas and bon" (42, with *fleas* repeated in the following line). When
stanza 2 of the Latin reports the dialogue between Mary and the angel, it
can do so without using introductory phrases because the opening words
of the two speeches echo the well-known speeches in their biblical form.
In contrast, the English poet had to be explicit in indicating who says
what (13-14 and 17). In this process of simplification, of reducing the
poem's texture to a lower level of originality and control, it is no wonder
that words and entire phrases should be repeated, that instances of word-
play should be totally lost, and that the stanzas should be full of words

[34] *IMEV* 888; *EL* 44.

and phrases that act merely as fillers: *iwis* (29), *mid þan* (37), *at time* (45), *al hut of hire sithte* (38), and others.

These tendencies of the English translation need not be judged entirely as a process of deterioration in poetic art. On the contrary, the English poem establishes its own tone and atmosphere, and what we have so far analyzed as failures could conceivably be part of poetic strategies which are simply different from what *Angelus ad Virginem* tried to achieve. I believe two major tendencies can be discerned. One is a shift in emphasis from Mary's virginity to Christ's redemption of mankind; the end of stanza 1 furnishes a good example of the difference, which in fact runs through all five stanzas. A second feature of the English version is the sweetening of its tone.[35] The Latin song is not entirely devoid of emotion and warmth, but this is expressed only in the last stanza and in a single word, *eya* (49).[36] In contrast, the English is filled with adjectives and adverbs which, without counterpart in either *Angelus ad Virginem* or Luke 1, emphasize the sweetness and light of the Annunciation: *swete* (2, 23), *blisful* (3), *faire* (4), *brith* (10), and especially *milde, mildeliche* (13, 14, 27 twice, cf. 50). But even if we grant the anonymous English poet a vision and purpose of his own, his verbal control and craftsmanship still occupy an inferior place. That the startling juxtaposition of joy and pain expressed in the Latin wordplay *post exiit / et iniit / conflictum* got lost in the translation may be blamed upon the differing structural resources of the English language or the translator's differing purpose; but to introduce at this point a line—"He bout us hut of pine" (47)—which had been used before in almost identical form (24) clearly indicates a limi-

---

[35] Such "sweetening" occurs also in Latin sequences and hymns from at least the late twelfth century on. A good example is *Mellis stilla, maris stella, / Cuius dulcor vincit mella* (*AH* 9:87, fourteenth century). The best known and most popular Latin hymn that shows this feature is *Dulcis Iesu memoria* (or *Iesu dulcis memoria*), apparently written in England toward the end of the twelfth century; see André Wilmart, *Le "Jubilus" dit de saint Bernard* (Rome, 1944). It draws heavily on Saint Bernard (cf. the name of Jesus is "honey in my mouth," etc.; *In Cantica*, sermo 15, 6; but see also Revelation 10.9-10). Another Englishman, Alexander Nequam, wrote a commentary on the Song of Songs which likewise has a good deal of such sweetness to it: "dum dulcissimam ymaginem Crucifixi . . . conspicio," etc.; see Richard W. Hunt, *The School and the Cloister. The Life and Writings of Alexander Nequam (1157-1217)*, ed. and rev. Margaret Gibson (Oxford, 1984), p. 107, and his comment on the difference of Alexander's tone from that of Anselm and later English commentators, ibid., n. 56.

[36] A collection of religious and secular passages which contain this interjection (of classical origin) can be found in Dimitri Scheludko, "Beiträge zur Entstehungsgeschichte der altprovenzalischen Lyrik. Die Volksliedertheorie," *ZFSL* 52 (1929), 230-32.

tation on the writer's part; and the same must be said of the somewhat clumsy repetitions of *milde*.

If, however, *Gabriel fram evene-king* is read on its own, without direct comparison with its Latin model, one must grant in all fairness that it does represent an achievement which is not altogether negligible, for the poet has managed to create a verbal structure that fits the given, rather complicated musical form extremely well and, at the same time, remains an *English* poem whose lines follow vernacular speech rhythms and whose vocabulary is native and simple. The following lines, for example,

> In hire was Crist biloken anon,
> Suth God, soth man ine fleas and bon,
> And of hir fleas
> Iboren was
> At time   (41-45)

are deceptive in their artlessness: they are simple, yet compact; there is nothing farfetched in their wording, and they move forward without awkward hesitation. Clearly, this is an achievement of its own, different from the intellectual vigor of *Angelus ad Virginem*, but also different from the artificial preciousness and declamatory stance of a later age, such as in:

> Myldyste of moode and mekyst of maydyns alle,
> O modyrs mercyfullyst, most chast þat euer was wyfe,
> Worschypfullyst of women þat were, 3et be, or schalle,
> Parfytst of a prayowre, þe best þat euyr bare lyue,
> Whose salutacyon was fyrste ioye of thy fyve,
> Whan Gabriel seyde, "Hayle, Mary, ful of grace,"—
> Wyth þe wheche worde þe Holy Gost as blyue
> Wythyn þi chest hath chosyn a ioyful place.[37]

The main poetic characteristics of *Gabriel fram evene-king* occur also in the slightly earlier English rendering of another Latin composition, *Stabat iuxta Christi crucem*.[38] This "regular sequence," too, was translated at least twice. Of the earlier translation the four opening stanzas have been lost. Their Latin counterpart introduces Christ's mother standing beneath his cross and seeing his wounds. The poem then continues:

[37] *RL XV* 31, st. 1.
[38] The Latin sequence has been discussed and critically edited by Dobson, pp. 146-48.

1. Os verendum litum sputis
   Et flagellis rupta cutis
     Et tot rivi sanguinis,
   Probra, risus et quae restant
   Orbitati tela praestant   5
     Et dolori virginis.

2. Tempus nacta trux natura
   Nunc exposcit sua jura,
     Nunc dolores acuit,
   Nunc extorquet cum usura   10
   Gemitus, quos paritura
     Naturae detinuit.

3. Nunc, nunc parit, nunc scit vere
   Quam maternum sit dolere,
     Quam amarum parere.   15
   Nunc se dolor orbitati
   Dilatus in partu nati
     Praesentat in funere.

4. Nunc fit mater, sed doloris,
   Servat tamen hic pudoris   20
     Virginalis gratiam,
   Nam pudicos gestus foris
   Non deflorat vis doloris
     Intus urens anxiam.

5. Triduanus ergo fletus   25
   Laeta demum est deletus
     Surgentis victoria.
   Laeta lucet spes dolenti
   Leto namque resurgenti
     Conresurgunt omnia.   30

6. Christi novus hic natalis
   Formam partus virginalis
     Clauso servat tumulo,
   Hinc processit, hinc surrexit,
   Hinc et inde Christus exit   35
     Intacto signaculo.

[39] Text reproduced from *AH* 8:58.

43

7. Eja mater, eja laeta,
   Fletus tui nox expleta
      Lucescit in gaudium.
   Nostrae quoque laetum mane   40
   Nocti plus quam triduanae
      Tuum redde filium.[39]

(Translation of the Latin)

1. His venerable face smeared with spittle, and the skin cut by the scourges, and so many streams of blood. Reproaches, laughter, and the rest furnish the weapons to [increase] the Virgin's bereavement and pain.

2. Grim nature, which has reached its time, now demands its right, now sharpens her pains, now wrings from her with interest the sighs that she withheld from nature when she gave birth.

3. Now, now she is giving birth, now she knows truly how painful it is to be a mother, how bitter to give birth; now, as she has become bereft, the pain that had been deferred at the birth of her child presents itself in his death.

4. Now she becomes a mother, but of sorrow; yet here she keeps the beauty of her maidenly modesty; for the power of her pain, while it burns her in her distress within, does not deflower her modest features without.

5. Thus her three days' weeping is finally quenched by the joyful victory of her rising [son]. Joyful hope shines on her in her suffering, for all things rise together with him who is rising from death.

6. This new birth of Christ keeps the form of her virgin birth, since the tomb remained closed. From here he came forth, from here he has risen, from here and from there Christ has come forth with the seal left untouched.

7. O mother, o happy one, the night of your weeping which has finished dawns into joy. Bring your son as the happy morning also to our night, which is longer than three days.

1. Þat leueli leor wid spald ischent,   spittle
   Þat feire fel wid scurges rend—   skin
      Þe blod out stremed oueral.
   Skoarn, upbraid, and schome speche,
   Al hit was to sorhes eche—   5   increase
      I woa þu was biluken al.

2. I þat blisful bearnes buirde   birth
   Wrong wes wroht to wommone wirde,   destiny
     Ah kuinde craued nou þe riht.
   Þenne þu loch, ah nou þu wep,   10
   Þi wa wes waken þat tenne slep—
     Childing-pine haues te nou picht.   pierced

3. Nou þu moostes, lauedi, lere
   Wmmone wo, þat barnes bere,
     Þa bitter and ta bale þrehes;   15   throes
   For in his dead þe wo þu ȝulde
   In childing þat tu þole schulde
     Þurd modres kuindeliche lahes.   laws

4. Ah, lauedi, þah þu wonges wete,
   Þah þe were wo at unimete,   20
     Þine loates weren lasteles;   guile; blameless
   Þi wep ne wemmede noht þin heau   blemished; complexion
   Þat made þi leor ful louk and lew—   cheek; feeble; pale
     Swa sari wmmon neuer neas.

5. Ah, þi kare was ouer-comen,   25
   Þe þridde dai þi ioie comen,
     Ded and deuel driuen doun
   Þwen þi sone risen wes
   To þine wele and ure peas—
     Blisse he brocte in icha toun.   30

6. Þi luue sone uprisinge
   Was selli liik to his birdinge—
     Bi-twene twa his litel schead—   is; distinction
   For, so gleam glidis þurt þe glas,
   Of þi bodi born he was,   35
     And þurt þe hoale þurch he gload.[40]   coffin?

7. Milde moder, maiden oa,   always
   Of al þi kare come þou þoa
     Þwen þi sone rise wes.
   Leuedi, bring us out of wa,   40

[40] This stanza expresses the common notion that just as Christ was born without physical injury to his mother, so he rose out of his tomb without breaking it.

Of sinne, of sorhe, of sich al-swoa,
To blisse þat his endeles.
Amen.[41]

This English rendering represents a remarkable artistic achievement. Like *Gabriel fram evene-king* it uses a heavily native vocabulary, full of such Old English words as *leor, fel, wirde, childing,* or *schead* that were to disappear before long. With them come such popular expressions or idioms as *in icha toun* (30). Yet despite this simple diction the verbal texture of at least some of its stanzas is considerably more carefully wrought than that of *Gabriel fram evene-king* and parallels, occasionally even surpasses, that of its Latin model. Stanza 1, for example, reveals a surprising combination of close translation and free rendering with the creation of different poetic effects, such as the alliteration in lines 1, 2, and 4, or the decorative adjectives *leueli* and *feire*. While lines 1 and 2 have lost the syntactic chiasmus of the Latin (*os . . . sputis / flagellis . . . cutis*), they have gained a syntactic parallelism which, with its heavy tread, is perhaps even more effective in appealing to the hearer's emotion than is the Latin model. This parallelism continues into line 3, which then changes the somewhat cold substantive structure of the Latin into a much more powerful verb structure whose oppressiveness is further increased by its long and dark vowel sounds. The following line replaces the general *quae restant* with the particular *schome speche*, and the two final lines, by refusing to follow the complicated image of their model, manage to render its difficult construction with ease and thus close the stanza satisfactorily.

Similar comments can be made about other stanzas and lines of this poem. It is evident that the English poet worked hard and successfully at imitating the verbal and syntactic artistry of his source with the linguistic resources of his own language, and he did so without falling into slavish dependency. Thus, the anaphora with *nunc* in stanza 2 is replaced by the antithesis of *Þenne—nou* in line 10, or the antithetical juxtaposition *fletus Laeta* (lines 25-26) is imitated in the syntactic parallelism of *þi kare—þi ioie*. The general antithesis of the poem between Good-Friday suffering and Easter joy, which is in Latin somewhat feebly introduced by *ergo,* is actually heightened in English with the initial *Ah* of line 25. Though the wordplay of *laeta—leto* in stanza 5 is lost, the English poem has plenty of verbal decoration of its own.

[41] *IMEV* *52. Text taken from *EL* 4.

There are, however, several spots where the English poet was clearly incapable of following his model. Stanza 4 is a good case in point. After developing the notion that in her suffering beneath the cross Mary paid nature that due (i.e., the pangs of childbirth) from which she had been exempted at the nativity of her son (sts. 2-3),[42] in stanza 4 the sequence continues this thought by announcing Mary's new title, *mater doloris*, and actually gives the concept a twist by stating that Mary's newly acquired motherhood of sorrow in no way destroyed her pristine virginity. This notion is of course not limited to our sequence and has been the subject for artistic expression from the hands of Michelangelo and many others. What is so amazing about the Latin sequence is its use of such boldly specific terms as *deflorare* and *urens*. The English here simply falls flat; it does translate the thought, in lines 19-21, but then tries to explain it in prosaic terms (22) and ends up with a lame generality (24) that actually misses the point of the stanza.

The same observation must be made about the poem's last stanza. The Latin sequence here for the first time addresses Mary directly, and it ends, in its final sentence, with a petition. In doing so, it plays delightfully with the antitheses of sorrow vs. joy, of night vs. day, and of Mary's joy vs. ours. The English rendering does exactly the same in its substance: it speaks of Mary's joy and petitions her for her help. But what a difference in terms of imagery and diction: the verbal play is lost, the image of night vs. day is abandoned, and the final prayer, which in Latin refers specifically to the experience of Easter morning, loses this strong coherence with the preceding stanzas altogether by dissolving into three lines of pious platitudes. Instead of undergoing a final poetic upswing as the Latin sequence does, the English rendering ends in rhetorical flatness.

It is worth noting that the thought as well as the diction of that final sentence: "bring us out of wa, / Of sinne, of sorh, of sich alswoa, / To blisse þat his endeles," are strongly reminiscent of medieval preaching. A favorite way to end a sermon was by making a reference to heaven and its future joys, and then adding: "Vn-to þe wiche blis brynge vs he þat. . . ."[43] While this form of closure does not necessarily prove the influ-

---

[42] While the Latin creates a certain tension between these two stanzas, in that 6 poses, as it were, a riddle that is solved in 7, the English loses that tension by making things clear already in st. 6.

[43] Woodburn O. Ross (ed.), *Middle English Sermons*, EETS 209 (London, 1940), 206/ 28. The sermon will be discussed in the following chapter.

ence of preaching on this particular poem, it is unmistakable that in finishing his stanza the poet reached for verbal material that was nearest at hand, and that happened to be the closing formula common in sermons.

In summary, then, this early rendering of *Stabat iuxta Christi crucem* is characterized by a good deal of verbal skill and care, aimed at re-creating in English some of the rhetorical beauty of its model. At the same time, its poet could or would not follow the most daring flights of thought, wordplay, and imagery of the Latin. In the English there is a tendency to simplify and to explain what is most sophisticated in its source. To this we must add another, very different tendency. The art of *Stabat iuxta Christi crucem*—and beyond it that of the best medieval Latin hymns and sequences, as we have seen—is predominantly intellectual, even cerebral. But in the English rendering, as well as in other English poems that derive from the Latin hymn tradition, the basic tendency is rather an appeal to the audience's emotions. In discussing *Gabriel fram evene-king* I spoke of a sweetening of its tone. The rendering of *Stabat iuxta Christi crucem* shows a different way to heighten the poem's emotional appeal. Whereas the Latin sequence postpones its direct address of the Virgin until the last stanza (*Eja mater . . . tui*), the English addresses her from the very beginning on (at least as the text has been preserved): "'i woa þu was biluken al'" (line 6). In fact, in its English rendition the Latin sequence has become an address of the Sorrowful Mother. As a result, the English poem has gained an aura of intimacy, sympathy, and compassion between Mary and the poem's speaker which parallels the great intimacy between Mary and Gabriel that we noticed in *Gabriel fram evene-king*.[44]

This tendency to establish an intimate emotional relationship between two characters finds its fullest realization in several dialogue lyrics, a genre that may well have been created by English poets. A fine example is the hymn *Stond wel, moder, vnder rode*, which has been preserved in six codices from ca. 1270 on and is in two cases accompanied by music.[45] The text is not closely derived from any known Latin or French model.[46] Nonetheless, it stands in the tradition of poems that deal with

[44] See also the analysis given by Woolf, p. 244.

[45] *IMEV* 3211, fully discussed by Dobson, pp. 152-60.

[46] The music of *Stond wel*, however, was closely adapted from *Stabat iuxta Christi crucem*, and it may well be that the sequence form of the latter, in which the two halves of each stanza were set to the same tune which changed from stanza to stanza, served as the catalyst to create the regular dialogue of *Stond wel*, as is suggested by Dobson, p. 154.

Mary's suffering beneath the cross and utilizes several topoi of this tradition. Like *Stabat iuxta Christi crucem*, for example, it gives a list of Christ's wounds and sufferings as seen by his mother; the sword of pain predicted by Simeon is mentioned;[47] Mary's suffering is declared to be more painful to Christ than his own wounds; her grief beneath the cross makes Mary fully a mother, but without loss of virginity; and the poem ends with the joy of Easter. In addition, *Stond wel, moder* even uses certain rhyme-words that seem to have become standard ingredients in English poems on this theme, especially *swungen* / *stungen* (lines 22-23).[48] But this traditional material is here used to create a dialogue: in alternating stanza halves Christ addresses his mother from the cross in an attempt to console her, and Mary replies in lament, questioning the possibility of consolation. In discussing the background of this dialogue, Carleton Brown pointed to several Latin prose meditations on Christ's Passion variously attributed to Anselm or Bernard of Clairvaux.[49] In one, Christ speaks at some length to Mary, in another, "Anselm" asks the Virgin about details of the Passion and "Mary" gives the desired account, including occasional reports of what Christ or other people had said to her. In none of these texts, however, is there any real *dialogue*, any sustained exchange of speeches between Christ and the Virgin. The English poem *Stond wel, moder* not only offers such an exchange of speeches but, in addition, creates an inner tension between the two speakers. While Christ tries to console his mother, the latter seemingly fails to understand the necessity for his suffering. Their dialogue is consistently built upon a pattern of opposition between "You should" and "How can I?" Thus the poem begins:

> "Stond wel, moder, vnder rode,
> Bihold þi child wyth glade mode,
>   Blyþe moder mittu ben."
> "Svne, quu may bliþe stonden?   4   who

---

[47] Cf. Luke 2.35. In *Stabat* it is only alluded to (*tela*), lines 4-6 of the Latin text printed above, but it is explicitly mentioned for example in *Planctus ante nescia* (*AH* 20:199, st. 6; Dobson, pp. 116-20).

[48] *Þe milde lomb*, *EL* 45, lines 17-18; and the very popular *Quanne Hic se on rode* (*IMEV* 3964-66), *EL* 34-37.

[49] Brown, *EL*, p. 204. The popularity of the two treatises and their vernacular derivatives are briefly discussed in Woolf, pp. 247-48. Another possible literary model for the dialogue form is the Latin sequence *Qui per viam pergitis*, discussed by Karl Young, *The Drama of the Medieval Church* (Oxford, 1933), 1:500-503.

Hi se þin feet, Hi se þin honden,
Nayled to þe harde tre.''[50]

The dramatic opposition that exists between lines 3 and 4 runs through-
out the poem. One may well ask whether there is a resolution to this ten-
sion or antithesis between the two speakers, a note of understanding or
resignation on Mary's part, as Christian theology and meditation would
require. One may find such a note in line 52: ''Sune, Y wyle wi' the fun-
den'' (''Son, I will go with thee''); but if this line is intended to express
acceptance and resignation, that effect is immediately canceled by the
next two lines, in which Mary reverts to her earlier complaint at the
greatness of her suffering, so that her desire to go with Christ is really no
more than a restatement of her earlier request, ''Let me deyn þe bi-
foren'' (36), a rhetorical commonplace to express great suffering. It is
true that in the full versions of the poem the dialogue is followed by a
narrative stanza speaking of Mary's Easter joy. But within the dialogue
proper it is not at all clear whether or not Mary comes to understand and
accept the need for her son's death.

However this may be, the significant feature of *Stond wel, moder* is
that in it an English poet has utilized the dialogue form in lyric poetry in
order to create two different personae whose different characters he ex-
plores as well as the intellectual and emotional tension between them.
The use of the dialogue form for such a purpose is not unique in medieval
lyric poetry,[51] but it seems to have held a special place in the vernacular
religious lyric of medieval England. There are some external indications
that this utilization of the dialogue form was the work of preachers or was
at least particularly dear to them. *Stond wel, moder* has been preserved,
whole or in part, in six manuscripts. Two of them are larger anthologies
that are famous for their gathering together a number of English poems
with French and Latin ones; their provenance, early association, and pur-
poses are matters of great controversy.[52] A third codex (Royal 12.E.i) is
a theological miscellany made up of originally separate booklets, which

[50] *EL* 49B.

[51] *Iam dulcis amica venito* of the Cambridge Songs is one well-known example, Dietmar
von Eist's *Uf der linden obene* is another. For recent comments on the *Wechsel* as an ''in-
digenous type'' of German poetry, see Olive Sayce, *The Medieval German Lyric 1150-
1300. The Development of Its Themes and Forms in Their European Context* (Oxford,
1982), p. 23.

[52] Bodleian Library, MS. Digby 86, and British Library, MS. Harley 2253; on their
character, see above, pp. 6-8.

reveals little about the poem's function and context. In Cambridge, St. John's College MS. 111, however, *Stond wel, moder* appears with the Latin text and the music of *Stabat iuxta Christi crucem* at the end of a variety of theological extracts and notes which may have been gathered for use in preaching. Dublin, Trinity College MS. 301, of the late thirteenth century, is another theological miscellany with sermons (fols. 30-100), though here the text of *Stond wel, moder* has no close internal relation to the surrounding context—it may simply have been entered to fill a blank page. In contrast, the sixth manuscript (Royal 8.F.ii) shows positively that, and how, the poem was used by preachers. Here the opening stanza is cited within a Latin sermon that deals with Mary's joys and sorrows.[53] "When the Blessed Virgin stood by the cross," the preacher exclaims, "and saw her beloved only son nailed to the wood and between two thieves in front of such a crowd, no one should doubt that she suffered the greatest pain in seeing him." Then he cites Luke 2.35, together with Origen's exegesis of the verse, and continues:

Unde secundum sanctos dolor Beate Virginis in morte filii excellebat [MS. excellabat] dolorem cuiuscumque martyris. Unde cum in quodam cantu dicatur in persona filii ad Beatam Virginem sic:
>Stond wel, moder, under rode,
>Byholt þy sone wyth glade mode,
>>Blize moder miȝt tu ben,

respondetur sic in persona matris:
>Sone, hou may Hi bliþe stonde,
>I se þi fet, I se þi honde
>>Nayled to þat harde tre,

quasi diceret: non possum esse leta. Set post istum dolorem secutum est gaudium resurreccionis. Unde dicitur:
>Gaude, quia tui nati,
>Quem dolebas mortem pati,
>>Fulget resurreccio.

(Whence according to the saints the Blessed Virgin's grief at the death of her son surpassed that of any martyr. Therefore, when in a certain song it is said, in the person of her son speaking to the Blessed Virgin: "Stond . . . ," the response is given in the person of his mother: "Sone . . . ," as if she were saying, I cannot be joyful. But after this grief followed the joy of his resurrection. Whence it is said: "Rejoice,

[53] Apparently the beginning of the sermon stood on fol. 179v and has been cut off.

for the resurrection of your son, for whom you grieved when he suffered death, now comes in splendor.'')[54]

The passage is instructive on several accounts. Apart from giving us a first example of the form in which English lyrics appear in Latin sermons, it throws some light on the form and popularity of the English poem. Following the pattern of his sermon, the preacher here opposes Mary's joy at the Resurrection to her sorrow beneath the cross. He could have easily quoted in English lines 55-57 of *Stond wel, moder*: ''When he ros, þan fel þi sorwe . . .''; but instead he cites a half-stanza from a *Latin* hymn on the joys of Mary.[55] This suggests that at least this preacher knew only the dialogue part of *Stond wel, moder* but not the two final narrative stanzas, which do not occur in all manuscripts. More importantly, this passage is one indication among many that it was specifically preachers who took a deep interest in the dialogue between Christ and Mary (or other personages) at the crucifixion. Indeed, such a dialogue formed a popular topos of preaching, particularly in sermons on the Passion, as we shall discover in a fourteenth-century collection of preaching verses (ch. 5). Dialogues between Christ and Mary hold of course also a particular dramatic potential and may, as has been suggested, have been the specific link between medieval preaching and play-acting. Although such a connection is quite plausible, it must be said that concrete evidence for it comes primarily from Italy,[56] and even there the genetic relation between preaching and the early drama seems not to be beyond critical question.[57]

In commenting on *Stond wel, moder* I pointed to its failure to bring the dialogue and the tension between its speakers to a resolution. The speeches do not really go anywhere; they are somewhat repetitious and

[54] British Library, MS. Royal 8.F.ii, fol. 180; partially printed by Brown, *EL*, p. 204. The hand may be dated to ca. 1300 or a little earlier. The quoted excerpt is followed by another of Mary's sorrows.

[55] The quoted half-stanza occurs (with variants for *dolebas*) in several sequences on the joys of Mary, all beginning *Gaude Virgo, Mater Christi*. See *AH* 31:172, 176, 188.

[56] See especially Vincenzo De Bartholomaeis, *Origini della poesia drammatica italiana*, second edition (Torino, 1952), pp. 326-31, summarizing and restating his views of the ''sermoni semidrammatici.''

[57] For example, Carlo Delcorno writes: ''Purtroppo i rapporti tra pulpito e scena restano ancora vaghi e incerti, nonostante gli studi del D'Ancona e del De Bartholomaeis'' in ''*Ars praedicandi* e *Ars memorativa* nell' esperienza di san Bernardino da Siena,'' *Bullettino Abbruzzese di storia patria* 70 (1980), 91, repeated in ''L'*ars praedicandi* di Bernardino da Siena,'' *Lettere italiane* 4 (1980), 449.

could easily be expanded into further stanzas. One might object that I am expecting too much from what is primarily a musical composition and a text that seeks, above all, to elicit emotions of sorrow and compassion. To this I would reply that the Latin sequences in whose wake the English poem appears show no such lack of control. And further, the same artistic shortcoming appears in many other English lyrics of the same period. A good example is *I-blessed beo þu, lauedi, ful of houene blisse*.[58] It is a prayer to Mary for her intercession, spoken by a penitent persona who acknowledges his sinfulness and asks for grace. This theme appears in the first stanza, and it runs without much alteration through the entire poem. Apart from changing the direct address from Mary to Christ in the last stanza, there is no progression, no structure that would guide the poem's thought. The poem says the same thing over and over: it could end after one or two stanzas or conversely continue in the same vein for several pages. In fact, the two versions in which the poem has been preserved show major differences in the text of the stanzas they contain as well as in their order. Carleton Brown suggested that this argues for oral transmission of the poem.[59] I would add that it also indicates strongly that in this kind of composition the number and sequence of stanzas do not really matter.

This is what I would call the "expandable lyric," whose structural features are confined to the repetition of a chosen stanza form.[60] The corpus of early English religious lyrics contains a number of such poems; beside *I-blessed beo þu* and similar "penitential lyrics"[61] stand other Marian hymns, such as *For on þat is so feir and brist*,[62] and especially

---

[58] *IMEV* 1407; *EL* 55. [59] *EL*, pp. 210-11.

[60] It is most likely that the music which accompanied sequences and hymns exerted a strong control over the form of the text. As noted earlier, in sequences the melody changes with each pair of versicles, whereas in (genuine) hymns each stanza is sung to the same melody. Obviously, the latter genre easily allowed additions and insertions of new stanzas to the original composition. A beautiful illustration can be found in *Dulcis Iesu memoria*. Its original form, as reconstructed by André Wilmart (op. cit.), had 42 stanzas of the same metrical form, and in one early manuscript the *jubilus* is accompanied by music in sequence form. Whether or not one agrees with Wilmart and Heinrich Lausberg (*Hymnologische und hagiographische Studien. I. Der Hymnus "Jesu dulcis memoria"* [Munich, 1967]) on their view that the original *Dulcis Iesu memoria* has a clear, controlled structure, the text of the poem seems quickly to have become separated from the music and in the course of its immense popularity suffered all kinds of accretions (see Lausberg, p. 57) which certainly destroyed that original structure and left it an "expandable lyric."

[61] For example, *Iesu for þi muchele miht* (*IMEV* 1705; *EL* 84).

[62] *IMEV* 2645; *EL* 17.

the English versions of *Dulcis Iesu memoria*.[63] One of them, *Swete Ihesu, king of blysse*, for instance, consists of what later spiritual writers would call pious ejaculations of the following type:

> Suete Ihesu, myn huerte gleem,
> Bryhtore þen þe sonne beem,
> Ybore þou were in Bedleheem—
> Þou make me here þi suete dreem![64]   music

One might detect in the poem a progression of references to the Nativity (st. 4), Passion (8), and future glory (12), but this forms the frailest of threads to string a series of petitions on.

What these expandable lyrics have in common besides their formlessness is their concentration on the speaking persona. They are not concerned with events of salvation history, whether it is Christ's Passion or Mary's joys or her intercession, but instead focus on a penitent "I" who—it is not unfair to say—wallows in generalities. In his study of Notker, Wolfram von den Steinen wrote that the earlier medieval sequence "blossomed out of blissful self-forgetfulness. It had to wilt as soon as people could only think of saving their dear little soul."[65] The expandable lyric furnishes a precise illustration of this very loss of intellectual substance and artistic form once the medieval Latin sequence ceased to exert its formative influence.

This, however, does not mean that an English lyric *had* to wander helplessly once it left the guiding hand of Latin hymns and sequences. A good poet could indeed work the best of this and other traditions into a new work of great verbal beauty. Such is the case with the following poem:

> 1. Nv Yh she blostme sprynge,
>   Hic herde a fuheles song.
>   A swete longinge
>   Myn herte þureþhut sprong,   4
>   Þat is of luue newe,
>   Þat is so swete and trewe
>   Hyt gladiet al my song;
>   Hic wot mid ywisse   8

---

[63] See Woolf, pp. 173-75.
[64] *IMEV* 3236; *RL XIV* 7, st. 4.
[65] *Notker der Dichter und seine geistige Welt* (Bern, 1948), 1:88-89.

My lyf an heke my blysse
Is al þar-hon ylong.

2. Of Iesu Crist Hi synge,
Þat is so fayr and fre,   12
Swetest of alle þynge;
Hys oþwe Hic oʒe wel boe,
Wl fer he me soþte,
Myd hard he me boþte   16
Wyþ wnde to and þree,
Wel sore he was yswnge
And for me myd spere istunge,
Ynayled to þe tree.   20

3. Wan Hic my-self stond
And myd herte ysee,
Yþerled fetd and onde
Wyt grete neyles þree—   24
Blody was hys eved,
Of hym nas novt byleved
Þet of pyne were vre—
Wel oþte myn herte,   28
Al for hys lvue smerte,
Syc and sory be.

4. Away! þat Hy ne can
To hym tvrne al my þovt   32
And makien hym my lefman
Þat þvs me haued hy-bovt—
Wyt pine and sorewhe longe,
Wyt wnde depe and stronge—   36
Of luue ne can Hy novt.
Hys blod fel to þe grvnde
Hut of ys swete wnde,
Þat of pyne hvs hauet hy-brovt.   40

5. Iesu, lefman suete,
Þv hyef me strenghte and myþt   *give*
Longinge sore and ofte
To servi þe aryþt,   44
And lene pine drye   *grant*

Al for þe swete Marie,
Þat art so fayr and bryþt.

. . . .

6. Iesu, lefman swete,
   Ih sende þe þis songe   52
   And wel ofte Ih þe grete
   And bydde þe among;
   Hyf me sone lete,
   And myne sennes bete   56
   Þat Ih haue do þe wrong,
   At myne lyues hende
   Wan Ih shal henne wende,
   Iesu, me hvnder-fonge! Amen.[66]

This poem draws on a variety of traditions. Stanzas 2-4 utilize verbal
material that is almost formulaic in poems on Christ's Passion. There is,
for instance, the rhyme *yswnge* / *istunge* (18-19) which we have found
in English lyrics derived from *Stabat iuxta Christi crucem*, or the phrase
"Wyþ wnde to and þree" (17) which occurs in other Passion lyrics.[67]
Like the lyrics discussed earlier, *Nv Yh she* combines a light rhythm and
intricate metrical pattern with a very simple and entirely Anglo-Saxon
vocabulary. It also shows the sweetening of tone found in *Gabriel fram
evene-king* and other poems: in its six stanzas, the word *swete* occurs six
times.

   In addition to these elements, however, this poem presents several fea-
tures not yet encountered in the course of our discussion. Foremost is the
nature introduction of stanza 1. To create a seasonal image, a short de-
scriptive statement about characteristic features of spring or winter, and
then to turn from it to the speaker and his emotions, was one of the most
common ways to begin a medieval poem. The device existed long before
the flourishing of medieval European song, and it can be found also in
some Ambrosian hymns.[68] But its great vogue during the later Middle

---

[66] *IMEV* 3963. The poem has been preserved in two manuscripts, which show some ma-
jor variations in the number and order of the stanzas; see Brown, *EL*, pp. 215-16. I follow
the earlier MS. Royal 2.F.viii, of the late thirteenth century, whose stanza arrangement is
much superior, as edited in *EL* 63.

[67] In *EL* 15, line 20; *EL* 54, line 36; and *RL XIV* 52, line 4.

[68] Of the many studies of the nature introduction two may be mentioned: Rosemond
Tuve, *Seasons and Months: Studies in a Tradition of Middle English Poetry* (Paris, 1933);
Roger Dragonetti, *La Technique poétique des trouvères dans la chanson courtoise*
(Bruges, 1960), pp. 163-93.

Ages seems to be due to the eager use made of it in secular love songs. Medieval French religious lyrics, which do not appear to rank high in formal and rhetorical inventiveness,[69] drew very heavily on secular poetry for nature introductions and similar devices (such as the *pastourelle* opening). In English, several very early lyrics are nothing but nature introductions without sequels: *Mirie it is while sumer ilast, Foweles in þe frith*, and what may well be the earliest Middle English religious lyric that has been preserved:

> Nou goth sonne vnder wod,—
> Me reweth, Marie, þi faire rode.
> Nou goþ sonne vnder tre,—
> Me reweþ, Marie, þi sone and þe.[70]

In the almost classical brevity of a couplet, here stated twice, this poem furnishes a perfect paradigm of the nature introduction: an objective picture from nature (sunset) is followed by a statement about the emotional state of the speaker (*me reweth*).

In contrast to *Nou goth sonne*, the opening stanza of *Nv Yh she* has a decided ring of the secular love song about it, with its evocation of opening blossoms, bird song, and love-longing.[71] Such a secular nature introduction was evidently a great favorite not only with religious poets but also with preachers. A fourteenth-century Latin sermon contains a lengthy story about an unnamed Cistercian abbot who led a very dissolute and irreligious life and fell into a grave sickness that rendered him immobile. After fourteen years he got better but soon returned to his former sins and "gave himself so much to gluttony, lechery, and worldly pomp that whores and ribalds made songs [*cantilenas*] about his indecent life." He could not bear to speak or to hear of God; yet when the name of the Blessed Virgin was mentioned, "he would lift his eyes with a sigh and raise his hands without saying any words." Then he fell gravely ill again and had a vision. "It seemed to him that he was in a field, where he saw Jesus Christ sitting in a high seat, from whose wounds streams of blood were flowing that were as fresh as on the day he was crucified. Near him to the right were the Blessed Virgin and angels and clerics; but to his left, devils and other condemned men. And below him he saw the

<hr>

[69] Pierre Bec, *La Lyrique française au moyen-âge (XIIe-XIIIe siècles)*, vol. 1: *Etudes* (Paris, 1977), pp. 142-43.

[70] Respectively: *IMEV* 2163, 864, and 2320. Text taken from *EL* 1.

[71] For parallels, see *EL* 62 (*IMEV* 360), 77 (*IMEV* 515), 81 (*IMEV* 1861), 82 (*IMEV* 1504), 86 (*IMEV* 4037).

deepest hell.'' The terrified abbot's prayer for a drop of mercy is rejected, since the time for mercy has passed. Then he turns to Mary and asks for her intercession, reminding her of the little signs of his love for her he had given and expressing profound grief at his sins. Christ first refuses her prayer, since the time for mercy is gone. But when Mary continues to pray, alleging that the blood Christ shed for sinners had originally been hers, Christ yields and allows the abbot three days of respite, after which he will live eternally with Mary. The story then concludes:

> But the abbot, after he had come to his senses and reported what had been done for him by Mary, was taken from this light after three days and, through the merits of the Blessed Virgin, was granted eternal light. Therefore, this abbot could have spoken that English [saying or song], as it were in the person of mankind:
>
> *þe dew of Aueril*—that is, the grace and goodness of the Holy Spirit;
> *Hauetȝ y-maked þe grene lef to sprynge*—that is, the Blessed Virgin;
> *My sorow is gon*—that is, punishment, through [her] merits;
> *Mi ioye is comen*—that is, the blissful life, through the Son of God;
> *Ich herde a foul synge*—that is, an angel, namely ''Ave Maria.''[72]

These English lines, which echo the sentiment, imagery, and some of the actual wording of *Nv Yh she*, are clearly a non-religious nature introduction which the preacher of this sermon has appropriated for his conversion story and provided with a brief moralizing commentary.

The nature introduction is not the only innovative feature that in *Nv Yh she* is combined with elements stemming from the medieval hymn tradition. With it goes the *envoi*, the closing device in which the poet sends his beloved (''lefman swete'') his poem (''Ih sende þe þis songe'') and his greetings (''Ih þe grete'') and prays for the good graces and mercy of his beloved (''and bydde þe,'' all in st. 6). The *envoi* was a standard device in Provencal *canzos* and probably spread from there to other European literatures.[73] Yet another and very different structural device ap-

---

[72] ''Abbas vero ad se rediens que gesta fuerant sibi per Mariam referens ab hac luce subtractus est post triduum, lucem adeptus meritis Beate Virginis sempiternam. Unde poterat abbas ille quasi in persona humani generis dicere illud Anglicum: þe dew of Aueril, idest gracia et bonitas Spiritus Sancti; / hauetȝ y-maked þe grene lef to sprynge, idest Beatam Virginem; / my sorow is gon, idest pena pro meritis, / mi ioye is comen, scilicet per Dei Filium vita beata; / Ich herde a foul synge, idest angelum, scilicet Ave Maria.'' Worcester Cathedral MS. F.126, fol. 248. This passage will be further discussed in ch. 7.

[73] On the *envoi* (*reprise, tornada*) as a formal element and motif in the medieval love

pears in stanza 3 of *Nv Yh she*, the "when-then" formula, which seems to have had native origins.[74]

But of much greater interest is the concentration on the speaking "I," the personal voice that pervades this poem from beginning to end. The first person singular pronoun forms the second word of the lyric—where it actually creeps into and refocuses the nature image, which by tradition should be objective, detached from the speaker—and it runs through the text to the second word from the end. It was just such concentration on the speaker that led to formlessness in *I-blessed beo þu, lauedi* and other expandable lyrics. Not so here. While *Nv Yh she* steadfastly retains this, as it were, center of consciousness, it yet progresses through a variety of emotions and stages to a clear goal, the final prayer for eternal bliss. Stanza 1 introduces the speaker's joy and love; we learn of his emotion, but its object is left undetermined, and in fact the spring opening may be calculated to raise a momentary false expectation in the song's listeners. Stanza 2, however, clarifies the object and cause of the speaker's emotion, which is Christ and particularly Christ's redemptive suffering. But the visualization of Christ's Passion suggests to the reflecting speaker that he ought to feel sorrow and pity (st. 3); and realizing his shortcoming, his incapacity to respond to Christ's great love with equal intensity, he is led to lament his insufficiency (st. 4). Yet sadness gives way to confident prayer for the strength to love and live well and for the final union with his beloved (sts. 5-6). By thus combining the speaker's consciousness ("I see, I heard, I know," and so forth) with an objectification of his emotion in its external causes (the crucifixion), and by firmly controlling the poem's movement of thought, this poem avoids altogether the repetitions and the formlessness we noted in other "penitential" lyrics. Instead, it achieves a masterful poetic exploration of different facets of religious emotion and a progressive movement through them, which is intense yet linguistically so simple.

In the early English religious lyrics we have examined, much of the intellectual vigor and verbal sophistication of medieval Latin sequences and hymns, such as *Ave praeclara*, *Angelus ad Virginem*, and *Stabat mater*, were lost in the process of translation. Yet such losses in verbal art-

---

chanson, see Dragonetti, *Technique poétique*, pp. 304-17. Some references to similar dedicatory passages in medieval Latin epistolary poetry are given by Dimitri Scheludko, "Beiträge zur Entstehungsgeschichte der altprovenzalischen Lyrik," *Archivum Romanicum* 15 (1931), 161-62.

[74] This structural formula is further discussed below, ch. 6, pp. 198-200.

istry, poetic wit, and structural control were—at least partially—compensated by gains in simplicity and the creation of a more intimate tone with the help of an everyday vocabulary and the dialogue form. In *Nv Yh she*, these gains are increased by the use of several formal elements from different poetic traditions and by a firmly controlled concentration on the speaking "I." The poem was evidently created without a direct Latin model, but it achieves an artistic expression of religious emotion which, while different in kind, closely approaches that of *Ave praeclara* in degree.

3

The Sermon

as an Art

Form

The rhetorical and literary context in which preachers' verses were used and for which they were created is the peculiar form of sermon which, throughout Western Europe, came into being in the late twelfth and early thirteenth century.[1] It is now known by various names, none of which is, for different reasons, wholly satisfactory. The label "modern sermon" echoes medieval usage itself, yet medieval writers who employed it drew the line between old and modern at different points.[2] The term "university sermon" reflects the historical fact that the new type of preaching apparently originated at the major universities, Paris and Oxford,[3] where masters used it and students learned its features; but in due course of time "university sermons" were preached elsewhere as well and did not remain restricted to the milieu indicated by the name. Another term, "thematic sermon," relies on the distinctive

---

[1] There is no modern comprehensive and authoritative historical study of the scholastic sermon, or for that matter of preaching in the Middle Ages. Short accounts of the scholastic sermon appear in James J. Murphy, *Rhetoric in the Middle Ages* (Berkeley, Los Angeles, London, 1974, pp. 269-355); Th.-M. Charland, *Artes praedicandi. Contribution à l'histoire de la rhétorique au moyen âge* (Paris, 1936); Johannes Baptist Schneyer, *Geschichte der katholischen Predigt* (Freiburg im Breisgau, 1969); and Jean Longère, *La prédication médiévale* (Paris, 1983).

[2] For instance, in his *De modo componendi sermones* (1340), Thomas Waleys considers as "modern" usage only sermons in which the division is preceded by an *introductio thematis* (p. 356), while other medieval as well as modern writers call "modern" any sermon that has a *thema* as its foundation and a division. *De modo componendi* has been edited by Charland, *Artes*, pp. 327-403, and will henceforth be referred to as "Waleys" followed by page numbers.

[3] An awareness of this fact, as well as of the differences in the techniques practiced at the two universities, pervades the *Forma praedicandi* by Robert of Basevorn (1322); see especially p. 244. The *Forma* has been edited by Charland, *Artes*, pp. 233-323, and translated by Leopold Krul, O.S.B., in James J. Murphy (ed.), *Three Medieval Rhetorical Arts* (Berkeley, Los Angeles, London, 1971), pp. 114-215. References to "Basevorn" in the following are to Charland's edition, and the translations are my own.

characteristic that the newer kind of sermon was based on and developed from a "theme," that is, a scriptural text, in ways that will be described presently; yet the term continues to mislead critics into believing that such sermons center on abstract themes, such as pride or the coming of Antichrist. Somewhat better perhaps is the label "scholastic sermon," because it not only suggests a period (post-1200) and milieu (the university) in which this sermon form originated but also implies certain formal characteristics associated with the mental habits and techniques of scholasticism, such as the constant urge to prove everything by a scriptural or patristic "authority" and to progress by way of fixed schemata with divisions and subdivisions; yet again, despite such learned features the "scholastic" sermon form was apparently also used before non-learned, popular audiences. But whatever the inadequacy in any of these labels, their common aim is to differentiate this newer sermon form from older structures used in preaching. In the older form, the "homily," the preacher would simply retell the gospel pericope for the day and add whatever doctrinal or moral lessons he deemed appropriate. At its structural best, a homily can be said to have three parts or, better, steps: narrative of the gospel, allegorical exegesis, and moral exegesis, as they can be found in the Lambeth Homilies,[4] the so-called Kentish Sermons,[5] the French homilies of Maurice de Sully,[6] the Wycliffite sermons,[7] and elsewhere. In contrast, the scholastic sermon is based on a single word, phrase, or sentence—the "theme"—out of which the preacher develops a long verbal structure by distinguishing several meanings of his verbal base and dividing and developing it according to rhetorical principles. The result is a prose work endowed with a variety of consciously sought artistic features.

But can such a verbal structure really be called art—a work that is at once expressive, imaginative, and esthetically pleasing?[8] Are late me-

---

[4] Richard Morris (ed.), *Old English Homilies*, EETS 29 and 34 (London, 1867-68).

[5] Richard Morris (ed.), *An Old English Miscellany*, EETS 49 (London, 1872), pp. 26-36.

[6] C. A. Robson, *Maurice of Sully and the Medieval Vernacular Homily* (Oxford, 1952).

[7] Anne Hudson (ed.), *English Wycliffite Sermons*, vol. I (Oxford, 1983). Three more volumes are to follow.

[8] A resounding No to my question can be heard in the following: "The result of preaching was to make it a pleasing dessert prized by the people, which neither the length of the sermon nor the most astringent criticisms nor the abstractness of its subject matter could ruin. Brave audience, mediocre in their devotion, credulous, and without zeal, hooked onto the words of talking machines who used impersonal recipes often tried and who played with

dieval sermons not characterized by an excessive formalism that relies on trite schemata and ubiquitous commonplaces, to the point that a preacher could build his sermon mechanically out of neatly labeled materials he would find in a variety of handbooks, according to a ready-made and tried recipe?[9] Did not such an enterprise per force exclude or even stifle the slightest amount of originality and imagination? And last but not least, was not a preacher's striving after art, his employment of artistic elements, severely censured by men in authority and theoreticians? Is not all of this so well known as to prevent one from calling the medieval sermon an art form? Well enough known it is—as much as a caricature by a political cartoonist.

Such reductionist statements and views distort historical reality: they remain unaware of the great amount of variation one encounters in preserved texts and of the coexistence, in one and the same cultural milieu, of contradictory viewpoints. They are also little concerned about the generic conditions and features of specific texts. A preacher's handbook is not a sermon; and a sermon preserved for us in manuscript is not necessarily what was actually spoken from the pulpit or heard in the pews. Concerning the alleged lack of originality, for example, we had perhaps better listen to the assessment of the scholastic sermon given by one of its greatest contemporary students:

> Probably the majority of the sermons that have come down to us were written as models, as sample sermons, pure literature for the development of sermons that were to be close to and full of real life. The authors of such sermons either omitted their personal experience as well as the coloring of particular times and places which they used in their preaching, leaving only the generally relevant thought structures, as we surmise it to have happened for instance in the sermons by John of Abbéville; or else they wrote down, in the first place, only sketches which were more or less detailed, and left it up to the individual preachers to fill out and develop such skeletons with personal experience, with material from real life, with references to specific times and places. One must not blame scholastic preaching for these schematic

---

number symbolism or with the icy subtleties of scholasticism!'' Jacques Toussaert, *Sentiment religieux en Flandre à la fin du Moyen-Age* (Paris, 1963), p. 79. I trust it is clear that I would detach myself from this assessment of popular preaching.

[9] For a recent expression of this view, see Janet Coleman, *English Literature in History, 1350-1400. Medieval Readers and Writers* (London, 1981), especially pp. 193-95.

features found in many sermon collections. Medieval preaching was not that abstract and far from reality![10]

Schneyer's view is totally confirmed by the literature with which he was least familiar, sermons made in England after 1350. The range from a mere sermon skeleton to fully developed sermon is very wide and covers a number of intermediate stages, all of which are represented in surviving manuscripts; and sermons that are fully developed do indeed show a good deal of the life and individual experience mentioned by Schneyer. This wide range in the degree of elaboration within actual complete sermons is paralleled by great differences in their shape, texture, and content. Reading a dozen sermons on the same feast or text would at once reveal how differently and uniquely various preachers solved their common task. It would further show that originality in medieval sermon-making is not to be sought in the use of individual details, as for instance the seven deadly sins, or biblical *figurae* of a sinner's hope for God's mercy, or the four kinds of backbiting, which are indeed commonplace topics, but rather in their *compositio*, in the differing ways in which these building blocks were assembled into the larger structure.

As to the condemnation of striving for art in preaching, it is again quite true that some authoritative writers spoke more or less harshly or cuttingly against those who would "saffron" their "predicacioun"[11] with rhetorical figures. Roger Bacon's words will serve as a good example. In discussing poorly educated priests of his day, he tells us that many try to supply what they failed to learn at the university, by borrowing "the booklets of young friars, who have invented boundless artistry in their preaching by means of divisions, harmony, and verbal agreement, in which is neither loftiness of speech nor much wisdom, but rather an infinite childish foolishness and dragging down of the words of God."[12] Another preacher aims his criticism at the audience's craving for rhetorical artistry:

> There are many who, when they go to a sermon, do not [pay attention to the spiritual food God gives us through his preachers], nor do they care about what the preacher is saying but how he does it. And if the sermon is nicely provided with rhymes, if the theme is nicely divided, if the friar speaks well, develops his sermon nicely, and comes to a

[10] Schneyer, *Geschichte*, pp. 185-86.

[11] Chaucer, *The Pardoner's Tale*, VI.345.

[12] Roger Bacon, *Opus tertium*, 75; in John S. Brewer (ed.), *Fratris Rogeri Bacon Opera quaedam hactenus inedita*, Rolls Series (London, 1859), p. 309.

pleasing conclusion, they say: "How well that friar has preached; what a beautiful sermon he has given!"

And the anonymous writer continues to compare such an audience to rustics who come to town for a feast. When they go to get a shave, the master barber gives them to an apprentice, who cuts them badly. But when they look in the mirror, they see "painted pictures on one side, and the windows and marble fronts of the houses across the street on the other," so that they forget all about their cuts.[13]

But misuse of a good thing is no argument against its reasonable employment, as Thomas Aquinas pointed out at some length in his defense of the new mendicant orders.[14] Among medieval theorists on preaching, too, the occasional condemnation of "elegant and polished words"[15] and of rhythm and rhyme "which are made to tickle the ears rather than edify the soul"[16] is neatly balanced by the sensible commendation of eloquence in the *Forma praedicandi* written by Robert of Basevorn (1322):

> It seems to me absolutely worthy of rejection what certain people say, namely that preaching must not be brightened with the false colors of verbal figures of speech . . . For who would hesitate to say that both together, namely wisdom and eloquence, move more strongly than either one by itself? . . . Clearly it is better to be eloquent than simply to lack all good altogether.[17]

Robert of Basevorn's treatise is instructive because it actually goes beyond the utility argument which lies behind these remarks and which was similarly made by Thomas Aquinas and others.[18] For Basevorn shows approval and appreciation of genuinely artistic elements in preaching by

[13] From a Latin sermon in Paris, Bibliothèque Nationale, MS. lat. 14961, cited in B. Hauréau, *Notices et extraits de quelques manuscrits latins de la Bibliothèque Nationale*, vol. IV (Paris, 1892), pp. 139-40.

[14] *Contra impugnantes Dei cultum et religionem*, 12; in vol. XV of the Parma edition of his *Opera omnia* (Parma, 1864), pp. 54-56.

[15] Jacques de Vitry, quoted in Thomas Frederick Crane, *The Exempla . . . of Jacques de Vitry* (London, 1890), p. xli, note: "Relictis enim verbis curiosis et politis . . ."

[16] Alanus of Lille, *Summa de arte praedicatoria*, 1 (PL 210:112). On Alanus's practice, see *Verses*, pp. 67-68.

[17] Basevorn, p. 248 (ch. 13).

[18] "But the mark of a good preacher is to be concerned with useful things that stimulate [the audience's] fervor, and by going over and reflecting on his material to throw out what is less useful and keep only useful matter." Humbertus de Romanis, O.P., *De eruditione religiosorum praedicatorum*, I.i.6, ed. Josephus Catalanus (Rome, 1739), p. 15.

his continuous use of *curiosus* and derived words,[19] which may be translated as "elegant" or "artistic."[20] The word occurs at least thirty-five times in the ninety pages of his edited text and strikingly reveals Basevorn's dominant concern with elements of art and formal beauty.

In order to discuss the major artistic features of late medieval sermons, it is necessary to review their structural principles and the pertinent terminology.[21] The scholastic sermon is based upon a theme (*thema*): a word or string of words usually taken from Scripture, though it could also be a liturgical or other authoritative text. From this theme the preacher derives a number of meanings or topics which are formulated in a concise division of the theme (*divisio* or *partitio thematis*). Each of these meanings or topics then forms the subject of the sermon's main parts (*pars principalis, membrum principale*). For example, a Middle English sermon for the First Sunday of Lent uses as its theme the words "If you are the Son of God, speak" (Matthew 4.3). From this sentence the preacher takes the single term "speak" to build his sermon on. He divides it into the following three parts:

$$
\text{Speke}
\begin{cases}
\text{þat God resceyve þe to grace} \\
\quad \text{whils þat þou art for þi synnes sorowyng;} \\
\text{þat God for-ȝeue þi trespas} \\
\quad \text{whils þou art þi-self of þi synnes shryvynge;} \\
\text{þat whils þou makes sethe for þi synnes} \\
\quad \text{God for-ȝeueþ þe is punyshyng.}^{22}
\end{cases}
$$

The three topics for his sermon, thus, are *sorowyng* for one's sins, *shryvynge* (making confession), and *makyng sethe* (making satisfaction), that

[19] Medieval Latin *curiositas* can of course also indicate a negative quality, curiosity or a vain striving after effects. As such it appears in Basevorn, pp. 244 and 316.

[20] Other words used to designate rhetorical elegance and beauty are: *artificialiter* (pp. 233, 247), *subtilitas* (260 and passim), *luculenter* (246), *redolentia* (247).

[21] Besides the accounts in Murphy, *Rhetoric*, and Charland, *Artes* (see note 1), the following contain good descriptions of the scholastic sermon structure: Woodburn O. Ross (ed.), *Middle English Sermons*, EETS 209 (London, 1940), pp. xliii-lv; Etienne Gilson, "Michel Menot et la technique du sermon médiéval," in *Les idées et les lettres* (Paris, 1932), pp. 93-154; Dorothea Roth, *Die mittelalterliche Predigttheorie und das "Manuale curatorum" des Johann Ulrich Surgant* (Basel and Stuttgart, 1956); and several articles by Harry Caplan, collected by Anne King and Helen North (eds.), *Of Eloquence. Studies in Ancient and Mediaeval Rhetoric* (Ithaca, N.Y., 1970).

[22] Ross, *Middle English Sermons*, Sermon 42, p. 271, lines 8-13. Further references to sermons edited by Ross will be given either by sermon or simply by page and line numbers (e.g., 271/8-13).

is to say, contrition, confession, and satisfaction or penance, the three standard parts of the sacrament of Penance, a topic eminently suited for the beginning of Lent. Each of these three topics is then utilized for a part in the development (*processus*) of the sermon. Extracting various topics from a biblical word in this fashion may strike us as fanciful, but in fact preachers were taught and required to justify such derivations with a biblical authority. This was done in the *confirmatio*, which could be given either immediately after the division or near the beginning of the respective principal. The sermon on "Speak" uses the latter method. To justify his deriving the (second) topic of confession from the term *speke*, for instance, the preacher quotes Psalm 31.5: "I said I will confess my injustice to the Lord, and you have forgiven the wickedness of my sin" (277/4-5). We may notice in passing that the division on *speke* quoted above shows syntactic and verbal parallelism in its three members as well as end-rhyme. The latter was evidently so important to the preacher that in order to achieve it (by means of the participle or gerund in *-ing*) he sacrificed the expected word order of the third line which, if it were completely parallel to lines 1 and 2, should end with *makes sethe* (or *sethmakyng*).

The cited sermon is therefore built on one term from which it derives its principal parts by a threefold division. A different pattern occurs in the following case, where the division utilizes all three terms of the theme, *Panis dat vitam* ("The bread gives life," cf. John 6.33):

> A fode of manys sustynnyng　　　　　*—panis*;
> an tokynyng of frendschype and louyng*—dat*;
> an fulfyllyng of vre saulls ȝernyng　　*—vitam*.[23]

The three aspects of the Eucharist thus derived—that it is food for the soul, a token of God's love and friendship, and the fulfillment of our deepest desires—then become the topics for the sermon's principal parts.

For the development of his principals the preacher could use a number of techniques. Of particular interest here is subdividing the topic of the principal. Thus, in the sermon on "Speak" the first principal, dealing with contrition, is developed by way of implicitly asking why we should be sorry, what true sorrow is, and what may impede it (271/14-276/39). Each member of this subdivision may of course in its turn be further divided. Thus, the question why we should be sorry is answered by refer-

---

[23] Worcester Cathedral, MS. F.10, fol. 29v.

ence to the four occasions on which Christ wept, each of which is applied to the human condition in general (271/19-274/3); and the impediments to contrition are said to be three (delight of sin, despair, and hope for a long life), which are proven with a variety of authorities from Scripture, the Fathers, and a medieval Latin commonplace (the "Four Sorrowful Things"; 275/4-276/39).

These essential parts of the scholastic sermon—theme, division, and development—could be augmented by one or two additions at the beginning of the sermon. Thus, the entire sermon could be preceded by a protheme or antetheme, which—in addition to its purpose of letting latecomers settle down before the beginning of the sermon's main part, like the overture to an opera[24]—might explain the nature of the respective feast day[25] or deal with the office of preaching.[26] The protheme could even have its own theme, different from that of the sermon itself. Another way of expanding was the "introduction of the theme" (*introductio thematis*), just before the division, which similarly could speak of a variety of things more or less closely connected with the sermon's theme. Theorists of scholastic preaching, both medieval and modern, have given us formal indications by which the reader or listener should be able to distinguish such introductory parts. Thus, the *protheme* normally leads to a *prayer* or an invitation to say the Our Father and Hail Mary,[27] which is followed by the *announcement of the theme*, which in turn may be followed by the *introduction of the theme*, at the end of which the theme is *repeated* and finally *divided*. In practice, however, a reader of medieval sermons will encounter a very great and sometimes puzzling diversity of structures that change from author to author, even from sermon to sermon;[28] as the author of one art of preaching says:

---

[24] See Humbertus de Romanis, *De eruditione*, I.vi.44 (p. 75).

[25] Thus commonly in the sermons of John Mirk's *Festial*, ed. Theodor Erbe, EETS, es, 96 (London, 1905); see for example Sermon 41, on Corpus Christi.

[26] Many examples of prothemes dealing with the character of a preacher and his office can be found in the following MSS: Cambridge University Library Kk.4.24 (fol. 128v, for instance); London, British Library Harley 331 (e.g., fol. 80); Oxford, Bodleian Library 649 (fols. 164-166); Balliol College 149 (fol. 90); Worcester Cathedral F.10 (fol. 27 and following sermons); and others. In *Die Unterweisung der Gemeinde über die Predigt bei scholastischen Predigern* (Munich, 1968), Schneyer has collected and analyzed material on the office of preaching from a large number of prothemes found in nearly forty MSS.

[27] Waleys, for example, speaks as if the protheme's very function was to lead to the prayer: *De modo*, p. 350.

[28] See for instance the analysis in Ross, pp. li-lv.

"One can hardly find two preachers delivering their own sermons who agree with each other in every aspect of sermon making."[29] With respect to these optional parts that can appear before the sermon division, it may therefore be more practical and realistic to speak simply of "introductory matter."

Even the simplified account I have given points to the fact that the scholastic sermon was a complex and complicated verbal structure, whose principles and rules were formulated and exemplified in a host of technical treatises, the arts of preaching.[30] One may reasonably wonder whether such structural complexity was in fact used in actual preaching. Schneyer expresses some skepticism in this matter: "Scholastic preaching before the people disregarded the network of rules given by these textbooks and only admitted their basic principles."[31] But after making due allowance for the fact that the precise form in which medieval sermons were delivered is irretrievable, I would point out that surviving sermons that have the length and fullness one might expect to find in oral delivery are built precisely on the pattern taught by *artes praedicandi*. Not only do they have introductory matter and divisions and subdivisions, but they further show an awareness of the significance of these structural elements by referring to them in the sermon or in marginalia.[32] Remarks made by the preacher, such as "Now I come to the second part" or "In order to prove this with an example from nature I might say," occur frequently in Latin sermons; and the Middle English texts edited by Ross likewise contain such references as "as I seid in myn anteteme" (275/9-10), "to shewe you a ground of my teme" (163/23), "the second poynt" (209/33), "oure second principall" (234/12-13), "for declaracion of þis is holy scripture" (245/39), and "I may þan perfitely conclude" (259/34). It would seem, therefore, that preachers practiced what their handbooks taught.

[29] Waleys, p. 329; similarly, p. 355. Basevorn likewise says, "There are almost as many different ways of preaching as there are able preachers" (p. 243, ch. 6); and he discusses 24 different forms of the "modern" sermon (cf. p. 319, ch. 50).

[30] For a list, see Harry Caplan, *Mediaeval "Artes Praedicandi." A Hand-List*, Cornell Studies in Classical Philology, XXIV (Ithaca, N.Y., 1934); and *Mediaeval. . . . A Supplementary Hand-List*. Ibid., XXV (1936). Further: Susan Gallick, "*Artes praedicandi*: Early Printed Editions," *MS* 39 (1977), 477-89.

[31] Schneyer, *Die Unterweisung*, p. 12.

[32] The detailed rubrication of the parts of a scholastic sermon can be seen in the first two sermons edited in D. M. Grisdale (ed.), *Three Middle English Sermons from the Worcester Chapter Manuscript F.10* (Leeds, 1939).

The question whether such complexity and refinement were employed in actual sermon delivery also has a sociological aspect, that of the preacher's audience. Should one not carefully distinguish between learned, elegant preaching before learned audiences, such as university students or the clergy, and much more simple sermons destined for the uneducated? There is good evidence that such a distinction was drawn, even with respect to the sermons' subject matter. Robert Holcot, for instance, puts it this way:

> It should be noted that there is a difference in the Church among the teachers who feed the people with the word of God, for some feed them with five loaves, others with seven. Simple preachers who are strong in their faith and devotion, though less educated in school learning, feed with five loaves. Through preaching the five points of Christ's Passion they edify the hearts of simple people sufficiently. In their person does the Apostle speak in 1 Corinthians 14 when he says: "In the Church I want to speak five words with my understanding, that I may instruct others" [1 Cor. 14.19]. These words are: what to believe, what to do, what to fear, what to keep from, and what to desire; that is to say: the twelve articles of faith, the Ten Commandments, the seven deadly sins, the pains of hell, and the joys of paradise.—Others there are who feed God's people with seven loaves. Seven is the number of universality,[33] and such are the subtle doctors learned in all things and taught by that mystical book which is written inside and outside and sealed with seven seals [cf. Revelation 5.1].[34]

In the use of formal elements, too, medieval theorists advise different approaches for different audiences. A macaronic sermon, for example, recommends that for an audience of clerics points should be proved with Scriptural authorities, but for gentle folk with "reasons," and for the uneducated with examples or *exempla*.[35] Similarly, the art of preaching attributed to Bonaventure gives the following counsel:

---

[33] *Universitatis*, a pun on "university."

[34] Robert Holcot, *Super libros Sapientiae*, edition of Hagenau, 1494 (reprinted Frankfurt am Main, 1974), lectio 96.

[35] "Auake, son þat slepest, and ich scal þe teche one þre wyse, and þat vor þre manners men þat cometh to sermone prechinge: clerekes, hyredmen, and leuuede men. To clerekes me scal scenny by holy wryt, to hyredmen by skyle and reyson, to leuuede men bi open and souþe vorbisne." Sermo *Hora est iam nos de somno surgere*, British Library, MS. Harley 505, fol. 15.

One should choose between the division from within and from without the theme one has selected, according to the need of one's audience. We must divide our theme in one way when we preach before the clergy, in the other when we preach to the people; for those grasp the matter more quickly, these more slowly.[36]

But these are a theorist's words, whereas reality in all likelihood never was so clearcut. About the last quoted piece of advice a modern student of university sermons has commented: "This is not a rigorous principle, for while the university sermons of 1230-31 are always addressed to clerics, we find in them both kinds of division."[37] And the macaronic sermon cited before continuously uses all three modes of proof, making it thus clear (as was already implied in the quoted sentence) that it addressed itself to a mixed audience. It would only be realistic to surmise that on a given Sunday towards the end of the fourteenth century all kinds of sermons could be heard in different churches, ranging from the sophisticated scholastic sermon with divisions and subdivisions to the simple homily[38] and the straightforward exposition of catechetical matter, the "five loaves" and similar topics that preachers were required by synodal decrees to present to their parishes as often as four times a year.[39] A collection of vernacular sermons, such as that edited by Ross, gathers precisely such a wide variety of sermons, from catechetical pieces (for instance, Nos. 2, 3, 5, 9, etc.) to full scholastic sermons (for instance, Nos. 14, 32, 35, 36, 41, 42, etc.), the latter embracing diverse pat-

[36] Pseudo-Bonaventure, *Ars concionandi*, in Bonaventure, *Opera omnia*, ed. Patres Collegii a S. Bonaventura (Quaracchi, 1882-1902), 9:9. For the difference between *divisio intra* and *extra*, see below, pp. 89ff.

[37] M. M. Davy, *Les Sermons universitaires parisiens de 1230-1231. Contribution à l'histoire de la prédication médiévale*. Etudes de philosophie médiévale, XV (Paris, 1931), p. 36.

[38] The *Ars componendi sermones* by Ranulph Higden (1340-50) speaks of "modern usage" which in "speaking to the people takes a lengthy theme from the Gospel and in developing the sermon expounds the Gospel by its sections ('particulas') without any subdivision." Ed. Margaret M. Jennings, C.S.J., Ph.D. dissertation, Bryn Mawr College, 1970, pp. 95-96. This seems to approximate the homily style, although Higden says that such preachers divide their theme into three (parts). The homily style, called *postillatio*, is recognized as one way of "dividing the theme" in the treatise by Simon Alcok, ed. Mary Fuentes Boynton, *HTR* 34 (1941), 216. Waleys was aware that in Italy the homily was the preferred form of preaching to the people (p. 344).

[39] See for example the *Instituta* by Roger de Weseham, bishop of Coventry, 1245-56, in C. R. Cheney (ed.), *English Synodalia of the Thirteenth Century* (Oxford, 1941), pp. 149-52.

terns.[40] And further, the audiences at these different kinds of sermon were probably very mixed in social standing and educational background, so that scholastic sermons with all their complexity and artistic elements might indeed have been given before congregations that included both learned and "lewd."

In applying these principles and rules of sermon construction, late medieval preachers created compositions that display several features of a distinctively artistic quality. I am here not thinking of rhetorical devices that are useful to capture the audience's attention and willingness to listen,[41] but of elements whose intended effect is esthetic pleasure. Of course, the tension between the useful and the pleasurable runs through many statements by theorists on sermon-making, and as we saw earlier, wiser heads found good reasons for reconciling the two sides of the dichotomy. But there is also evidence for a willingness to accept the pleasurable for its own value. At least some theorists consciously and approvingly taught ways that would produce delight. With respect to one such device, Thomas Waleys declared: "What use such rhythmic devices have I do not see, unless it is that they delight the ears of those who hear them. . . . I do not dare, nor am I able, to forbid it, since even in Holy Scripture some writings are found to be in meter." Indeed, Waleys did not only not dare to forbid this, but actually compiled a rhyming dictionary for the use of preachers.[42] Quite apart from such theoretical statements, one can find four major artistic features present in the scholastic sermon that distinguish it as a work of art: structural control, verbal concordance, variation, and decoration.

Structural control shows itself in the creation of an ordered whole out of parts that are clearly and logically related and articulated. This is achieved, as we have seen, primarily by dividing a term or concept and then further subdividing some or all of its members. The divisions are explicitly set out and customarily formulated with verbal and syntactic parallelism and end-rhyme, whether in Latin or in English. The parts of the sermon which are thus generated are linked together by clear and re-

---

[40] Cf. Ross, pp. liv-lv.

[41] Basevorn treats of "alluring the ear" in chapter 24 (pp. 260-62).

[42] Waleys, p. 373. On rhyming dictionaries see further below, p. 85 and n. 73. Thomas de Tuderto expresses himself similarly: "Rithmus sic debet esse formatus quod quadam sui melodia et dulcedine auditorum alliciat aures" ("End-rhyme should be formed in such a way that through its melody and sweetness it tickles the audience's ears"), *Ars sermocinandi*, Vatican Library, MS. Palat. 668, fol. 207v.

peated marking devices. The simplest of these are ordinal numbers. Thus, in the Middle English sermon on "Speak" the preacher concludes his first principal part with "And þus for þe first principall" and continues at once with "I seid for the secounde . . ." (276/39-277/1). The end of the second principal is similarly marked: "Þe wiche [is] þe entent of oure secound principall" (283/10-11). These English formulas imitate such Latin ones as *Dixi pro secundo*, which are ubiquitous. In introducing a new principal with "I seid for þe secounde," the preacher must of course also repeat the respective member of the division in its entirety or at least by its key term. A skillful preacher would do the same at the end of the principal part as well, so that the ordering of parts became clear not merely by their mechanical numbering but—more elegantly—by the repetition of key terms and concepts. The following excerpts will illustrate this procedure:

> [Division, second line:] Speke þat God for-ȝeue þi trespas whils þou art þi-self of þi synnes shryvynge. (271/10-11)
> [Beginning of second principal:] I seid for þe secounde þat ȝiff þou be Goddes child, þou shuldest speke þat God wipe avey þi trespase whils þou arte þe of þi synnes shryvynge. (277/1-3)
> [End of second principal:] Lat vs þan all amend vs and shryve vs to þe prest, þat haþ þis poure and dignite, and so shall we haue forȝeuenes of oure synnes and speke as þe children of God, þe wiche [is] þe entent of oure secound principall. (283/8-11)

While repeating the key terms at the end of a part, the preacher also had to find a natural and smooth transition from the subject matter he had just been discussing, which in the quoted sermon is a longish digression on the dignity of the priesthood (280/1-283/7). The last quotation achieves this very well. We might also notice the slight but pleasing variation in word choice at the beginning of the second principal from *for-ȝeue* to *wipe avey*.

The end of the entire sermon posed a special challenge, because here a good preacher might not merely conclude his last principal in the way described but in addition tie together all the principals and refer back to the division, perhaps even to his protheme. Arts of preaching call this procedure *unitio*,[43] and English preachers apparently named it the

---

[43] Basevorn, pp. 306-7 (ch. 46). Other *artes* call it *connexio* or *colligatio* (MS. Arezzo 325, fol. 50v), *conglutinacio* or *concatenacio* (British Library, Addit. MS. 24361, fol. 63).

"knot" of the sermon. I have elsewhere given an example from a fif-
teenth-century macaronic text;[44] a different sermon speaks similarly of
"knyttyng and combryng of þese thre particles," though here the refer-
ence is to the three members in the division itself.[45] Our sermon on
"Speak" lacks such a *unitio*, but we shall presently find an example in
another Middle English sermon.

The repetition of key terms from the sermon theme and the division is
thus a major device in the creation of a unified structure. But the under-
lying principle of repeating identical or very similar words throughout
the sermon has a further application. When speaking of the sermon di-
vision, we noted that the meanings a preacher extracted from one or sev-
eral of the terms contained in the theme had to be "confirmed," that is,
the preacher had to show good reason for his deriving a particular mean-
ing from a particular term. For this he relied on an authoritative quota-
tion, which would normally be taken from Scripture but could also come
from the Fathers or elsewhere. This authority had somehow to combine
the derived meaning and the term. Now, the relation between the words
of this confirming authority and the terms of the theme and division could
be an agreement in sense only (*concordantia realis*) or one of sense and
the actual words in question (*concordantia realis et vocalis*). The latter
is perfectly achieved in the second principal of the Middle English ser-
mon used above:

> [Second member of division:] Speke þat God for-ȝeue þi trespas whils
> þou art þi-self of þi synnes shryvynge. (271/10-11)
> [Confirmatio:] "Dixi confitebor iniusticiam meam Domino, et tu re-
> misisti impietatem peccati mei." (277/4-5)

Here Psalm 31.5 "confirms" the connection the preacher has established
between speaking (*dixi*), God's forgiveness (*Domino . . . remisisti*),
trespass (*iniusticiam meam*), shriving (*confitebor*), and one's sins (*im-
pietatem peccati mei*). I have quoted the psalm verse in Latin in order to
illustrate a perfect and ideal confirmation. In his English translation the
preacher actually omits *dixi* from the quotation itself (it occurs of course
in the preacher's own words):

---

[44] "Chaucer and the Language of Contemporary Preaching," *SP* 73 (1976), 160.

[45] Oxford, Bodleian Library, MS. Laud Misc. 706, fol. 159v. This sermon has been ed-
ited by Patrick Joseph Horner, F.S.C., "An Edition of Five Medieval Sermons from MS.
Laud Misc. 706," unpubl. Ph.D. dissertation, State University of New York at Albany,
1975, pp 147-79.

The prophete seiþ þat he wold shryve hym of is wronge lyvynge, and he seis sicurly þat God haþ for3eue hym is trespasse (277/6-8),

so that the confirmation agrees verbally only with the respective member of the division, not the divided term from the theme (*speke*), by repeating the key words *shryve, God haþ for3eue,* and *trespasse.* (*Wrong lyvynge* for *synnes* would be *concordantia realis* only.) This degree of parallelism in the confirmation was deemed sufficient. It likewise appears in the other two principals of our sermon. Thus, the first member of the division: "speke þat God resceyve þe to grace whils þat þou art for þi synnes sorowyng" is confirmed with Psalm 50.19: "God will not dispise a sorefull and a lowly herte" (271/16-17).

The device of verbal concordance—which of course was never to be used in violation of the lexical meaning the texts had[46]—appears not only at or in relation to the sermon's main division but would be further used throughout the entire sermon, with the subdivisions as well as in the sermon's introductory matter and conclusion. In addition to its confirming function, the device could further serve to generate and develop material for the sermon. In illustration of this Robert of Basevorn cites the example of a sermon on Saint John with the theme *Justus de angustia liberatus est* ("The just man is delivered out of distress," Proverbs 11.8). The theme is divided into three parts, whose first, on *justus,* speaks of Saint John's holiness. This is confirmed with Proverbs 4.18, *Justorum semita quasi lux splendens procedit* ("The path of the just goes forward as a shining light"). The quotation is then used as the text for a subdivision into three parts, which derive from *lux* (John's virginity), *splendens* (his teaching), and *procedit* (his martyrdom), each of course again confirmed with other Scriptural passages that contain these words in some form together with *justus* or *justitia.*[47] On this mode of invention Basevorn bestows the praise of "greatest elegance," *maxima curiositas.* In Middle English sermons, matters normally progress more simply. Nonetheless, whether a sermon contains only four or five authorities with *concordantia vocalis* or two dozen,[48] the repetition of key words binds the parts of a long prose structure tightly together and creates a unity not only of abstract meaning but also of physical sound. If read by the eye from

[46] Cf. Basevorn, pp. 252-53 (ch. 18).

[47] Ibid., pp. 280-81 (ch. 35).

[48] A longish sermon on *Hoc est signum federis* ("This is the sign of covenant," Gen. 9.12), in Worcester Cathedral, MS. F.126, fols. 247-249v, for example, contains at least 23 scriptural quotations with the word *signum* besides the theme.

the printed page, such repetition may seem a mere formal trick,[49] mechanical and boring; but if picked up by the ear in an oral discourse, its periodic reappearance like that of a musical motif in a sonata or symphony may well become a source of esthetic delight.

In music, motifs and themes are of course not merely repeated but developed, changed, modulated. The principle of variation was similarly recognized by medieval handbooks on sermon-making as another source of delight and was applied by the sermon-makers as well. The great preoccupation with modes of dilation or amplification on the part of classical and medieval rhetoricians is well known. It is fully shared by medieval arts of preaching, most of which present a number of different methods and give either short lists or more extensive discussions involving up to twenty or more *modi amplificandi*. In addition to developing a topic by means of division, these methods include defining a term and giving its etymology (with subsequent moralization); distinguishing various meanings of a word, including the spiritual sense of the object it designates; adducing authoritative quotations; listing the properties, aspects, or parts of natural objects and concepts; giving illustrative similes; telling long stories, with or without moralization; and much else. All of this, of course, had the primary purpose to prove and to illustrate the doctrinal or moral point under discussion. The great variety of such means, and the very broad range of material that could be used within them, especially with similes and narrative *exempla*,[50] is well known from page after page of fully developed scholastic sermons. With such a wide diversity of means on hand, preachers would naturally aim at variation in developing their sermons. One principal might be developed with a number of learned or philosophical-scientific authorities, while another could contain a biblical narrative with moralization, and a third an *exemplum* from contemporary life. Clearly, the possibilities are nearly unlimited, and surviving sermons give ample evidence that skillful preachers did

---

[49] Notice, however, that Basevorn was not above recommending a particular rhetorical "trick" (*cautela*) when the preacher cannot find an immediately fitting authority: p. 274. Father Krul translates *cautela* as "precaution," which misses the common meaning the word had acquired in medieval Latin. *Cautela* is similarly used in Waleys, p. 385.

[50] See my survey of these two devices as found in one preachers' handbook: "Vices, Virtues, and Popular Preaching," in *Medieval and Renaissance Studies. Proceedings of the Southeastern Institute of Medieval and Renaissance Studies, Summer 1974*, ed. Dale F. J. Randall (Durham, N.C., 1976), pp. 42-45. For the use of comic tales and jokes, see Wenzel, "The Joyous Art of Preaching; or, the Preacher and the Fabliau," *Anglia* 97 (1979), 304-25.

not simply pile illustration upon illustration but made a controlled, varied, and pleasing selection. This principle of variation can be found even behind some very minute details. In the Middle English sermon division quoted several pages ago, I called attention to the fact that in the third member the word order was reversed, which I there attributed to the desire of creating end-rhyme. This change might alternatively be credited to the preacher's desire to introduce a variation in the syntactic structure of his division members.

The presence of structural control, verbal concordance, and variation, and their appearance in the course of an actual sermon can be illustrated from a relatively simple Middle English sermon on the theme *Diliges Deum tuum* ("Thou shalt love thy God," Matthew 22.37). The sermon has a protheme (198/15-199/13), which begins "inductively":[51] since the soul forms a unity without parts, it cannot love objects that are mutually contrary in their nature (198/15-18). This generality is proven by an example from nature (19-24) and then applied to man's spiritual life: one cannot love sin and (the salvation of) one's soul (25-34). The point is confirmed with a quotation from Psalm 10.6, *Qui diligit iniquitatem odit animam suam* ("He who loves wickedness hates his own soul") and further with a passage from Saint Bernard (199/1-4) which repeats the key words "wicked" and "hate your soul" and is then briefly developed (4-13).

After the prayer and announcement of the theme (199/14-20), the preacher formally introduces his theme by explaining why man shall love his God; love is the "principal commandment" of the Law,[52] because love destroys every sin and is therefore "the principal way" to heaven (cf. 201/1). This point is stated at the beginning (199/21ff.), middle (200/18), and end (201/1-2) of the *introductio thematis*. It is introduced with a simile from nature attributed to Chrysostom (199/22-27) and then "proven" and developed with the biblical example of Mary Magdalene (199/28-200/7), a quotation from Saint Bernard (200/8-15), and, after midpoint, reference to common experience, namely, that a person who loves God is happy in both prosperity and adversity (200/21-37). In the course of this introduction, the preacher quotes two biblical verses that contain the verb *diligere* (200/2 and 32), and the citations from Bernard

---

[51] Basevorn and other authors of *artes praedicandi* offer a variety of ways to begin the protheme as well as the *introductio thematis*, including *inductive*: Basevorn, p. 269 (ch. 31).

[52] Cf. Matthew 22.38.

and Chrysostom similarly contain *amor* (200/10-11) and *loue* (199/25, no Latin). There is, thus, plenty of *concordantia vocalis* between the sermon's theme and its introductory matter.

After the theme has been repeated, it is divided (201/4-8). This particular sermon uses only a twofold *divisio* based on the two terms of its theme, which may be schematized as follows:

(1) And hertely likynge þat ys full besye in folowynge—*diliges*;
(2) a souerayn ȝefte of endeles rewardynge—*Deum tuum*.

Confirmation of the two members is given in the development of the respective parts.

The first principal develops the thought announced in the division, which it subdivides into two parts (201/9-12):

Love: (a) is a "full likynge";
      (b) naturally follows the object it desires.

Part 1a then develops the notion that in essence love is a matter of intention, desire, or direction of the will, not of external acts. It is therefore crucial for the moral quality of any action, and this is shown by love in good men (201/36-202/30) and in evil ones (202/31-203/39). Either case is confirmed with a biblical verse that contains the key terms: *Si iusticiam quis diligit . . .* (202/22-23, from Wisdom 8.7) and *Dilexit maledicci-onem . . .* (203/33-34, from Psalm 108.18). This part is then summed up (204/1-2) and at once followed by 1b (204/3-14), a much shorter section that contains only an example from nature and a confirming quotation, *Qui habet mandata mea et servat ea, ille est qui diligit me* (204/10-11, from John 14.21).

The second principal is not formally subdivided (204/15-206/22). It develops its topic that love, i.e. God, is the greatest gift of our eternal reward, first with a quotation from Saint Bernard (204/16-28) and next with a simile from life (204/29-205/2). This leads directly to the *confirmatio* for the second principal, *Quod oculus non vidit . . . diligentibus te* (205/3-4, from 1 Corinthians 1.9). At this point the preacher adds some further development by asking, "But how shall a man com here-to?" (5). The answer is, by confessing his sins and asking for God's mercy. This may seem like a new and unrelated topic, but the notion of God's forgiveness was in fact announced as early as the *introductio thematis*. The point is explained and illustrated with the warning image of the devil holding a sinner by his throat so that he cannot confess; and then follow two common *exempla* that illustrate the efficacy of shrift. The first (205/ 12-37) does this negatively, by having the spirit of a dead man appear to his curate and bewail his damnation for having failed to confess one sin, while the second illustrates the same lesson positively with the story of a repentant scholar who, too much ashamed to tell his sins to a priest, was asked to write them out. He did so, but when the slip of parchment got to the abbot, the writing had disappeared—a visible sign of how God's mercy can delete sin (206/4-22).

At this point the preacher concludes by summing up and leading to the mandatory closing formula:

> Loo, here þou may well see what sorowe o[f] herte is, and to aske mercy and forȝeuenes, how meche þis pleyseþ God, how it doþ a-wey all maner of synnes and bryngeþ a man owte of þe dewels boundes and makeþ hym able to com vn-to þe blis of heven when þat he goyþ oute of þis worlde. Vn-to þe wiche blis brynge vs he, þat for vs died on þe, et cetera.   (206/23-29)

The *unitio* does not succeed in explicitly tying together all of the sermon's parts, but it does combine 2b ("aske mercy and forȝeuenes") with the introduction of the theme ("doþ a-wey all maner of synnes" and "com vn-to þe blis of heven").

Though comparatively short and sparse, this sermon yet contains all the elements of a complete scholastic sermon. Its structure is clear and well marked. Verbal concordance binds the principal parts not only to the theme but further to the *introductio thematis* and the protheme, by means of seven biblical quotations (beyond the theme itself) that contain a form of the word *loue*. Other quotations from Augustine, Chrysostom, Bernard, and even Cicero (201/13-15) add further occurrences of *loue* which cement the sermon's structure. And variation in the development or proof of a point is achieved by alternating between authoritative quotation and example from nature or everyday experience, by opposition (good vs. bad people), by unfolding a generic concept (sinners) into some specific parts (lechers and covetous people, 202/34-203/21), and finally by, as it were, playing narratives on the same theme first in the minor and then in the major key.

The three artistic qualities so far considered are all architectonic in nature, similar to the structural features set by the groundplan of a cathedral, with its proportions and relations of parts to the whole, its repetition of structural elements in columns and bays, and the like. In contrast, the fourth quality, decoration, corresponds to the mosaics and frescoes and statues that embellish the interior spaces. Such decorative elements in preaching comprise all the figures of speech and rhetorical tricks taught by medieval arts of rhetoric, which do appear in the surviving sermons, though perhaps less profusely than one might think. One particular element of this kind is of prime relevance for this study: the use of verses. Both Latin and vernacular sermons employed short poems extensively, but preachers in the vernacular clearly went beyond what was normal practice in Latin sermons and would often use English verses where their models had a sentence in prose. Verses appear in the scholastic sermon with a number of different functions and can on that basis be classified as follows:

(1) *Renditions of the sermon theme*. After quoting the theme in Latin, many sermons translate it into English rhymes. Occasionally a preacher will furnish one translation in prose and another in verse. One of the Middle English sermons edited by Ross, for example, translates the theme *Erumpe et clama* (Galatians 4.27) into prose: "Breke oute and crye" and then continues:

> Or els þus: Breke owte and not blynne,
> And cry God mercy for þi synne. (218/2-4)

(2) *Renditions of the division*. As has already been shown in several quotations, in the cited Middle English sermon collection the division is commonly put in rhymed form, though here the results are metrically awkward, in contrast to other sermons that will be examined further on.

(3) *Prooftexts*. These are verses that give authoritative proof for a point made by the preacher. They are frequently translated from biblical verses (in prose) or from sentences by the Fathers and Doctors of the Church, as well as from medieval Latin verses. The confirming authorities on *diligere* in the sermon analyzed earlier, for example, might by a more talented preacher have been rendered in English verses rather than prose. Even native proverbs could be used to prove a point. For instance, worldly friendship may be likened to the friendship between dog and master—

> For: When þe hounde knawithe þe bone,   gnaws
> Þan of felishippe kepeþ he none.[53]   cares about

---

[53] Ross, 89/15-16. Cf. Bartlett Jere Whiting and Helen Wescott Whiting, *Proverbs, Sen-*

(4) *Message verses*. These items do not so much prove a point by authority as address an imaginary or real audience whom they warn or frighten or console. They have, in other words, a strong emotional appeal. The negative *exemplum* in the Middle English sermon on "Speak" ends with such a verse when the damned soul wails:

> I brene and euermore must
> For synne þat neuer man wiste! (205/35-37)[54]

Besides similar exclamations or appeals in *exempla*, message verses include inscriptions reportedly found on such objects as rings, boxes, paintings, and statues.[55] I would also place in this group appeals spoken by Christ on the cross or by the preacher calling attention to him, which address the audience with *behold, see, think,* or a similar command.

(5) *Prayers* also are occasionally formulated in verse. Some are based on liturgical models (hymns, sequences, antiphons), while others are freely formed by the sermon maker. Though not a standard ingredient of the scholastic sermon, they may occur at the end of a section by way of summary and devotional guidance.[56]

(6) *Memory verses*. By this I refer to versifications of material the audience was required to memorize, such as the Lord's Prayer, the Ten Commandments, the qualities of a good confession, and the like, without extending the term to the general appeal to memory that any kind of verse might have by virtue of being easily recalled. Strictly speaking, their proper purpose lies outside the specific rhetorical or structural functions within the sermon, although many of them have been preserved in handbooks for preaching or are quoted in sermons. An example is the hitherto unnoticed verse rendering of the (six or seven) circumstances of sin:

> 3yf þou wlt well schriue boen,
> Sixth kep þat I þe kene:
> Wo, wat, how, wenne, wy,
> Qwere, how oft I þe rede.[57]

---

tences, and Proverbial Phrases from English Writings Mainly before 1500* (Cambridge, Mass., 1968), H.596.

[54] Other message verses, in an *exemplum*, occur in Ross, 44-45.

[55] An example is Ross, 90/35-38.   [56] For example, Ross, 154/11-14.

[57] Worcester Cathedral, MS. F.126, fol. 111rb. The circumstances are usually summarized in the Latin hexameter: Quis, quid, ubi, quibus auxiliis, cur, quomodo, quando. Compare their discussion in *The Parson's Tale*, X.960-81. On memory verses see further below, p. 116.

More examples of these types of sermon verses can be found in an earlier study of a handbook for preachers,[58] where I also discussed their background and their appearance in surviving manuscripts; and the next chapter will provide further illustrations and examine their verbal artistry. At present I will focus on one of the listed functions for further analysis, the division.

My description and discussion of sermon structure may already have suggested how important and crucial to a well-made scholastic sermon the *divisio thematis* is. In fact, one treatise on sermon making goes so far as to identify preaching itself with the formal techniques of selecting and dividing a theme.[59] Another treatise, by the Englishman Simon Alcok, deals exclusively with "the way of dividing the theme" and offers more than forty different ways in which a term from the theme can be divided and expanded.[60] The reason for this emphasis is that the division "generates"[61] the subject matter of the scholastic sermon, by a technique we saw exemplified earlier in this chapter. The process of generation by division extends beyond the initial *divisio* through the entire sermon. Just as the sermon's principal topics are generated from the theme by means of the division, so can the subject matter within each principal part be generated by means of a subdivision, and material for any member of the subdivision in turn may be generated by means of a distinction. Consequently, the formal division of the theme is like the root from which the trunk and branches of a large tree grow, and medieval preachers refer to it indeed as *radix sermonis*.[62] This generative function of the

[58] *Verses*, pp. 69-86 and ch. 2 in general.

[59] "Predicacio est thematis assumpcio, eiusdem thematis diuisio, thematis diuisi subdiuisio, concordanciarum congrua cotacio, et auctoritatum adductarum clara et deuota explanacio"; W. O. Ross, "A Brief *Forma Praedicandi*," *MP* 34 (1936-37), 340-41.

[60] I count 45 ways, but one of them, *postillatio*, refers to the straightforward exposition of the Gospel or Epistle. See Mary Fuentes Boynton, "Simon Alcok on Expanding the Sermon," *HTR* 34 (1941), 201-17. The treatise begins with "Incipit tractatus de modo dividendi thema."

[61] "Per hec enim ampla loquendi materia generatur" ("Through these [i.e., distinctions, divisions, etymologies, and definitions] ample subject matter for the sermon is generated"); A. De Poorter, "Un manuel de prédication médiévale," *Revue néo-scolastique* 25 (1923), 203.

[62] Thus, the division is frequently marked *radix sermonis* in the margins of Bodleian Library MS. 649 (fols. 2v, 61, 75v, 114, 127). The tree image was further applied to the entire sermon structure; see Otto A. L. Dieter, "*Arbor Picta*: The Medieval Tree of Preaching," *QJS* 51 (1965), 123-44.

division was explicitly acknowledged by theorists,[63] and preachers likewise often remark that their purpose in making a division is to "invent" the sermon's subject matter.[64] One gets the sense that once a preacher had hit upon a good division of his theme and provided himself with fitting confirmatory quotations as required, the rest was plain sailing. This sense is confirmed by the arts of preaching. A fifteenth-century treatise by a Portuguese Franciscan, for example, occupies 66 printed pages, of which 54 are devoted to what I have called the sermon's introductory matter leading to the division.[65] Actual sermons made in England bear out the same point. Many of them carefully work out the introductory matter including the division, and then deal with the remainder of the sermon in a highly abbreviated, sketchy form. Besides some examples from Merton College MS. 248 we shall consider later, a good illustration comes from an Easter sermon on *Viderunt revolutum lapidem* ("They saw the stone rolled back," Mark 16.4). Here the preacher begins with a long protheme on the four ages of the world, in the course of which he refers to the famous Moor Maiden "carol."[66] This protheme occupies 125 lines of text. The following *introductio thematis* and *divisio* in Latin (here a manifold one) take up 48 lines, and the English rendition of the *divisio* another 17. For the remainder of the sermon—what we would consider its main body—this manuscript offers a mere 8 lines of sketchy notes on how the sermon might be developed. As these simply refer to stories and similes, it is obvious that the real thought structure of the full sermon was felt to have been sufficiently laid out in the division. A similar concentration on the introductory matter appears in the sermon out-

---

[63] For instance: "Moderni . . . suas predicaciones communiter dividunt in tres partes. Prima / vocatur introductio, secunda dicitur thematis introductio, tercia appellatur distinctio et prosecutio. Iste autem modus inventus est ad habendum et ad inveniendum copiam materie ad predicandum" ("Modern preachers . . . commonly divide their sermons into three parts. The first is called introduction, the second introduction of the theme, and the third distinction [i.e., division] and development. This format was invented in order to have and to find plenty of material for preaching"). The writer adds two further purposes of this form of the sermon: it helps the preacher's memory, and it makes him methodical (*disertum*) so that he always knows how far along he is. *Ars praedicandi* in Vatican Library, MS. Ottob. lat. 396, fol. 40v-41 (Caplan No. 84).

[64] "Divisio pro materia sermonis," or "pro materia sermonis invenio tria." Examples can be found below, pp. 94-98.

[65] Albert G. Hauf, "El *Ars Praedicandi* de Fr. Alfonso d'Alprao, O.F.M. Aportación al estudio de la teoría de la predicación en la península Ibérica," *AFH* 72 (1979), 233-329.

lines attached to *Fasciculus morum*. They normally offer an introduction and division, followed by no more than references to sections in the handbook that might be used for the sermon's development.[67]

This fundamental importance of the division for the scholastic sermon is underscored by its being regularly embellished with two devices of ornamentation: parallelism of its members (*consonantia*) and end-rhyme (*cadentia*). It is at this point that devices we would consider "poetic" were consciously used and cultivated in Latin prose sermons. In teaching this practice, arts of preaching list a number of metrical patterns they deem appropriate, and furnish illustrative examples. These are various forms of *cursus*, the widely used ornament of classical and medieval Latin prose, whose exposition in the handbooks calls for the technical vocabulary of Greek and Roman metrics, especially the names of various metrical feet.[68] The application of these ornamental devices in the sermon would then lead to such divisions as,

> Status prudenter praelibandus,
> Actus ferventer frequentandus,
> Modus clementer moderandus.[69]

Naturally, some smart clerics recently graduated from Paris or Oxford might on occasion overshoot their mark and produce something like the following division of three things that are necessary for salvation:

> Fortitudo patientiae insuperabilis animarum roborantis,
> Rectitudo justitiae inobliquabilis aspectum illustrantis,
> Pulcritudo munditiae inviolabilis subditum decorantis.[70]

The theorist who gives this example condemns it as so much "foliage without fruit" and advises not to go beyond three terms for each member of the division. It is precisely such *rhythmorum melodiae et consonantiae metrorum*[71] whose excessive deployment was chastised by responsible preachers and Church authorities. On the other hand, a moderate

[66] Cf. Wenzel, "The Moor Maiden—A Contemporary View," *Speculum* 49 (1974), 69-74. The sermon appears in Worcester Cathedral, MS. F.126, fols. 145rb-146ra.

[67] For an example, see *Verses*, pp. 47-48.

[68] See for example Basevorn, pp. 321-23 (ch. 50, on *coloratio*). For the use of rhyme in Latin prose, see Karl Polheim, *Die lateinische Reimprosa* (Berlin, 1925; second edition, 1963), who discusses its use in sermons especially on pp. 383-92 and 455-59.

[69] Basevorn, p. 321 (ch. 50).

[70] Gérard du Pescher, *Ars faciendi sermones*; ed. Ferdinand M. Delorme, O.F.M., *Antonianum* 19 (1944), 198.

use of the same rhymed divisions was taught as an essential part of the scholastic sermon and used everywhere. Their use was generally justified as being a help to the preacher's memory. ''He who wishes to make a useful and good division of his theme,'' says one theorist, ''does not need to pay attention to rhymes, unless he derives from this help for his memory.'' Yet in the following sentence the same writer goes on to allow rhymes alternately ''for some other pious reason.''[72] And the French author who condemns the excessive illustration quoted above later speaks of ''beautiful words'' he wants his readers to use in their divisions and then provides long lists of adjectives, nouns, and other parts of speech, that have the same ending—a rhyming dictionary, in other words, for the use of preachers.[73]

It will not surprise us, then, to find the same practice followed in the vernacular. Many sermons written in Latin contain an additional English rendition of their division, so that the same section of the sermon appears in two languages side by side—often a most helpful state of affairs for the modern reader who might otherwise be left totally baffled by the quirks of Middle English orthography and by the results of apparent incomprehension on the part of medieval scribes. Frequently the division is the only place at which some English verses or prose phrases appear in a Latin manuscript; and they may appear only at great and irregular intervals from each other, so that searching for them requires examination of every page. The sermons ascribed to Robert Holcot, for instance, contain a total of four English divisions scattered over 119 sermons and 199 folios.[74] One can even observe how English divisions gradually crept into the Latin text a scribe was copying. In a set of Latin sermons attributed (probably erroneously) to Doctor Rypyndon, some English divisions and distinctions first show up as marginal additions; only after some 80 folios do they get incorporated in the body of the text.[75]

[71] Alanus of Lille, *Summa de arte praedicatoria*, 1 (PL 210:112).

[72] ''Volens autem utiliter et bene uti divisione thematis, non est necessarium intendere rithimis, nisi ex hoc iuvetur in memoria. . . . Ubi autem quis velit eum ad rithimos deducere pia intensione, ut scilicet melius iuvetur memoria vel alio pio motivo, bene potest.'' Vatican Library, MS. Ottob. lat. 396, fol. 43.

[73] Delorme, op. cit., pp. 187-97. The purpose of these lists has been discussed by David L. D'Avray, ''The Wordlists in the *Ars faciendi sermones* of Geraldus de Piscario,'' *FranS* 16 (1978), 184-93. Thomas Waleys similarly collected rhyme words; see *De modo*, pp. 372-75.

[74] Cambridge, Peterhouse MS. 210, fols. 1, 32, 128, and 139.

[75] Manchester, John Rylands Library, MS. Lat. 367, fols. 199-317v. Another example

It is generally assumed that during the fourteenth and fifteenth centuries most if not all the popular preaching in England was done in English. At the same time, however, scribes continued to write down sermons in Latin, and fresh sermons were in fact still composed in the learned language.[76] The appearance of English divisions in otherwise Latin texts, and beyond this the existence of texts in which the two languages are even more intimately mixed, poses questions about the language used in actual preaching that are far from answered. Nonetheless it seems reasonable to imagine that when a preacher delivered a sermon in the vernacular, he might have memorized a Latin outline in advance or perhaps carried a written text with him into the pulpit. At this point, he could apparently rely upon his skill to extemporize from the outline with the necessary prooftexts and some *exempla* and the like. But the formulation of English verses could not be left up to the inspiration of the moment. Hence, English divisions had to be created and inserted into Latin sermon texts. The state of the manuscripts, then, itself reveals what importance preachers gave to a carefully structured and ornamented *divisio thematis*.

Many times such English divisions appear as no more than vernacular rhyme-words added to the Latin:

Intelligatis pro processu sermonis quod Christus in passione sua inter alia reliquit homini quatriplex exemplum sequendum, scilicet:
>vite quam duxit, *lad*,
>amoris quem precepit, *bad*,
>pene quam habuit, *had*,
>doctrine quam legit, *rad*.[77]

(Let us understand then, for the development of the sermon, that among other things in his Passion Christ left man a fourfold example that he should follow, namely of the life he led, of the love he commanded, of the suffering he endured, and of the teaching he gave.)

---

is Cambridge, Gonville and Caius College MS. 221, of the mid-thirteenth century, which contains Latin sermons with some English rhymed divisions added in the lower margins (fols. 22, 24, 24v).

[76] As for instance the sermon cycle in MS. Rylands Lat. 367, fols. 1-197v, ascribed to Radulphus de Attoun (or Acton), probably of the fourteenth century. These sermons contain no English.

[77] British Library, MS. Harley 331, fol. 81v.

But much more frequent than single words are English phrases or sentences, which may either occur together with the respective Latin division, or stand by themselves without corresponding Latin, or be mixed in with Latin words. In any of these situations, what mattered were the rhyme-words, as the following example with its changing mixture of the two languages demonstrates:

> *Amicus noster dormit . . .* In quibus verbis tria possunt notari:
> Primo a thyng þat es spedfull—*amicus noster*;
> secundo a thyng þat es drydfull—mors, que intelligitur in
>   *dormit*.
> Bot for owre frend þat was spydful has mette dede þat es
>   drydful, þerfor is þe thryd thyng nedful, scilicet suffragia
>   ecclesie. Et potest addi quartum þat es helpyng and med-
>   ful, scilicet implecio suffragiorum.[78]

Sermons entirely preserved in English may, of course, have rhymed divisions also, as we have seen earlier. And in some Latin sermons of the fifteenth century it becomes apparent that the division was first made in English and then translated into Latin, as is the case with the following subdivision:

> Sum commys to confession os þe craw cryes;
> and sum commys to confession os þe fals man leys;
> sum commys to confession os þe dedman deys;
> and sum commys to confession os a wyse man hys enmie spyes.

The corresponding Latin lines, which occur only in the (Latin) development of these four ways in which people make their confession, have neither parallelism nor end-rhyme.[79]

The mixture of the two languages in the sermon division leads to some

---

[78] Cambridge, Jesus College MS. 13, part vi, fol. 119v.

[79] "Aliqui veniunt ad confessionem sicut corvus clamat . . . , sicut viri falsi et iniusti a tramite veritatis delirant . . . , sicut homo in puncto mortis moritur . . . , sicut sapiens homo percipit inimicum suum." British Library, MS. Harley 2388, fol. 83. The relation of Latin to English in this manuscript, however, is not consistently the same. On fol. 89, for instance, a Latin division is "Englished" (*anglicabitur*). On the other hand, the Latin of these sermons reads like the second language of an Englishman, with such Anglicisms as *iam dierum* ("nowadays"), *unum sedendo* ("one sitting"), *non diu ex quo* ("not long ago"), and so forth.

interesting ramifications in the following example. This sermon begins in Latin (here translated):

> *There shall be one sheepfold and one shepherd* (John 10.16). . . . In these words the Church is commended in two ways: for the unity of its faith and for the uniqueness of its God. The first is indicated in the words *There shall be one sheepfold*; the second, in the subsequent words, *and one shepherd*. Those who are dispersed are gathered in the unity of faith, and by the uniqueness of God they are proven not to be gods. . . . These things can be clearly enough confirmed. But I pass on to divide the matter of this theme in a different way for people who are less educated; and I do so in their mother tongue. For that purpose, we must know that every Christian soul may be called a sheep, as can be well enough shown from today's Gospel in which my theme occurs. Therefore, every Christian who lives in the desert of this world must carefully watch and reflect on how he may protect his sheep from the wolves of this desert. And therefore I will teach you as well as I know how you may build a sheepfold for yourselves in which you can safely guard this sheep. As you know, a sheepfold must have four sides as its walls. In the same way, your sheepfold must have four walls.

At this point the manuscript changes to English: "The first wall of this fold shall be prudence, the second justice, the third fortitude, and the fourth temperance." The text continues, in English, to show four moral teachings that help in the construction of the sheepfold: these are such pieces of proverbial wisdom as, "Mine to thee and thine to me" (for justice) or:

> Loue me and Yche þe,
> And þenne schal we wrendes boe   friends

(for temperance); and the preachers adds four kinds of men who are about the walls and must be guarded against.[80] When the second division

---

[80] "*Fiet unum ovile et unus pastor*. Iohannis 10. . . . In quibus verbis ecclesia dupliciter commendatur, a sue fidei unitate et a Dei sui singularitate. Primum notatur cum dicitur *fiet unum ovile*; secundum cum infertur *et unus pastor*. In fidei unitate dispersi congregantur et a Dei singularitate dii non esse probantur. . . . Ista possunt probari satis clare, set transeo ad dividendum aliter materiam huius thematis personis minus litteratis, et hoc in lingua materna. Pro quo sciendum quod quelibet anima Christiana potest dici ovis, sicud potest satis ostendi ex ewangelio hodierno ubi thema habet locum. Et ideo quilibet Christianus in de-

is completed, the text reverts to Latin and then develops the construction of the sheepfold in that language.

This text clearly reveals that in late fourteenth-century England sermons were preached in Latin as well as in English, whether the two languages were used on separate occasions or, as one might infer from the quoted passage, on one and the same occasion. Besides, the choice of language depended on the nature of the audience. And further, the nature of the audience also determined the kind of division the preacher might use, for in the quoted sermon the two divisions belong to different types. The first *divisio thematis*, technically called *divisio intra*, derives its members directly from the verbal matter of the theme: *unum*, *ovile* (signifying the Church), and *pastor* (signifying God). It can be schematized thus:

$$\text{Ecclesia commendatur} \begin{cases} \text{a sue fidei unitate}\text{—}\textit{fiet unum ovile}; \\ \\ \text{a Dei sui singularitate}\text{—}\textit{et unus pastor}. \end{cases}$$

The other kind, called *divisio extra*, derives its members not from within the verbal form of the theme but from without, i.e., by dividing a concept that is contained in or suggested by the theme. In our sermon, the biblical ''sheepfold'' suggests a (spiritual) building, whose four walls are moralized as the four cardinal virtues. In this case, the *divisio extra* is explicitly offered for use before *personis minus litteratis*, following thus the advice given by Pseudo-Bonaventure.[81]

The *divisio extra* gave a preacher a much greater freedom with respect to his theme, which had important consequences for his constructing the formal division because it led directly to divisions of great length and complexity. These stand at the far end of a wide and richly diversified range of rhymed English divisions. The simplest members of this range contain no more than the pertinent English rhyme-words:

---

serto huius mundi constitutus habet se diligenter inspicere et considerare qualiter a lupis huius deserti ovem suam custodiat. Et ideo ut potero docebo vos ad presens quomodo unum ovile vobis construatis in quo secure hanc ovem custodire possitis. Ovile, sicud scitis, habere debet quatuor latera quasi quatuor muros. Sic ergo habeat ovile tuum quatuor muros. . . . þe firste wald of þis wold sal be sleiȝþe [*interlinear*: prudencia], þe oþer sal bee rythfulnesse [*interlinear*: iusticia], þe thridde sal be strenþe [*interlinear*: fortitudo], þe ferþe sal bee mytfulnesse [*interlinear*: temperancia].'' Worcester Cathedral, MS. F.126, fol. 194.

[81] See above, p. 71.

Agnus qui in medio troni est reget eos (Rev. 7.17). . . . In quibus ver-
bis tria possumus videre que decent quemlibet regem in sua introni-
zacione, videlicet,
> quod sit vnlothfull,
>> wurshipfull,
>>> wytffull.[82]

That English appears so sparsely in this division, incidentally, does not
mean that this preacher or scribe was shy of using his native tongue, for
in the course of this sermon occur an English quatrain from the hymn
Vexilla regis prodeunt (st. 5), a versified dialogue of Christ and the devils
at the Harrowing of Hell (translating *Attollite portas*, Psalm 23.7-8), and
at least six couplets translating biblical quotations which show that Christ
is the lamb offered for us.[83] A similarly minimal amount of English ap-
pears in another division:

Ecce nunc tempus acceptabile . . . (2 Corinthians 6.2).
> of gostyly fyȝtyng,
> of gostly helyng,
> of gostly syngyng,
> of gostly sowyng.[84]

Here again the sparsity of the division contrasts with much greater verbal
richness in a subdivision, appearing in part three of the sermon, which
specifies how a sinner should (four qualities) and should not (two quali-
ties, the text breaking off before the two expected final qualities are men-
tioned) "sing" in confession:

> As þe nyȝthyngale in þe þorne,
> As þe turtyl in þe morne,
> As þe cok agayn þe day,
> As þe þrowstyl in þe May (vel as þe lauerok),
> As þe crowe in hys flyȝth,
> As þe oule in þe nyȝth.[85]

When English divisions extend beyond the rhyme-word, the verbal
processes employed are of the most diverse nature. To illustrate this di-

---

[82] Bodleian Library MS. Lat. th. d. 1, fol. 167. The sermon was preached at Lynn in
1431.

[83] Respectively: *IMEV* 3490.6; 3825.5; the biblical quotations remain unlisted.

[84] Cambridge University Library, MS. Kk.4.24, fol. 180v.

[85] Ibid., foi. 184r-v. The lines appear only separately in their respective sections.

versity I will quote three divisions that deal with the same subject, Christ's three (or four) comings. In the first, the rhyme-words are expanded by a modifier:

> *Tu es qui venturus es?* Matthei 11 . . . Pro processu sermonis sciendum est quod triplex est adventus Christi, de quo modo est loquendum, videlicet in mundum, in mentem, et ad finale iudicium.
>
> In mundum be oure keende takyng,   <small>by taking our nature</small>
> in mente[m] be grace and good leuyng,
> et ad iudicium be vniuerseel demyng.[86]

The second example not only has longer phrases (which are translated from Latin) but, being a fourfold division, allows this preacher to introduce a change in the rhyme-words:

> *Ecce venio cito*, Apocalipsis 10 . . .
> In maydenes breste,
> In mannys soule for reste.
> To hel payne to slake,
> Et venit into þis world a dome to take.[87]

This actually is only a distinction used in the introductory matter. The proper *divisio thematis* (here very much *extra*) focuses on Christ's coming for judgment and lists seven parts of the medieval judicial process, which then furnish the structure for moralized treatment in the sermon:

> Opyn warnyng,
> Loud callyng,
> þe iustyse on be benche y-set,
> þe felon ys forþe y-fet,
> þe seriauntes þe harmys rekyn,
> þe dosen þe soþ tellyn,
> And þe iuges þe dome delyn.[88]

The final example is one of the rare English divisions in Holcot's sermons. It is characterized, more than the two previous divisions, by its close imitation of a Latin pattern in its syntactic parallelism as well as end-rhyme:

---

[86] Cambridge, Jesus College, MS. 13, part vi, fol. 91v.
[87] Cambridge University Library, MS. Kk.4.24, fol. 234v.
[88] Ibid., fol. 235.

Venit tibi mansuetus, Matthei 21 . . .
Anglice: [He come] myghtyli and frendly, þe helpyng;
he come wyttily and bodyli, þe warnyng;
he come to þe trustely and frendly, þe vnderfongyng.[89]

The following *divisio intra* is similarly close to its Latin model and handles its verbal material with differing processes of both shortening and expansion:

Sedet a dextris Dei, Marci ultimo [i.e., Mark 16.19] . . . , in quibus tria:

[Requies] favoris post fatigacionem—*sedet*,
Anglice: Rest after long swynkynge;
Linies (?)[90] honoris post confusionem—*a dextris*,
Anglice: Worshipe after gret lowynge;   humiliation
Merces amoris post prestolacionem—*Dei*,
Anglice: Mede of alle oure loue-longynge.[91]

This Ascension sermon holds a further interest because it has been preserved in at least two other manuscripts which show variations that are characteristic of the partly oral transmission of such texts and of the freedom their users must have felt to add or delete material *ad libitum*.[92] This freedom extends to the division; in one of the other manuscripts it has only two parts, but then a second division is added to it:

Vel sic: In þis wordis we may se þat—
Crist had rest at hys nede, cum dicitur quod *sedit*,
and Crist had worschyp for hys mede, et ideo *sedet a dextris Dei*.[93]

Such offers of alternatives within one and same sermon are not infrequent. One further example is the following *divisio thematis intra* into

---

[89] Cambridge, Peterhouse MS. 210, fol. 1.

[90] I fail to make sense of this word. *Linies* might mean "anointing" but seems not to be recorded in the standard dictionaries. The other two manuscripts (see the following note) omit the initial word in the three members of the Latin division.

[91] Worcester Cathedral, MS. F.126, fol. 148.

[92] Cambridge University Library, MS. Ii.3.8, fols. cxxxvii-138; London, St. Paul's Cathedral MS. 8, fol. 199. The normal introduction beginning "Boni rumores letificant cor" is, in Worcester F.126, preceded by a protheme, "Wlgariter dicitur: Cum poteris quod vis . . ." Here the entire sermon occupies fols. 147vb-148va.

[93] Cambridge University Library, MS. Ii.3.8., fol. cxxxvii; printed by Stemmler, No. 37.

92

two parts, for whose second member the writer gives two different forms:

Ambulate in dileccione [Eph. 5.2] . . .
> What nedys a pilgryme do þat wyll sped hym smert? *Ambulare*.
> What nedes a man [do] that will plese wyþe hert?
>> well [*read* vel] sic: What nedes a rewin do that wyll
>> stand in quert? *Habere dileccionem et diligere*.[94]

The just quoted example has brought us to divisions whose members are complete sentences and form long lines. Here, too, one finds much variety in pattern and verbal form, from which I select three illustrations. The first translates a Latin *divisio extra* of the theme *Fecit Levi convivium magnum Iesu in domo sua* ("Levi made Jesus a great banquet in his house," Luke 5.29). The sermon speaks of four kinds of people involved in making a banquet: messengers who invite the guests, damsels who receive them, friends who sit down with them, and servants who wait on them, and these four groups are then moralized to form the following division:

> Invitant ergo fides, pietas, et benevolencia.
> Recipiunt spes, humilitas, et continencia.
> Recumbant pauper[i]es, caritas, et paciencia.
> Ministrant sanctitas, zelus, et modestia.
>> Vs preyen bileue, god wille, and pite.
>> Vs kepen god hope, mekenesse, and kastite.
>> Vus sit by pouert, wisdom, and god louy[n]g.
>> Vus seruen clannesse, ryth, and feyr bery[n]g.[95]

The next example comes from a sermon on the feast of Corpus Christi. Here the preacher gives first an elegant Latin division of "bread":

> Triplex, amatissimi, panis spiritualiter in sacra reperitur scriptura:
>> Panis commendabilis sustentans fatigatos . . . ,
>> Panis admirabilis recreans educatos . . . ,
>> Panis delectabilis [MS. delicabilis] exponens figuratos.

The members of the division are at once confirmed with references to biblical figures. Then the preacher puts the division into English. In

---

[94] Oxford, Balliol College, MS. 149, fol. 73.
[95] British Library, MS. Harley 7322, fol. 184.

doing so he creates a quatrain whose last line repeats the theme, which is then followed by three long lines based upon the Latin division:

> Ideo citato themate nostri sermonis dixi *Hic est panis*, ubi supra.
>> Whan Crist for vs wold be ded,
>> He made his body of þis hed [*read* bred?].
>> Þan schal Y schew wyth good rede
>> How Iesu Crist þan ys þys bred.

> Sic: Þys ys bred to preyse þat susteyneth þe wery and makyth hym
>> strong to wend.
>> Þys ys bred meruelous þat God wold to hys folke fro heuyn send.
>> Þat ys bred best of al þat bryngyth hem þat hyt eten to ioy wyt-
>> owten eny ende.[96]

An equally skillful way of laying out the *materia sermonis* occurs a few folios later in the same manuscript. Here the theme—*Ascendit Deus in iubilo* (''God is ascended with jubilation,'' Psalm 4.6)—leads at once to an initial distinction of four kinds of men whose task it is to ''ascend'':

> Ascendunt enim communiter: doctores studii, ductores prelii, judices regnorum, et reges eorum. Anglice sic:
>> Maystres þat ben ordeynyd for to teche,
>> Werryours þat goen to take wreche,
>> Domesmen þat ben sweryn to kype ryʒth,
>> And kyngus and lordys þat ben of myʒth.

These four professions, the preacher continues in Latin, may all be applied to Christ:

> Christus est magister scientissimus, preliator fortissimus, iudex equissimus, et dominus potentissimus, et per consequens sibi competit ascendere. Quapropter de ipso merito dicere possum quod—
>> Primo ascendit as a mayster þat hem tauʒth
>>> þat were leude and vnkunnyng.
>> Ascendit secundo as a werriour þat ys pray y-kauʒth
>>> and ouercome woo and anger.
>> Ascendit tercio as a juge þat demeth wel sore
>>> hem þat ben in syn dwellyng.

---

[96] Cambridge University Library, MS. Kk.4.24, fol. 173.

> Et ascendit quarto as a kyng for to reyne euermore
> and men to mede after here beryng.
> Et hec materia sermonis.[97]

The English lines thus follow the schema set by the Latin division. In the first quatrain, the change of rhyme-word (*teche . . . ry3th*) may be modeled on the similar change in the Latin (*studii . . . regnorum*), but in the second set of English lines the preacher has independently managed to break up the monotony of the Latin parallel phrases and has expanded them into much looser but genuinely English verses with double rhymes.

There remains for consideration a final technique of sermon construction which leads to very complex divisions. A sermon on *Redde racionem* ("Give an account," Luke 16.2) first advances a very short *divisio thematis intra*, in Latin and English:

> In quibus duo breviter denotantur, videlicet:
>> racionalis exaccio —*redde*;
>> et terribilis satisfaccio —*racionem.*
> Anglice: a sky[l]ful askynge,
>> and a dredful 3uldynge.

After confirming this much with scriptural authorities, the preacher then generates further matter for his sermon which runs as follows in modern English:

> The more a person receives to spend, the more useful it is for him to be very careful in his expenditures, because the account he will have to render of them will be so much more strict. But everything we have, we have received from someone else (1 Corinthians 4.7). . . . Therefore, we shall have to render a strict account. Now we have received three kinds of goods from the Lord for our spending, namely the goods of nature, of fortune, and of grace. But since it is natural for us to act with reason, it is a good thing to so spend our natural goods that we may give of them a reasonable account. And since the goods of fortune, that is, worldly possessions, must not be gathered in excess, nor must we put our hope in them, for they come by chance and go by chance, therefore they must be spent courteously (*curialiter*) so that we may be able to give of them a faithful account. And the goods of grace must be spent in such a way that we be able to give of them a

[97] Ibid., fol. 186.

safe account. . . . Therefore, I can say in English, as to the matter of this sermon:

So byset þi god of kunde
Of god of hap þou salt be hende } ut possis racionem reddere { skilfulliche
þi god of grace so salt þu spende treweliche
syker-
liche.[98]

The procedure illustrated in this paragraph is technically known as *declaratio partium*:[99] the first division (here, what we are to give an account for: the three kinds of goods) is followed by a second (how we are to account for them), and this process may continue to a third and fourth division.[100] In the subsequent development, the corresponding members of the several divisions (first, second, etc.) would then be tied together in precisely the way that is graphically demonstrated by the quoted macaronic lines.

The result of such a *declaratio partium* with *colligatio* is three or four successive divisions, which may appear to readers who are unfamiliar with the techniques of scholastic sermon construction as so many stanzas of a poem. "How Christ Shall Come," mentioned at the beginning of this book, is such a case, to which I will add two further examples. The first appears in a sermon on *Ambulate* ("Walk!" Ephesians 5.2). Here we find three divisions, each of three members, which deal with the manner of walking, the way we should take, and the reward which walking thus brings us:

[98] "Pro materia est advertendum quod quanto plura homo percipit expendenda, tanto utilius est ut se in expensis habeat cauciorem, quia districcior est racione . . . Set nos omnia que habemus recepimus ab alio, sicud dicit Apostolus Ad Corinthios 4 . . . Igitur districtam racionem reddituri. Recepimus enim a Domino tria bonorum genera expendenda, videlicet bona nature, bona fortune, et bona gracie. Set quia naturale est nobis habere racionem, ideo bonum est ut expendamus bona nature ut de eis poterimus racionabiliter reddere racionem. Et quia bona fortune, videlicet illa temporalia, non sunt nimis colligenda nec in eis spes ponenda, quia fortunate adveniunt et fortunate recedunt, idem sunt expendenda curialiter, ut possimus reddere racionem fideliter. Et bona gracie sunt expendenda ut secure poterimus reddere racionem . . . Dicatur igitur Anglice sic pro materia: . . ." Worcester Cathedral, MS. F.126, fol. 193.

[99] Basevorn, chs. 34-38.

[100] In the example, a third division is added, on our being reconciled to God; it is given only in Latin, and it links the first member to the second, and the second to the third: "Si racionabiliter expenderimus, fideliter reconci[li]abimur; et si fideliter expenderimus, secure reconciliabimur."

Ambulate inquam tripliciter in via triplici et habebitis tria.
  Primo ambulate:
    redeliche withouten lettyng,
    wyseliche withouten stumlyng,
    sothliche withowten faynyng.
  Sic ergo ambulate tripliciter, et in via triplici:
    In þe wey of penance and of butturness,
    in þe wey of obedience and of lownesse,
    in þe wey of loue and of swettnesse.
  Sic ergo in via triplici, et habebitis tria:
    Walke and haue bliss withowten sorowyng.
    Walke and haue worschip [withowten] fletthyng.   change
    Walke and haue mede withowten endyng.

The next sentence, which begins the first principal, then ties the corresponding members together: "Primo ambulate in via penitencie et acerbitatis celeriter sine tardacione, et habebitis gaudium sine desolacione."[101]

In contrast, my final example, taken from a sermon on *Iesu, fili David, miserere mei*" ("Jesus, son of David, have mercy on me," Mark 10.47), gives the division in Latin:

In quibus verbis [Iesus] a tribus commendatur:
  a potestate ineffabili,
  ab equitate inflexibili,
  a bonitate inenarrabili.
Pro processu dicatur sic:
  Iesu salvator omnium, miserere mei,
  Iesu redemptor gencium, miserere mei,
  Iesu largitor munerum, miserere mei.
Iesu, filii David, miserere mei.
  Fili inquam David vigore potentissime, miserere mei.
  Fili inquam David nitore splendi[di]ssime, miserere mei.
  Fili inquam David virore clementissime, miserere mei.
Iesu filii David, miserere mei—
  mei inquam implo- / rantis perfectam humilitatem,
  mei inquam recordantis propriam calamitatem,
  mei inquam affectantis ad tuam maiestatem.[102]

---

[101] Oxford, Magdalen College MS. 93, fol. 148.
[102] Oxford, Merton College MS. 248, fol. 66.

Here the initial distinction (*a potestate,* etc.) is followed with a threefold *declaratio partium.* Each of these *declarationes* "divides" one of the three terms contained in the theme: *Iesu, Fili David,* and [*miserere*] *mei,* into three parts. The individual lines in the three divisions of course agree logically with the respective line of the initial distinction; thus, the first lines of the divisions go with *potestas ineffabilis,* and so forth. After confirming all this, the text changes to English:

> Iesu þat al þis world haþ wroʒt haue merci on me. Iesu þat wiþ þi blod vs bouʒt. Iesu þat ʒaf vs whanne we adde noʒt. Iesu David sone, etc. David sone ful of miʒt, haue etc. David sone fair to siʒt. David sone þat mengeþ merci wiþ riʒt. Haue merci on me and mak me mek to þe. And mak me þenche on þe. And bring me to þe þat longeþ to þe þat wolde ben at þe. Iesu, etc.

Because it is written in a highly abbreviated form, the English rendition is difficult to unravel, but a moment's attention will show that it contains rhymed English material for all nine lines of the complex Latin division, as well as a translation of the theme (*Iesu, David sone,* etc.). Inadvertent readers might find here a fragmentary Middle English hymn or even carol with refrain:

> Iesu þat al þis world haþ wroʒt,
> Iesu þat wiþ þe blod vs bouʒt,
> Iesu þat ʒaf vs whanne we adde noʒt—
>   Haue merci on me.
> Iesu, David sone, haue merci on me.

But in fact the English lines are directly derived from the Latin sermon division and furnish the structural blueprint for the sermon's principal parts. This is made quite clear by the preacher himself when he continues:

> Prosequatur ergo sic: Iesu þat al þis world had wroʒt, David sone ful of myʒt, haue merci on me and mak me mek to þe; et isto modo concluendo [*read* circulando *or* colligando] prosequitur sermo.

(Let the development then be as follows . . . ; and by tying the members together in this fashion, the sermon is developed.)[103]

---

[103] Oxford, Merton College MS. 248, fol. 66v.

In the manuscript the text of this sermon ends at this point. By setting forth its most important, basic material, the preacher or scribe has put down all that is needed to guide him or others.

Though the English divisions of various shapes and types we have surveyed make use of some artistic devices (parallelism and end-rhyme), they can hardly be called works of great verbal art. It would seem that the formal constraints set for them by their Latin models, as well as their sermon function, work against any display of poetic skills that might endow them with lively diction, imagery, rhetorical figures, and the like—qualities we found so amply present in Latin and English hymns. These rhymed divisions are versified prose rather than genuine poems. But where the constraints of a sermon *divisio* no longer apply, one can frequently find an immediate move towards greater craftsmanship, and the lines begin metrically to breathe. This is often the case in subdivisions and even more so in distinctions. An example has already occurred in the lines on various singing birds. These still preserve syntactic parallelism but vary the rhyme scheme more pleasingly. Yet even in rendering their main divisions some preachers clearly took pains to make them agreeable to the ear. A sermon on *Vocati estis* ("You are called," 1 Peter 2.21), for instance, sets up four things to which we are called. Its Latin division is endowed with nearly total syntactic parallelism and trisyllabic end-rhyme:

> Ad stadium pugne fortioris,
> ad domum scole melioris,
> ad scannum regis melioris,
> ad aulam mense lautioris.

The immediately following English rendition, however, abandons this monotony and introduces a change in the rhyme as well as in the metric pattern between the first and the second couplets:

> To a feld of daynty fyȝtyng,
> To a scole of holy techyng,
> To a dome dredful,
> And to a mele blesful.[104]

---

[104] Cambridge University Library, MS. Kk.4.24, fol. 227v; previously quoted in *Verses*, p. 79.

Quatrains with similar characteristics occur elsewhere in the same and in other manuscripts.[105] On rare occasions one might even find a more developed stanza form used for the division, as in this case from a Latin sermon by John of Waldeby on the theme *Abiit Iesus trans mare* ("Jesus went over the sea," John 6.1):

> Corrupciun of synne
> Þat we han fallun inne
> We schul now forsake—*trans mare*.
> Þe sacrament of penaunce
> Schal be oure delyueraunce
> And so amendus make—*abiit Iesus*.[106]

And as we have seen, complex sermon divisions may lead to three or four units with different rhyme schemes which look much like so many stanzas of a poem.

But it must be said that even such longer structures or stanza-like divisions do not deserve much praise for verbal craftsmanship. As a rule, their rhyme-words betray great poverty of linguistic resources and imagination, for such rhymes as blode/rode/fode, dede/spede/mede, synne/ynne/blynne, sesoun/tresoun/resoun, make/take/sake, adjectives in *-ful*, and participles or gerunds in *-ing* are ubiquitous to the point of being quite predictable. Nevertheless, as the examination of formal techniques of sermon construction and of the presence of artistic qualities in actual sermons has shown, the sermon division was the *locus par excellence* in late medieval preaching which demanded the application of "poetic" skills, primarily versification. It presented the occasion for a widespread, lively, and diversified artistic activity among preachers which led to the production of rhymes and verses in the vernacular. Making rhymed sermon divisions was not the only opportunity a talented preacher had to create a poem;[107] but it certainly was a seedbed that could stimulate talent and lead to further growth.

---

[105] See the examples given in *Verses*, pp. 77-80.

[106] Bodleian Library, MS. Laud Misc. 77, fol. 77v; "Unrecorded," No. 10.

[107] Nor was it historically the earliest use of English verses in sermons, because rhymed English proverbs appear in Latin sermon manuscripts earlier than divisions. See *Verses*, pp. 93-98.

4

The Oeuvre
of Friar John
# of Grimestone

In order to build the kind of verbal structure analyzed in the preceding chapter, individual preachers needed expert guidance as well as handy depositories of the materials from which sermons could be composed. This need was supplied by a wide variety of preaching tools.[1] *Artes praedicandi*, formal treatises on sermon construction, would teach the organization and structural principles of the scholastic sermon and indicate ways in which its parts could be generated and developed.[2] Collections of fully developed sermons would furnish models which a preacher might imitate or freely plunder. Briefer sermon *schemata* would provide outlines, perhaps with more detailed introductions, which the preacher could then adapt and fill in at his convenience. In contrast, other collections and handbooks would offer the actual verbal material to be used. Biblical concordances in alphabetical order indicated all the passages in Scripture where a particular word occurred, and collections of *distinctiones* gave the various real or allegorical meanings that a term, usually a biblical term, might carry. From the latter developed huge encyclopedias in which the properties of all things, from God to minerals, were listed and provided with moral interpretations. Finally, collections of *exempla*, arranged by topics and eventually in alphabetical order, would gather hundreds of stories with which a preacher could graphically illustrate his points.[3] These reference materials can be found

[1] See the surveys on preaching tools in Johannes Baptist Schneyer, *Geschichte der katholischen Predigt* (Freiburg i. Br., 1969), pp. 178-85; Richard H. Rouse and Mary A. Rouse, *Preachers, Florilegia and Sermons: Studies on the "Manipulus florum" of Thomas of Ireland* (Toronto, 1979), esp. chapter 1; and Homer G. Pfander, "The Mediaeval Friars and Some Alphabetical Reference Books for Sermons," *MAe* 3 (1934), 19-29. See also Christina von Nolcken, "Some Alphabetical Compendia and How Preachers Used Them in Fourteenth-Century England," *Viator* 12 (1981), 271-88.

[2] Cf. references in ch. 3.

[3] For the variety and development of *exempla* collections, see J.-Th. Welter, *L'exemplum dans la littérature religieuse et didactique du moyen âge* (Paris and Toulouse, 1927; repr. New York, 1973).

101

in various combinations in the great, voluminous handbooks for preachers written between the mid-thirteenth and the late fifteenth centuries. Such manuals were compiled in widely different forms and with different emphases: *Fasciculus morum*, for example, arranges its sermon material in a discursive treatment of the seven deadly sins and their opposite virtues,[4] whereas Bromyard's *Summa praedicantium* presents its subject matter in a large number of articles on theological subjects, like an alphabetical encyclopedia. Both books, and many others, however, share the same purpose of furnishing preachers with *materia praedicabilis*.

Of particular interest for the early English lyric and its relation to preaching is the handbook compiled by Friar John of Grimestone,[5] because the preaching material it collects—in Latin, as is usual for books of this kind—also contains some 240 poems in English. That preaching tools in Latin also preserve some vernacular verses is not unusual; the extraordinary interest of Grimestone's commonplace book lies in its exceeding its closest competitors by three or four times the number of English lyrics.[6]

This collection of commonplaces is arranged in 232 alphabetical articles, which run from *Abstinencia* to *Vestis*.[7] Its character may be seen from the following excerpt, the entire section on *Adulacio*, which occupies one page:

De adulacione. 3.

[1] "Adulacio est fallaci laude seduccio," Augustinus.
[2] Item: "Ypocrisis est virtutum simulacione et arte inclusiva vicii."

---

[4] *Verses*, ch. 1.

[5] Edward Wilson, *A Descriptive Index of the English Lyrics in John of Grimestone's Preaching Book*, Medium Aevum Monographs, n.s., II (Oxford, 1973), p. xiii. For the sake of brevity and consistency, I refer to Friar John of Grimestone simply as "Grimestone." We know next to nothing about him, including whether he was the author of these or any poems or merely their collector or a scribe. In this and the following chapter I will speak of Grimestone as if he were the author of at least most of these poems, but the question of his authorship remains open.

[6] British Library, MS. Harley 7322 contains some 80 English verses; *Fasciculus morum*, 61.

[7] The topics of the entries are listed in an alphabetical index, which specifies 232 topics, though the text seems to have three or four more. The last three articles listed in the index (*Usura*, *Vita*, and *Vestis*), however, are missing in the text, which ends—apparently incomplete—with *Via Christi*.

[3] Gregorius: "Qu[i] vite sue testem in celo habet, testimonium hominum non debet timere in terra."

[4] Item: "Si laudibus letamur et vituperacionibus frangimur, gloriam nostram non in nobis sed in ore ponimus aliorum."

[5] Seneca: "Cum omnia habeant divites, vix habent aliquem qui eis verum dicat."

[6] Gregorius: "Nemo potest in una eadem re omnipotenti Deo et hostibus eius gratus existere."

[7] Ignacius: "Hii qui me laudant pocius flagellant."

[8] Gregorius: "Serpentes astuti sunt, sed in malo; enim semper aspiciunt quomodo mordent, et cum morderint, quomodo se ocultent."

[9] Crisostomus: "Adulator omnis virtutis inimicus est."

[10] Ieronimus: "Palpantes adulatores quasi hostes fuge."

[11] Item: "Isto tempore maxime regnat vicium adulacionis, et ita fit ut qui adulari nescit aut invidus aut superbus reputatur."

[12] Augustinus: "Nichil sic probat amicum sicud oneris amici portacio [MS. portare]."

[13] Bernardus: "Verbum glorie, noli me tangere."

[14] Ysidorus: "Sicud bene constitutus non metuit aliene lingue convicium, ita et qui laudatur ab alio non debet errorem aliene laudis attendere, sed magis unusquisque testimonium consciencie sue querat cui plus ipse presens est quam ille qui eum laudat."

[15] Augustinus: "Lingue adulancium alligant animas in peccatis."

[16] Item ait: "Plus nocet lingua adulatoris quam gladius peccatoris."

[17] Unde quidam philosophus cuidam sibi adulanti sic ait: "Nihil proficis, adulator, quia intelligo et scio quid loqueris."

[18] Augustinus: "Oleum demulcens lingua adulatoris est que mentes a rigore veritatis emollit ad noxia."

[19] Unde Psalmo 11: "Disperdat Dominus universa labia dolosa."

[20] Ieremie 12: "Ne credas eis cum locuti fuerint tibi bona."

[21] Augustinus *De consensu evangelistarum*: "Qui facile credit, levis est corde."

[22] Ysaie 3: "Qui te bonum dicunt, ipsi te decipiunt."

[23] Augustinus: "Non acerba sed blanda verba timebis."
[The following text written in two columns. Col. a:]
[24] Non satis est totum mellitis credere verbis.
　　Ex hoc melle solet pestis amare sequi.
[25] Raro credatur cuiquam si multa loquatur.
　　Unde relatori tu semper credere noli.
[26] Non bene creduntur nimium qui blanda locuntur.
　　Decipiuntur aves per cantus semper suaves.
[27] Þei ben nouth wel for to leouen
　　Þat with manie wordis wil quemen.
　　For often deceyued þe briddes be
　　With sundri songes an loueli gle.
[Column b. Two lines blank next to Non satis.]
[28. *Next to* Raro:] Late lef him þat michil spekt,
　　　　　For gret spekere treuthe brekt.
[29. *Next to* Non bene:] Nota quod mercatores abscondunt merces
　　　　　suas male solventibus. Sic iusti bona sua adulatoribus.
[30. *Next to* Þat with:] Si vis ditari vel ut propheta vocari
　　　　　Discas adulari quia tales sunt modo cari.
[31] ȝef þu wilt ben riche or cleped holi,
　　Ler to flateren, for þei ben laten wel bi.
[End of page; end of section.][8]

On Flattery. 3.

[1] "Flattery is seduction by means of deceitful praise," Augustine.
[2] Further: "It is hypocrisy by means of simulating the virtues and hedging in the vices."
[3] Gregory: "He who has a witness to his life in heaven need not fear the testimony of men on earth."

---

[8] Edinburgh, National Library of Scotland, MS. Advocates 18.7.21, fol. 13. In the manuscript, the items are not numbered. They are written continuously through 23. Items 24-31—all verses except 29—are written as verse and in two columns, as indicated. In the margin appear most of the names of the authorities quoted. To the left of 27 and to the right of 28 appears a cross. Item 29 is marked "exemplum. nota." Items 27-31 seem to have been written in different ink and with a different pen than 1-26. This, as well as the changing spatial relation of Latin source and English translation (25/28, 26/27, and 30/31) and the blank space left next to 24, suggests that the material in Grimestone's commonplace book was entered at different times. This suggestion is borne out by marginal additions throughout the volume and by entire sections that were apparently added later. The English

[4] Likewise: "If we are highly pleased by praise and broken by censure, we place our honor not in ourselves but in the mouth of others."

[5] Seneca: "While rich people have all things, they hardly have anyone who tells them the truth."

[6] Gregory: "No-one can in one and the same matter be pleasing to both Almighty God and his enemies."

[7] Ignatius: "People who praise me rather scourge me."

[8] Gregory: "Serpents are shrewd, but in an evil way, for they are always on the lookout how they may bite, and when they have bitten, how they may hide."

[9] Chrysostom: "The flatterer is an enemy to every virtue."

[10] Jerome: "Flee coaxing flatterers like enemies."

[11] Further: "In our time the vice of flattery is most powerful, and so it comes that one who does not know how to flatter is held to be either envious or proud."

[12] Augustine: "Nothing tests a friend so much as carrying his friend's burden."

[13] Bernard: "Word of glory, do not touch me!"

[14] Isidore: "As a well-ordered person does not fear the insult that comes from another man's tongue, so must a person who is being praised by another not heed the error of external praise but rather seek the testimony of his own conscience, which is nearer to him than the man who praises him."

[15] Augustine: "The tongues of flatterers tie down souls in their sins."

[16] He says further: "The tongue of a flatterer does more harm than the sword of a sinner [*read*: a persecutor]."

[17] Whence a philosopher said to someone who was flattering him: "You don't get anywhere, flatterer, because I understand and know what you are saying."

[18] Augustine: "A flatterer's tongue is a softening oil which relaxes minds from the rigor of truth to harmful things."

[19] Hence Psalm 11: "May the Lord destroy all deceitful lips."

---

verses quoted here and throughout the following chapters have been checked against the text of Grimestone's manuscript. Abbreviations are silently expanded. The ampersand is expanded to *an* or *and*, following Grimestone's apparent practice when he writes out the full form. The *nomen sacrum*, written *Jhu, ihu,* or *iᵘ*, is consistently expanded to *Iesu*.

[20] Jeremiah 12: "Do not believe them when they have spoken good things of you."

[21] Augustine, *On the Agreement of the Evangelists*: "He who believes easily is light of heart."

[22] Isaiah 3: "They who call you good deceive you."

[23] Augustine: "You must not fear harsh words but smooth ones."

[24] "It will not do to trust honeyed words. From such honey usually comes a bitter disease."

[25] "A man who talks much must be trusted little. Do not always believe a tale-teller."

[26] "People who talk too pleasantly are not easily trusted. Birds are always beguiled with sweet songs."

[27] "Þei ben nouth . . . ."

[28] "Late lef him . . . ."

[29] Notice that merchants hide their wares from people who do not pay promptly; thus just men hide their good points from flatterers.

[30] "If you wish to get rich or be called a prophet, you must learn how to flatter, for these are now highly prized."

[31] "ȝef þu wilt . . . ."

The English verses of this entry are representative of the 246 English verse items which appear sprinkled throughout the volume. Of these, seven occur twice, so that the book contains a total of 239 separate English poems. These are distributed somewhat unevenly. Many articles contain no English at all (such as those on Christ's Advent, Baptism, Contemplation, Chastity, Envy, etc.). Among the 75 articles with English verses, most have between one and four items each, while only a handful contain five to eight poems.[9] Sharply different in this respect are the sections devoted to death and to the Passion of Christ, which contain 22 and 63 English poems respectively. Both were favorite topics in late medieval preaching, but the great emphasis on Christ's Passion in Grimestone's lyrical output is peculiar.[10] Many of Grimestone's poems

---

[9] *Cupiditas* and *Luxuria*, five each; *Superbia* and *Tempus*, six each; *Peccatum*, eight.

[10] The numbers here given refer to the actual items included in a particular section. Further items on the same subject may occur in different sections. Thus, the number of poems dealing with death can be increased to 28; see my analysis in "Pestilence and Middle English Literature: Friar John Grimestone's Poems on Death," in *The Black Death. The Impact of the Fourteenth-Century Plague*, ed. Daniel Williman (Binghamton, N.Y., 1982), pp. 130-59.

consist of only one or two couplets, but several of them are considerably longer and organized in stanzas, reaching as many as 196 lines (the ABC poem, 198).[11]

This remarkable body of English verses clearly written for use in preaching allows us, in this and the following chapter, to examine closely the processes involved in creating such verses, their function in preaching, and the degree and kinds of verbal artistry their creator strove for and achieved.

The verbal processes employed in creating Grimestone's preaching verses show the same wide variety we observed in their subject matter, length, and metrical form. They range from translation through various degrees of expansion to free creation. A large number of Grimestone's poems—in fact, a little over fifty percent—are the result of directly translating a Latin text, which is usually cited in the handbook immediately before the English verse rendition.[12] Thus, Ecclesiasticus 3.32: *Cor sapiens et intelligibile abstinebit se a peccatis* ("A wise and understanding heart will abstain from sins") is rendered as:

> Þe wise herte and vnderstondingge
> Sal kepen himselue fro senningge.   (12)

The translation is literal to a fault. Less so is the following rendering of 1 Peter 2.24: *Peccata nostra ipse pertulit in corpore suo super lignum* ("He himself has borne our sins in his body on the cross"), which both omits material in its source and adds to it:

> On þe tre he hatȝ iborn
> Oure sennes for wiche we weren forlorn.   (24)[13]

---

[11] In this and the following chapters, Grimestone's verses will be identified by the numbers they have been given in Wilson's *Descriptive Index*. Twenty-three of them, usually longer and poetically more interesting items, were edited by Carleton Brown in *RL XIV*, nos. 55-76. They are: Grimestone 4 (Brown 55), 5 (56), 6 (57), 7 (58), 8 (59), 34 (60), 107 (61), 174 (62), 177 (63), 178 (64), 180 (65), 184 (66), 185 (67), 186 (68), 201 (69), 202 (70), 203 (71), 205 (72), 208 (73), 211 (74), 213 and 215 (75), and 214 (76).

[12] Wilson normally gives only the first line in the case of Latin verses and rearranges the order of Latin source and English translation, placing the source text after the English poem. I identify sources in the following notes only where Wilson has not given them.

[13] Both Latin source text and identification appear in the lower margin of fol. 18. They are followed by the remark, *Verte wlgariter*. The vernacular translation was then written in the lower margin of fol. 18v.

Now and then Grimestone translated not merely a single verse from Scripture but an entire passage, as in his verses on the Beatitudes (38, from Matthew 5.3-10) or on the signs of charity (47, from 1 Corinthians 13.4-8). Besides biblical verses, Grimestone also translated a number of prose sentences from Latin Church Fathers. Again, some render their sources fairly closely, as for instance the following item attributed to Augustine but in reality by Isidore:

> Augustinus: "Tale est ieiunium sine elemosina qualis sine oleo lucerna." (Fasting without almsgiving is like a lamp without oil.)
> Þat fastingge withouten elemesse is of mith
> As is þe lampe withoten olie an lith. (95)

Others, in contrast, treat their cited models more freely, as does the following authority against the sin of *accidia*:

> Anselmus libro *De redempcione generis humane*: "O lignum aridum, quid respondebis illa die, cum exigetur a te omne tempus tibi impensum," etc. (O dry wood, what will you answer on that day when an account for all the time that was given to you will be demanded of you, etc.)
> Þe slauwe man is but a driȝe tre þat no froit will beren.
> Of al is time in þis werld at þe dom he sal ansueren.
> And afterward han helle pine but penance mou him weren.
> (21)[14]

The majority of Latin texts which have thus been translated, however, are not prose passages from Scripture or the Fathers but medieval Latin verses, usually in the form of hexameters or distichs. In drawing on this rich tradition and handing it on in vernacular garb, Grimestone followed a custom that was common among preachers and talented verse-makers of the later Middle Ages.[15] His sources, many of which can also be found in other sermon handbooks or collections, usually appear together with the English rendition, and in several cases where no such source for an English poem is identified in the respective article, one still suspects that Grimestone's verse is a translation from a Latin text. On occasion Grimestone manages to render an entire hexameter in a single English line, but more often he transforms each Latin verse into a couplet, as was

---

[14] The source is Anselm, *Meditatio 1*; F. S. Schmitt (ed.), *S. Anselmi Cantuariensis Archiepiscopi Opera omnia*, vol. III (Edinburgh, 1946), p. 77, lines 38-40.
[15] See *Verses*, esp. pp. 87-100.

the more common procedure among his fellow preachers. The resulting lines are of very different quality:

> Gustato pomo, etc. [i.e., nullus transit sine morte;
> Heu misera sorte labitur omnis homo.][16]

(After the apple had been tasted, nobody passes on without death; alas, every man sinks down in his wretched fate.)

After þat þe appel was eten, withouten detȝ passed non of alle.
Allas for þat wrecched hap þat to mankinde was falle. (144)

Here the attempt to render each Latin verse by one English line makes for a very uneven couplet. But where each Latin verse is cast into a separate couplet, the result is considerably more successful:

> Et ideo versus: Si Venerem vitare velis, loca, tempora fuge.
> Si venis, ipsa venit; si fugis, ipsa fugit.[17]

(And therefore these verses: "If you want to avoid Venus, flee the respective places and times. If you come, she comes; if you flee, she flees.")

> Ȝif þu wilt flen lecherie,
> Fle time an stede an cumpanie.
> Ȝif þu fle, senne folwet nouth;
> Ȝif þu vnbide, sche comth vnsouth. (99)

Beyond merely translating, Grimestone often expands the verbal material of his source. Apart from simply adding words and phrases in order to fill out the metrical pattern—of which we have already seen several examples—Grimestone often expands his source material to create additional lines. In the following case he first translates a sentence from Philippians 2.7, *Seipsum exinanivit, formam servi accipiens* ("He has emptied himself, taking on the form of a slave"), and then expands it in a quatrain that refers to a specific moment in Christ's Passion:

> He þat was al heuene with him þat al hat wrouth,
> Als a wreche he hat him lowed an mad himself as nouth.
> A þrallis robe þei han him taken,
> Pat Lord of mith þat hadde no nede,

---

[16] Walther, *Prov* 10501.
[17] Under *Luxuria*. Wilson misreads the abbreviation for *ipsa* as *tempora*.

It semet he hadde himself forsaken
To ben clad in mannis wede. (166)

A very different situation occurs in a poem from the section on *Lingua*. Here the source is an entire Latin stanza:

Cor lingue capud est sicud vir femine,
Ut eius copula fetetur famine.
Mecatur igitur in verbi germine
Quod non concipitur ex corde [*read* cordis?] semine.[18]

(The heart is the head of the tongue, as a man is the head of his wife, so that by union with him she may teem with words. Therefore, she commits adultery in producing a word which is not conceived from the seed of the heart.)

Grimestone translates the first line, but then abandons the following pro-creative imagery and explains the tongue's subordination to the rule of the heart in much more prosaic terms:

Als a clerk withnesset, of wisdom þat can:
Herte of tunge meister is, as man of womman,
Þat þe tunge no word speken ne sulde,
But as þe herte assentede an seyde þat he wolde. (102)

The process of thus expanding an authoritative saying can lead to longer poems in which the Latin text furnishes only the germ out of which the poet has developed foliage and blossoms without counterpart in his source. Nr. 174, for example, versifies Christ's prayer to his Father in Gethsemane. It utilizes two biblical verses, which are first quoted before the English lines:

"Pater, si fieri potest," etc. ["transfer calicem hunc a me"] (Mark 14.35-36).
"Et iterum: Si vis ut bibam," etc. ["fiat voluntas tua"] (cf. Matthew 26.42),

and which then appear in fairly close translation as lines 3-4 and 5-7. But Grimestone has expanded this biblical core into two memorable quatrains by developing the image of drinking the chalice:

---

[18] Stanza 52 of Walter of Wimborne, *De palpone*; *The Poems of Walter of Wimborne*, ed. A. G. Rigg (Toronto, 1978), p. 47.

A sory beuerech it is an sore it is a-bouth.   bought
Nou in þis sarpe time þis brewing hat me brouth.
Fader, if it mowe ben don als I haue be-south,
Do awey þis beuerich, þat I ne drink et nouth.

And if it mowe no betre ben, for alle mannis gilth,
Þat it ne muste nede þat my blod be spilth,
Suete Fader, I am þi sone, þi wil be ful-filt!
I am her, þin owen child, I wil don as þu wilt. (174)

Similar cases include the free development of the *Ave Maria* (33), of a prose sentence attributed to Saint Bernard in which the Virgin beneath the cross addresses the Jews (34), of one of Christ's Seven Words on the Cross (187), of phrases from the *Improperia* (205), and others. In all these, a Latin source text is cited before and incorporated into the English verse translation. This process of expansion further appears in all the poems which deal with one of the meditative commonplaces discussed by Rosemary Woolf, such as that of Christ the Lover-Knight standing at the door of man's heart and asking to be allowed in (cf. Revelation 3.20; Nr. 186) or the various appeals of the suffering Christ based on *O vos omnes* (Lamentations 1.12, in 34) or *Vide, homo, quid pro te patior* (translated in 202; partially quoted and expanded in 204), whether the source text is actually cited in the manuscript before the English poem or not.

Somewhat different from expanding a verbal *auctoritas* is the process of versifying a conventional topos, though here of course, too, some verbal base would often have been readily available in the Latin tradition. This category comprises a variety of English poems, ranging from the simple formulation of the four objects of charity (87) or the four enemies of man (88 and 131) to the listing of the works of mercy (105) and the utilization of the ABC to structure a longer poem (198), and further to poems that relate the five senses to aspects of Christ's Passion (191) or set Christ's wounds against the seven deadly sins (199). In all of these, tradition furnished the poet not so much a specific text for translation and expansion as a commonplace pattern for free adaptation.

Of special interest in this connection is Number 219, which lists the seven deadly sins and then declares that "now" (modo) each of the vices is triumphant or considered a virtue: "Gula is sameles . . . , Invidia is holines . . . , Cupiditas is holden wis." This poem not only follows a learned Latin tradition, that of listing the seven chief vices, but at the same time reflects native backgrounds which will engage our attention more closely in a later chapter. As in this poem, Grimestone in general draws not only on Latin sources but also, at least to some extent, on native English ones. Of the latter, it is particularly native proverbs that he utilizes, occasionally by quoting them (120, a stanza from *The Proverbs of Hending*), more often by formulating them in his own way, as in the following case:

> Nu is vp, nou is doun;
> Nou is frend fo.
> Nou is out, nou is nouth   aught; naught
> Nou is al ago.   (9)[19]

The influence of proverbs or proverbial sayings and patterns can further be seen in items 3, 83, 91, 116, 117 and 132.[20] None of these verses is accompanied by a Latin source text.

Distinct from the processes of adaptation, expansion, and translation is that of free creation. Its products are not directly based on authoritative Latin texts or vernacular sayings, nor do they versify a readily discernible conventional pattern. Several poems of this kind are short and not . much different from translations in their tone and appearance, as the following warning by Death:

> Be-war, man, I come as þef
> To reuen þi lif þat is þe lef.   (110)

Others are longer and show considerably more inventiveness. Thus the devil's address of a slothful person seems to have been freely created for the unusual narrative context in which it appears:

> In a similar way does the devil act with whom we fight. He makes us look back to the world,[21] and then he strikes our head, that is, our reason, with some sin and kills us. For when the devil sees that you want to seek God and renounce the world, he at once offers you this advice:
> To pley3en an ragen is for þi pru.
> Wanne suldest þu pley3en betre þan nou?

---

[19] Also items 26 and 60, although the latter translates a Latin quotation.

[20] The presence of native elements specifically in Grimestone's death lyrics has been discussed in the essay cited above, note 10. For native elements in *Fasciculus morum*, see Wenzel, "The English Verses in the *Fasciculus morum*," in *Chaucer and Middle English Studies in honour of Rossell Hope Robbins*, ed. Beryl Rowland (London, 1974), pp. 230-48; and *Verses*, pp. 103-4.

[21] Cf. Luke 9.62.

Wan þu for helde of pley salt blinne   old age; cease
Þanne saltu amenden þe of þi senne.
An doute þe nouth to sennen mikil,   fear
For Godes merci was neuere fikil.   (20)
   This is the devil's advice. But listen to my advice: I find that the
dove has the following characteristics . . .[22]

Still other poems in this category are longer lyrics and include what critics have rightly selected as the finest pieces in Grimestone's oeuvre: his
lullabies (5, 8, 180), meditative lyrics (e.g., 201), or the dialogues between Christ and Mary (e.g., 181, 183, 185) that appear clustered in the
section on *Passio Christi*.

   But the term "free creation" must not be taken too literally, nor
should the preceding classification be accepted as rigorous. Many free
poems, especially the shorter ones, may upon further search turn out to
be derived from a Latin source that lies hidden in the context and has escaped the eyes of the few who have perused Grimestone's manuscript.
Others can perhaps be connected with an authoritative text—Latin or native—which has inspired them but is not quoted. In addition, as the dividing lines between classes cannot be drawn with absolute rigor, one
may debate at length whether a given English item belongs to one category rather than another. Lastly, even the longer lyrics are of course not
free creations in an absolute sense; hardly anything in poetry ever is.
Their major generic forms, such as prayer, dialogue, lullaby, or lament,
have parallels and models elsewhere, as for instance in the hymn tradition we discussed earlier; and their verbal substance is likewise to a large
extent taken from a common tradition. Nonetheless, within the range of
major and predominant types of literary processes which I have suggested can be discerned in Grimestone's output, the creation of free lyrics differs essentially from processes of translating, expansion, or versifying, and in these cases Grimestone shows himself to be a genuinely
creative artist.

   This raises the question of Grimestone's originality. Are the 239 English items in his book his own work, whether translated or freely created?

[22] "Simili modo facit diabolus cum quo pungnamus. Facit nos retro respicere, scilicet
ad mundum, et tunc percutit aliquo peccato capud, idest racionem nostram, et interficit.
Quia quando videt diabolus quod velles Deum querere et mundum abnegare, statim prebet
tibi tale consilium: 'To pley3en . . .' Istud est consilium diaboli. Sed audi consilium
meum: invenio quod columba est talis nature . . .'' Edinburgh, Advocates' Library MS.
18.7.21, fol. 16.

How many of them might be flowers he picked elsewhere? Since Grime-
stone himself gives no hint about the authorship of his English verses,
attempts at providing an answer are limited to searching for their appear-
ance in other manuscripts and then speculating on the findings. Thus,
following the listings in *Index* and *Supplement*, Wilson found that 25
verses in Grimestone's collection also appear in (''are shared with'')
other manuscripts,[23] to which two more poems can be added (87 and
164).[24] The majority of these 27 items appear in manuscripts that are
roughly contemporary with[25] or later than Grimestone's book. Using
these items for the purpose of determining Grimestone's originality,
however, is not very helpful because the exact dating of some of the most
important manuscripts, such as Harley 7322 and Merton 248, is at this
point quite uncertain, and because several items appear in later manu-
scripts but within works that were composed long before 1372.[26] The
question of originality thus requires further careful study of particular
manuscripts and even of individual verses. What can be said at this point
at least is that about half a dozen verses in Grimestone's work are also
attested in texts written as early as the late thirteenth century. These in-
clude part of a song found with music (200), a stanza from *The Proverbs
of Hending* (120), and several very popular meditative or proverbial
commonplaces including a version of the Decalogue (154, 239, 217, and
perhaps 186). This is a very small percentage of the 239 verses in the
collection; and even if one were to consider all the items Grimestone
shares with contemporary or later manuscripts as part of a large mass of
preachers' verses in English whose authorship is undeterminable and
which formed a sort of common property among preachers, this would
account for no more than ten percent of Grimestone's total output. The
available evidence relating to the question of his originality, then, allows
me to extend to his collection the result I have reached earlier with re-
spect to *Fasciculus morum*: ''Preaching aids composed in the fourteenth
century include some English verses that apparently were common prop-

---

[23] Wilson, *Descriptive Index*, p. xi.

[24] No. 87 appears also in *Fasciculus morum* (see *Verses*, nos. 24 and 51). No. 164 is also
in Lincoln Cathedral MS. 44, fol. 335v: see below, p. 120.

[25] Since Grimestone may have been of an advanced age in 1372, I include, as ''roughly
contemporary,'' manuscripts assigned to the second quarter and the middle of the cen-
tury—specifically MSS. Harley 7322 and Merton 248.

[26] Thus, all extant manuscripts of *Fasciculus morum* are later than 1372, yet the work
seems to have been composed shortly after 1300, including its English verses.

erty; but they also present a much larger number of verses that are unique to each work" and were in all likelihood composed by the author of the respective handbook.[27]

But whether original with Grimestone or not, and whatever their sources, these verses were clearly written for use in preaching. Precisely how would they have been used? It may be helpful to begin examining their specific purposes by distinguishing between their rhetorical modes and the literary functions within the concrete situation for which they were made, their *Sitz im Leben*. This distinction may be illustrated by recalling that the sequence *Ave praeclara* realizes the rhetorical modes of invocation, praise, and petition; at the same time, it is a composition created to be sung at a specific moment in the Mass. With respect to their rhetorical modes, Grimestone's verses are not so easy to analyze and to classify. Quite apart from their great number and diversity, individual poems, even short ones, may belong to more than one mode, and more importantly, it is nearly impossible to correlate a particular mode with a particular linguistic form. For example, poems that center on an imperative verb form may be thought to aim at exhortation or warning, and many unquestionably do just that. But others achieve such exhortation instead with a question or by means of the "blessed be those who . . ." formula, whereas conversely the imperative is in different poems used primarily to give information or to express an emotion. Despite these methodological difficulties, however, I think one can without undue simplification or falsification still speak of several major rhetorical modes present in Grimestone's work. Approximately ten items are prayers, addressing God and expressing a specific petition. Other poems give information and teach either a general truth (as proverbs often do) or a specific point of doctrine. Others instead appeal to man's will and exhort or warn. Finally, a number of poems are more concerned with emotions, whether joy or sorrow, resolve or compassion. Some of them simply express such emotion, whereas others more directly attempt to move the hearer to love, sorrow, fear, repentance, and the like. These main modes of teaching, exhorting, and moving may be contrasted to others that literature in general can have, such as telling a story (in epic poems, romances, or novels), depicting a scene (in descriptive passages), or representing an action or conflict (in drama or dialogue). These latter modes do occasionally appear in Grimestone's lyrics: 5 and 6, for instance, narrate

[27] *Verses*, p. 119.

Christ's life in its main outlines; 141 presents a debate between heart and eye, while other poems dealing with Christ's Passion are cast in the form of a dialogue between Christ and Mary; and several lyrics contain detailed descriptions of Christ's suffering (for example, 199 and 214). But I believe that in all these cases narrative, description, and dramatic conflict are subordinated to the major purposes of teaching, exhorting, and moving. Numerically, poems that teach by far outdistance the other groups; they form over half of the total of Grimestone's verses, while poems that exhort form less than a fourth, and poems dealing with emotion only about one sixth.[28]

To these three major rhetorical purposes must be added another, which lies behind and subsumes all of them: the intention that these verses should be remembered by their audience and should continue to affect mind and will beyond the moment at which they were spoken. Little imagination is needed to comprehend that the preacher's message that "death comes unexpected" will have a much greater emotional impact and be retained more easily if it is put into rhyme and rhythm, clothed in appropriate imagery, and spoken as a warning by personified Death himself:

> Be ware, man, I come as þef,
> To reuen þi lif þat is þe lef.   (110)

And the same is true of the suffering Christ's appeal for compassion and love, as in verse 170. I have argued elsewhere that to label such verses as mnemonic or "memory verses" or *aides-mémoire* is rather misleading, because their function in preaching goes beyond that of helping the preacher and his audience remember the structure of a sermon or a particular point of doctrine. Their ulterior intention is to affect the will and to move; and this relates them closely to the rhymed advertisement jingles and political slogans of our day, with which they share many specific purposes as well as linguistic and rhetorical devices.

In regard to their actual use in sermons, nearly all the verses collected

---

[28] In percentages: poems that express a general truth or give information, 52.5%; poems that exhort or warn, 23.3%; poems that express the speaker's emotion or attempt directly to move the listener, 15.8%; prayers, 4.2%. The remainder (4.2%) are verses I am unable thus to classify. I offer these figures, and indeed this entire classification, with some hesitancy. Its value lies only in showing the proportionate emphasis on the major rhetorical purposes.

in Grimestone's preaching tool can be quite readily related to one or more of the major sermon functions surveyed in the previous chapter. The following paragraphs will illustrate their use with specific examples. A number of Grimestone's verses actually appear in full sermons preserved in other manuscripts, in a linguistic form that is identical with or at least very similar to that given by Grimestone. Where we are not so fortunate, their use can still be demonstrated from sermons that quote their respective Latin source, which during the actual delivery might have been rendered in an English verse similar to that entered in Grimestone's collection.

The approximately 25 items which translate biblical verses could have easily been used for the theme of a sermon. Thus,

> Þis is my bodi, als ȝe mov se,
> Þat for ȝou sal peined be   (56)

translates *Hoc est corpus meum quod pro vobis tradetur* (1 Corinthians 11.24), a verse which was occasionally employed in sermons on the feast of Corpus Christi.[29]

But biblical verses could also be used as prooftexts within the development of a sermon, together with rhymed renditions of patristic authorities and medieval Latin verses and with vernacular proverbs. Grimestone's Englishing of Lamentations 5.15-16 (39)—a commonplace put into English rhymes in at least five different forms[30]—thus appears as a prooftext immediately after the theme in the following Palm Sunday sermon:

> *Mourning takes hold of the end of joy*, Proverbs 14. Dearly beloved, the words I have just spoken in Latin may be said in English as follows:
>   Worliche blysse and joye al so
>   Enditeȝ in sorwe and wo.
> For if we reflect on the joy we have lost through sin—we habbet ylore—and the wretchedness and tribulation to which we are born because of sin, I believe we can sing with Jeremiah his doleful song in this way:
>   Myn hertes joye is went away,
>   To wo and sorwe ys turne my play.

---

[29] For example: Cambridge University Library, MS. Kk.4.24, fols. 155-157v.
[30] Cf. *Verses*, p. 90.

Of myn heued þe garland ys afalle to grounde—
Þat I euer sengtheþe, weylaway þe stounde!
And why? Because *mourning takes hold of the end of joy*.[31]

A similar popular prooftext is the Pseudo-Bernardian commendation of Mary's intercessory power which gives sinners hope and confidence in God's mercy: "O man, you have safe access to God, for you have the Son before the Father, and his mother before the Son. The Son shows his Father his side and wounds; the mother shows her son her bosom and breasts. Therefore, no prayer can be refused where there are so many signs of love."[32] Grimestone's verse rendition in three couplets, *Man, siker helpe hast þu and prest* (155), is quoted nearly verbatim in a long macaronic sermon on Christ's Passion from the early fifteenth century. Near the end, as the preacher develops his third main part, namely that Christ has died in order "to restoryn vus to owr ryȝth," he dwells briefly on Christ's Seven Words on the Cross, the first of which, "Father, forgive them," shows God's boundless forgiveness, which is then further proven by the Pseudo-Bernardian commonplace:

Unde Bernardus: "Securum accessum . . . insignia."
    Suer help hast thou and prest,
    Qwer the modyr hyr sone schewyt hyr brest,
    The sone hys fadyr hus blode syde
    And alle hys wowndes opennyd wyde.

---

[31] "*Extrema gaudii luctus occupat*, Prov. 14. Karissimi, ista verba que nunc dixi in Latinis possunt sic dici in Anglico: 'Worliche . . .' Quia si consideremus gaudium quod per peccatum perdidimus—we habbet y-lore—et miseriam et angustiam to wych for senne we beþ y-bore, credo cum Ieremia propheta canere possumus cancionem doloris in hunc modum: 'Myn hertes joye . . .' Et quare? Quia *extrema gaudii luctus occupat*." Worcester Cathedral MS. F.126, fol. 29, not listed by Wilson or *IMEV*. The version of Grimestone 39: *Into sorwe and care turned is oure play* reverses the first two lines and shows some other verbal differences, but they are very minor, and both forms have identical rhyme-words; see the edition by Frank A. Patterson in *JEGP* 20 (1921), 275. A very similar version, *Al þe ioȝe of our herte nou is went awey*, with identical rhyme-words appears in MS. Harley 7322, fol. 153v, in a long moralization of an *exemplum*; ed. F. J. Furnivall, EETS 15:261.

[32] "O homo, securum accessum habes ad Deum. Habes Filium ante Patrem, matrem ante filium. Filius ostendit Patri latus et wlnera, mater filio pectus et ubera. Ideo non potest esse oracio repulsa ubi tot occurrunt caritatis insignia"; Grimestone 155. The source of the Latin is Arnaud de Bonneval, *De laudibus Beatae Mariae Virginis* (PL 189:1726), commonly attributed to Saint Bernard.

Ther no may be noo waryngge   refusal
Qwer is of loue so gret toknygge.[33]   sign

The homiletic use of native proverbial material can best be seen in the case of a stanza (120) that Grimestone took over from *The Proverbs of Hending*, a mid-thirteenth-century "elaboration of the sayings of the common people."[34] The stanza is quoted in a Latin treatise on the vices which begins with the words *Quoniam ut ait Sapiens*. Though not strictly a sermon, the context here still shows us how the stanza would have been employed in order to prove a moral point:

> For those who hold on to their sins and delay confession until their death are like a tree: for a long time, the farmer waits for it to bear fruit; but after a long wait it is cut down and thrown into the fire. In English:
>
> > Riche and pouer, yunge and halde,
> > To qwiles þu haueste þi wit in walde
> > þu sech þi saule bote.
> > For wane þu wenest alle / þir best,
> > Blisse and hele, ro and rest,
> > Pe ax is at þe rote.[35]

Since, as was noted in the preceding chapter, many prooftexts may alternately be classified as message verses, a number of Grimestone's verses could well have taken either one of these functions. Others, however, are unequivocally message verses. Number 59, for instance, has not been found outside Grimestone's commonplace book, but it expresses the moral of a widespread tale perfectly. *Fasciculus morum* tells of a certain backbiter who died without repentance:

> Then it happened that an acquaintance of his saw him in a horrible shape, with a fiery tongue that hung from his mouth to the earth, which he constantly gnawed and spat out, and then drew in again and spat out

---

[33] Cambridge, Jesus College MS. 13, part vi, fol. 90. The Grimestone text is edited in Woolf, p. 34. The same verse is quoted in the moralization of an *exemplum*, in MS. Harley 7322; see EETS 15:264.

[34] R. M. Wilson, *Early Middle English Literature*, third edition (London, 1968), p. 191.

[35] "Qui enim peccata [*MS.* parata] defendunt et usque ad mortem confiteri differunt, similes sunt arbori que diu expectatur ab agricola ut fructum faciat. Post diutinam vero expectacionem evellitur et in ignem mittitur. Anglice: 'Riche . . .' " Durham Cathedral MS. B.I.18, fol. 37r-v; also in British Library, MS. Harley 3823, fol. 129. On this work, see Wenzel, "The Source of Chaucer's Seven Deadly Sins," *Traditio* 30 (1974), 352-53.

once more, and thus a third and a fourth time. When his acquaintance asked him what this was about, he replied: "Since I took delight in backbiting while I was alive, I am now being tormented in this fashion." For by what a person sins, by that he is tormented.[36]

It might have been precisely this story that was in Grimestone's mind when he wrote verse 59:

A3en my felawes þat I haue spoken,
An with my tungge wroth hem wo,
In endeles fir it is nou wroken.
Allas, þat euere spak I so!

A special type of message verse is the address of Christ directed to mankind or a sinner. This type includes such commonplaces as *O vos omnes* (211), *Vide, homo, quid pro te patior* (202), or *In cruce sum pro te* (209), which were translated into English in multiple versions and are ubiquitous in sermons on the Passion. A particularly interesting address poem is Grimestone 164, which appears in a fifteenth-century sermon on *Memorare testamenti Altissimi* (Ecclesiasticus 28.9). Here Christ's legacy is said to have been written on his members on the cross. His feet are said to bear the message of his love for man:

For by "feet" love is indicated in Holy Scripture. With this foot the Son of God came to earth and walked in this world and ascended to heaven in order to prepare a lodging for us. Therefore, on this foot could have been written in English:
Hard gatys haue I gon,
Þat es sen of euerilkon,
To mac my frend o my fo.
Luf me, man, for all my wo![37]

---

[36] "Unde narratur de quodam detractore qui morte preventus simulavit se confiteri velle sed non fecit et mortuus est. Contigit postea quod quidam sibi notus ipsum vidit in forma horribili valde, linguam habentem igneam ab ore usque ad terram dependentem, quam continue corrosit et expuit et iterum resumpsit et expuit, et tercio et quarto. Quod cum alius quesisset, 'Quid est hoc?' respondit: 'Quia,' inquit, 'in detraccionibus dum vixi applaudebam, sic crucior,' quia per quod homo peccat, inde torquetur." Bodleian Library, MS. Rawlinson C.670, fol. 34. Tubach, No. 4907.

[37] "Per pedes enim amor in sacra scriptura designatur. Cum isto pede descendit Dei Filius et ambulavit hic in mundo, et cum eodem ascendit in celum ut nobis hospicium pararet. Unde in isto pede poterat sic scribi Anglice: 'Hard gatys . . .' " Lincoln Cathedral MS. 44, fol. 335v.

120

A final type of message verse, inscriptions on a statue or painting (*pictura*), is represented in at least two Grimestone verses. Verse 232 gives three inscriptions on a depiction of Holiness, as Grimestone himself indicates. Similarly but without explanatory context, 107 (*Merci abid an loke al day*) presents three inscriptions in couplets, followed by a four-line prayer for grace to recognize one's sins. These three couplets appear verbatim in a sermon, though in a different order, as inscriptions on a picture of *Pietas*:

> The pagans imagined that there were as many gods as there are virtues. Hence, among other gods, that of *Pietas* was depicted like a man who was holding in his hand a heart cut in two pieces. On one half was written in red letters as follows:
>
> 3if sinne nere, merci nere non.
> Wan Merci is cald, he comet anon.
>
> On the other half, thus:
>
> Þer Merci is rediest wer sinne is mest.
> Þer Merci is lattest were sinne is lest.
>
> And around that heart was written in letters of gold:
>
> Merci abidet and loket al dai
> Wan mon fro sinne wil torne away.[38]

Lists of the properties of such abstractions as Holiness or Mercy and equally of concrete objects occur also, albeit in a more condensed form, in verses that were designed to function as sermon divisions or distinctions. Grimestone's oeuvre contains a large number of them, on such topics as money (17), love (25; 47, based on 1 Corinthians 13.4-8), the Christian soul (32), cupidity (46), white color (48), children (50), the cross (51), and many others.[39] His couplet on the—rather idealized—characteristics of children, for example:

> Children ben litel, brith an schene, and eþe for to fillen,   easy
> Suetliche pley3ende, fre of 3ifte, and eþe for to stillen   (50)

---

[38] "Pagani finxerunt tot esse deos quot sunt virtutes. Unde inter alios deos deus pietatis depingebatur ad similitudinem hominis tenentis in manu sua cor scissum in duas partes. In una medietate sic literis rubeis scriptum fuit: '3if sinne . . .' In alia medietate sic: 'þer merci . . .' In circuitu circa cor aureis literis sic scribebatur: 'Merci abidet . . .' '' British Library, MS. Harley 7322, fol. 158. The source is Holcot, *Moralitates*, III.

[39] Nos. 57, 65, 71, 73, 82, 84, 111, 112, 142, 145, 151, 168, 169, 172, 212, 220, 221, 222, 233, 242, 246.

translates closely two accompanying Latin hexameters:

Sunt pueri parvi, puri, parvo saciati,
Ludunt conformes, cito dant, cito pacificantur.

(Children are little, pure, satisfied with little; they play together in harmony, give things away easily, and are quickly pacified.)[40]

This is a traditional *distinctio* on *puer* or *pueri* which was frequently used in sermons on the theme "There is a boy here who has five barley loaves and two fishes" (John 6.9), from the Gospel of the Fourth Sunday of Lent (in English also called "Loaf Sunday"), in which these properties of children were then held up seriatim against the seven deadly sins.[41] Other Grimestone verses are likewise *distinctiones* though this may not always be immediately obvious. Thus, verse 82, in the section on Grace, states:

Wanne þe sunne rist: þe day taket his lith,   Misericordia
    þeues taken here flith,   Demones
    þe deu ginnet springge,   Gracia
    [þe foules ginnen] singge. [Boni Christiani][42]

How such a verse could serve as a major sermon division may be seen from a long sermon on the theme "Who is she that goes forth as the dawn, fair as the moon, and clear as the sun?" (Canticles 6.9).[43] As the anonymous preacher begins the first principal part, he subdivides his key word, *aurora*, as follows:

First I say that she [i.e., Mary] was like the rising dawn in her entrance into the world, and this because of three properties of the dawn, which are these:
Hyt ys begynnyng of the dayes bry3thnesse.
Hyt ys lettyng of þe þeuys wykkydnesse.   hindring
And hyt ys lykyng and cause of gladnesse,

---

[40] The Latin is listed in Walther, *Prov* 30779. Wilson misreads the first word.

[41] For example: British Library, MS. Harley 2247, fols. 77v-78, and MS. Royal 18.B.xxv, fol. 50. In Bodleian Library, MS. Barlow 24, fol. 151, the Latin verse and its seven *conditiones* furnish the main structure for a sermon on Holy Innocents.

[42] The text is cropped; words in square brackets are my tentative emendations.

[43] For a summary of the sermon, see Wenzel, "Chaucer and the Language of Contemporary Preaching," *SP* 73 (1976), 158-60.

because at dawn people who are sick begin to feel better, and birds begin to sing and make much melody.[44]

The preacher then proceeds to develop each of these three parts at some length. Although this sermon utilizes a threefold distinction of *aurora* instead of Grimestone's fourfold one, both are substantively identical and quite traditional. Such employment as sermon divisions or distinctions could be shown for many other Grimestone verses. Even the three lines:

> Allas, Iesu, þi loue is lorn.
> Allas, Iesu, þi det is suorn.   death
> Allas, Iesu, þi bane is born (168)

which may strike us at first glance as an affectionate expression of compassion with Christ's suffering, probably served as a distinction on *heu*.[45] A sermon in Cambridge University Library, MS. Ii.3.8, on the theme *Heu, heu, heu*, employs just such a distinction, even though here the *alas* is spoken by sinful man who recognizes his condition.[46] Finally, Grimestone's collection also includes two examples of acrostics, on DEATH (112) and on AMEN (148), the first of which certainly is a distinction.[47]

The English versification of the Decalogue (217) I would place in the category of memory verses. The biblical Commandments were put into Latin hexameters in several different forms, most of them rendered in English, and one of them even in multiple translations. Though all these verse renderings usually appear only on flyleaves or in commonplace books separately from a direct sermon context, it is not difficult to imagine their place in actual sermons, because popular preachers customarily devoted an entire sermon of the annual cycle to the exposition of the Commandments.[48]

The remaining category of preaching verses, that of prayers, is also

---

[44] "Primo dico quod fuit quasi aurora consurgens in suo introitu in mundum, et hoc propter tres proprietates aurore, que sunt iste: 'Hyt ys . . . ,' quia qui sunt infirmi, in aurora incipiunt alleviari, et aves incipiunt cantare et facere magnam melodiam." Cambridge University Library, MS. Kk.4.24, fol. 244v. Notice that the precise images of Grimestone's lines—the day "takes its light," thieves "take to flight," etc.—also appear in the further development of this sermon, in Latin.

[45] In fact, *Heu* is written in Grimestone's manuscript to the left of the three lines.

[46] Erb, pp. 78-79. The sermon cites Ezekiel 6 as source of its theme.

[47] For the use of such acrostics, see *Verses*, pp. 57 and 152-53.

[48] For example: Woodburn O. Ross (ed.), *Middle English Sermons*, EETS 209 (London,

represented in Grimestone's collection. Among English verse prayers one may distinguish liturgical or para-liturgical prayers from those which have no clear liturgical connection and, as they are spoken in the first-person singular, can be called "personal." In Grimestone's collection the former group is represented by a version of the Lord's Prayer (135), a petition from the *Te Deum* (134), and a free expansion of the *Ave Maria* (33). The first and last of these were frequently recited in sermons at the end of the protheme. The petition from the *Te Deum*, translated in 134, is actually quoted in a fifteenth-century sermon on *Sic honorabitur* ("Thus shall he be honored," Esther 6.9), where it is differently translated and preceded by three more couplets that render *Tu rex gloriae . . . esse venturus.*[49] Besides these liturgical prayers, Grimestone's preaching tool contains four "personal" prayers (54, 106, 176, and 192).[50] Their first-person singular form as well as the apparent absence of Latin models might be thought to speak against their recitation in such a public act as a formal sermon. However, short vernacular prayers with these characteristics are in fact not unknown in late medieval preaching. A Passion sermon on *Amore langueo,* for example, concludes each of its seven parts on the signs of love-longing with a four-line prayer, such as the following:

> But since he suffered all this for our salvation, so that he might give us an example, you [singular] should direct your prayer to him and ask him that the torments he suffered may have an effect in your soul, etc., and you must say as follows:
>> Lord, þat suffredust hard torment
>> And on þe rood was al to-rent,
>> Let me suffir wo and pyne,
>> Þat Y may be oon of þyne.[51]

1940), No. 5; Theodor Erbe (ed.), *Mirk's Festial*, EETS, es, 96 (London, 1905), No. 23; MS. Harley 2247 and MS. Royal 18.B.xxv, sermon 30 (all in Middle English). MS. Harley 979, fol. 37v, in Latin. For Latin and English verse renderings of the Decalogue, see *Verses*, pp. 156-57.

[49] The four couplets begin *A Lord Crist, of heuene blisse þu art kynge* (*IMEV* 10) and were printed by Erb, pp. 73-74. The connection with the Latin source was not noticed by Erb, but a marginal note in the manuscript refers to the *Te Deum*.

[50] All four were edited by Rossell Hope Robbins, "Popular Prayers in Middle English Verse," *MP* 36 (1939), 345-46; but see Wilson's remarks on the last, 192.

[51] "Sed quia omnia ista sustinuit pro salute nostra, ut nobis exemplum daret, ideo facies sibi oracionem et rogabis quod tormenta que sustinuit habeant effectum in anima tua, etc., et dicas sibi: 'Lord . . .' " Cambridge University Library, MS. Kk.4.24, fol. 146v.

In its structure and tone, this and its companion prayers are indeed very much like Grimestone's "personal prayers," such as:

> Iesu, my suete with,
> Þat alle þingge hast wrouth,
> Þat come fro heuene lith
> An hast me dere bouth,
> Þu ʒeue me wil an mith
> To ben clene in þouth,
> To kepen þe o rith
> Þat I ne senne nouth. Amen.   (54)

Of course, such simple prayers or the versification of the Our Father need not have been made for use in normal preaching but could instead have been included in this collection to be readily at hand for catechetical instruction[52] or in giving a single person or a small group of religious guidance for meditation. As the preceding pages have shown, however, such verbal structures were in fact employed in formal sermons. It is further abundantly clear, I hope, that English verse renderings of such popular "meditative" commonplaces as *Candet nudatum pectus* (154)[53] or *O vos omnes* (211)[54] or "The Three Sorrowful Things" (239)[55] also had their place and specific rhetorical and structural functions in the late medieval sermon. This is true even of longer and more complex poems, as two final examples will demonstrate. Grimestone's *Herde maket halle* (130) is a version in four quatrains of the "Earth-Upon-Earth" commonplace which generated a large number of poems that show great variety in their verbal and metrical shape.[56] Though it may appear that such extensive poems could not have been used in preaching, I have in fact

---

[52] The Lord's Prayer and the Ten Commandments were among the basic matter parents and godparents were required to teach their children. English verse renderings of both are more readily found in catechetical handbooks than in sermons (e.g., *Speculum Christiani, Lay Folk's Catechism*). On the relation between preaching and catechetical manuals, see Vincent Gillespie, "*Doctrina* and *Predicacio*: The Design and Function of Some Pastoral Manuals," *Leeds Studies in English*, n.s., 11 (1980), 36-50.

[53] Discussed by Woolf, pp. 28-30 and passim. The English rendering (*IMEV* 4088) is quoted in an Easter sermon in Yale University Library, MS. 15, fol. 90.

[54] Grimestone's rendering of the commonplace is used, for instance, in Cambridge University Library, MS. Ii.3.8, fol. 59v; see Stemmler, No. 5.

[55] For its use, see *Verses*, pp. 85, 90, and 123, n. 48. *IMEV* 3711 also appears, in very garbled form, in Yale University Library, MS. 15, fol. 91r-v.

[56] The topic and its vernacular forms were surveyed by Hilda M. R. Murray, *The Middle English Poem, Erthe upon Erthe*, EETS 141 (London, 1911).

125

found an instance of just such use in a sermon on *Benedictus qui venit in nomine Domini* ("Blessed is he who comes in the name of the Lord," Luke 19.38). In developing the notion that true honor is not a matter of wealth and rank, the preacher at one point declares that noblemen who "on account of their noble lineage engage in carnal pleasures" must be taught to detest sin because riches and flowers and human rank pass away, because there is no significant difference between nobleman and commoner, and because after death everyone

> is given over to oblivion. Behold, "all things are vanity, every living person" (Psalm 38.6). And thus notice: "Wan erþe is on erþe." Therefore, because you are so mortal and corruptible, do not seek honor from this![57]

Though the "Earth-Upon-Earth" poem is here merely alluded to, in delivering the sermon the preacher may well have quoted the entire poem, especially since the imperative *nota* is frequently a signal in written sermons that the preacher should develop or quote or retell at greater length material that is only referred to. An even better case of quoting more complex vernacular poems concerns Grimestone 141, a debate between Eye and Heart, each of which are given three one-line speeches; their dispute is finally resolved in one couplet spoken by Reason. The entire mini-debate is quoted in a sermon extant in two manuscripts, where it "proves" the wisdom of guarding one's sight.[58]

Having thus seen their concrete function in sermons as well as the processes that were at work in their creation, we can now turn to an evaluation of Grimestone's verses as verbal art, as poetry. To begin with the verbal craftsmanship manifested in his translations: here Grimestone shows a preference for four-stress lines arranged in couplets or alternating rhymes which are characterized in general by a very simple language and sentence structure, native vocabulary, great economy, and fluency. Grimestone always tried to stay as close to his source as the structure of his native tongue would allow. The results are very literal and compact renditions, especially where his source is in verse. The following couplet illustrates this tendency well, even though it is an extreme case:

[57] "Et postea traditur oblivioni. Ecce 'universa vanitas, omnis homo vivens.' Ita nota: 'Wan . . .' Ergo ex quo tam mortalis et corruptibilis es, non queras de hoc honorem." Worcester Cathedral MS. F.126, fol. 12v.

[58] Pfander, pp. 49-51 (on MS. Merton 248); Stemmler, No. 9 (on Cambridge University Library, MS. Ii.3.8).

Ebrietas frangit quicquid sapientia tangit.
>   Drunkenchipe brekt
>   Al þat wisdom spekt.   (77)

Grimestone's attempt to give us no word beyond what his source offers produces a very tight couplet, whose lines are really too short to be pleasing.[59] More acceptable to English ears is the following:

> Quatuor ista: Timor, odium [*MS.* odio], dileccio, census,
> Sepe solent hominum rectos pervertere sensus.

(These four: fear, hatred, love, and property are often accustomed to turn the right minds of men.)

>   Dred an loue, hate an good
>   Turnen mannis with an maken him wod. (79)

In terms of economy, Grimestone here actually does better than his source, for the entire second hexameter is rendered in a phrase of three words ("turnen mannis with") whose meaning is then simply repeated in different terms ("and maken him wod"). In the first line, he has dropped the initial *quatuor ista*. He could just as well have kept the phrase and produced an absolutely literal translation:

>   These four: dred, loue, hate an god . . .

Instead, his actual rendering shows a sense of rhythm, fluency, and balance, which have turned the Latin hexameter into a genuinely English line.

When Grimestone translates a hexameter, he occasionally does so in only one line. In order to accommodate the entire content of their source, the English lines may then have six or seven stresses:

> Cum nihil auscultes set plurima vana loquaris,
>   Una tibi melius auris et ora duo.
> Nam gemina aures nobis deus, os dedit unum.
>   Nos audire decet plurima, pauca loqui.

> 3if þu wilt nouth here, but spekt wordis manie an veyne,
> Betre þu were to han on ere an mouþes to haan twey3e.
> For to eres God vus 3af, and mouth ne 3af but on.
> [Heren michil] an speken litel becomet wel ich wis man. (104)

---

[59] For another example, see 144, quoted above, p. 109.

But more normally Grimestone prefers to put each hexameter or pentameter into two English lines arranged in couplets or with alternating rhymes. This is the standard metrical pattern for his translations from prose texts as well:

> "Si cum viris femine habitant [*MS.* habitat], incendiarium diaboli non deerit," Ieronimus.
> ("If women live together with men, the devil's fire will not be absent," Jerome.)[60]
> Quil men an wemmen woniȝen togidere,
> Pe fendes brond sone comet þidere. (97)

In order to achieve balance and fluency Grimestone feels free to deviate from the syntactic structure in his source and its sequence of elements. In the following item, for example:

> Lex et natura, Christus, simul omnia iura
> Dampnant ingratum, plangunt illum fore natum,

(The [Mosaic] Law and nature, Christ, together with all [human] laws condemn the ungrateful person and lament that he was ever born)

the four halves of the two leonine hexameters are reordered, from *abcd* to *bcad*:

> Iesu Crist and al mankende
> Dampnen þe man þat is vnkende.
> An skil þat hat ben her aforn
> Hat weiled þat euere was he born. (90)

Such freedom vis-à-vis the syntactic structure of his source texts breaks the tight, occasionally even tortuous Latin sentences and makes their meaning clearer and more readily accessible.

The inflected nature of Latin creates possibilities for a very tight verbal structure and punning wordplay in Grimestone's sources, but also causes thereby the greatest difficulties for their translator. Grimestone has solved these problems remarkably well. The following verse, a typical representative of the *Sum quod eris* addresses and warnings from the dead, plays with various forms of *esse*, "to be" (and *ire*, "to go") in a way that was so dear to the later Middle Ages:

---

[60] The source is Pseudo-Jerome, *Epistula 42, Ad Oceanum de vita clericorum*, 3 (PL 30:289). The text is written on fol. 77 of Grimestone's MS., with a *signe de renvoi* that also appears before the translation on 76v.

Si quis eris qui transieris, sta, respice, plora!
Sum quod eris, fueramque quod es. Pro me, precor, ora!

(Whoever you are who is going by, stand, look, and weep: I am what you will be, and had been what you are. Pray for me, I pray!)

Grimestone has omitted the final request, and the space thereby gained allows him to render the message of the second hexameter more clearly, by using the demonstrative-plus-relative *suich as* in place of the indefinite relative *quod*, and by expanding the simple verb forms *fueram, sum*, and *eris* with a verbal phrase (*was I wone to be*) and two adverbs (*non* and *some*) respectively:

Watso þu art þat gost her be me,
Withstand an behold an wel beþenk þe,
Þat suich as þu art was I wone to be,
An suich as I am nou saltu sone be. (115)

Another warning of death's uncertainty is equally illustrative of this tendency towards linguistic clarification. In this case the particular problem for the translator lies in the incomplete, suspended predication in the first half of the Ovidian pentameter[61] (*Qui non est*, without subject complement), which is then followed by the antithesis of *hodie—cras*:

Et nocet et nocuit semper differre paratis.
Qui non est hodie, cras minus aptus erit.

(To delay does harm and always has done harm to those who are prepared. He who is not ready today will be less so tomorrow.)

Grimestone fully retains all the elements of the distich, including the antithesis of today/tomorrow. The suspended predication of the Latin is completed, and the somewhat vague reference of *aptus erit* has become very concrete, even with two different predicates that use idiomatic phrases. Though one may fault the repetition of the rhyme-word, the distich is rendered with great metrical fluency as a quatrain whose lines alternate between four and three stresses:

It doth harm an hat don harm
To putten forth þe time.
He þat kepth him nouth today fro harm
Tomorwen may gon to pine. (113)

---

[61] Ovid, *Remedia amoris*, 94.

129

The success with which Grimestone encodes the message of his Latin source into his native English is often total. Consider the following lines which formulate a penitent's acknowledgment of his sins, his prayer for forgiveness and his promise not to sin again:

> Þat I wrecche þat senful was
> Mouwe fynde merci an cum to gras,
> After þis day nou wil I blinne
> Forwarde maken with dedli senne. (49)

At first glance, this medieval Act of Contrition may seem to be entirely homegrown. But it is in fact accompanied by two Latin hexameters:

> Ut veniam, miser, adveniam de crimine fedus,
> Non feriam post hanc feriam cum crimine fedus.

(So that I, a wretch, dirty from sin, may come to grace, I shall not, after this day, make a pact with sin.)

The English lines have to be a translation of the Latin verses, for they render them literally step by step, although in a vernacular word order. The Latin hexameters contain a triple pun involving homophones belonging to different word classes (*venia*/grace—*venire*/to come; *fedus*/dirty—*fedus*/pact; *ferre*/to bring—*feria*/day [of the week]) as well as parallelism with antithesis in *de crimine*—*cum crimine*. Nothing of this rhetorical firework has been preserved or even attempted in Grimestone's translation. What his quatrain has gained, however, is clarity, absolute verbal and syntactic simplicity, fluency, and the deceptive appearance of being original and autochthonous. Another, though shorter, example of sacrificing brilliant wordplay in order to render the message clear and direct occurs in the following item:

> Tu caveas caveas, ne perias per eas!

(Beware of the pits, that you may not perish through them!)

> Fle þe dich of senne,
> Þat þu fal nouth þerinne! (143)

The phrase ''þe dich of senne'' merely translates *cavea*/pit, and expands it by drawing on its allegorical meaning. But ''þu fal nouth þerinne'' is a much freer rendering of the corresponding Latin; especially the choice of ''to fall into'' for *perire per* demonstrates Grimestone's willingness and ability to replace mere literal translation with more appropriate vernacular idioms. This tendency to use native idiomatic expressions can be found throughout his work. Two other examples are "ben begiled in is eyʒe" for *falsus erit* ("he will be deceived," 121) and the expansion of the "small pit" image with "doun to þe kne" in his rendition of the following pentameter:

> In modica fossa clauderis pellis et ossa.

> In a dep pitʒ doun to þe kne
> Sken an bon men solen closen þe. (122)

The inclination towards vernacular idioms occasionally yields an image that is startling and effective. In his verse on detraction:

> Si "nisi" non esset, perfectus quilibet esset.
>   Sed non sunt visi qui caruerunt "nisi."

(If it were not for the "but," everyone would be perfect. But none have been found who lacked the "but.")

> To eueri preysing is knit a knot.
> Þe preysing wer good ne wer þe "but."
> I ne woth neuere wer it may ben founde
> Þat with sum "but" it is ibounde. (58)

Grimestone translates the Latin distich fairly closely in lines 2-4, but he adds to it the faultfinder's "knot" in line 1, apparently an image of some currency in pulpit oratory.[62] The use of such images, however, is relatively rare; in this respect Grimestone's poems bear no comparison with the Pardoner's sermon against the three tavern sins which Chaucer has given us. This scarcity is characteristic even of Grimestone's longer lyrics.

If, in his desire to clarify and simplify Grimestone thus often loses the syntactic tightness of his source and such rhetorical devices as wordplay, parallelism, and antithesis, he as often succeeds in gaining an effectiveness of his own and in fact improves on his models. A minor but revealing instance is the following:

---

[62] For the popularity of the Latin distich, see Walther, *Prov* 28724. The image is used in Chaucer, *The Parson's Tale*, X.494. Grimestone 63 also uses the knot image, though here the image does not appear in the quoted source: "Tot fallunt extra, vix unquam creditur intra."

> Si prece vel precio potuisset mors superari [*MS*. superare],
> Aut prece vel precio morte careret homo.

(If death could be overcome by prayer or bribe, man would be free of death by prayer or bribe).

> ʒef preyʒer or mede
> Mith of detʒ maken meistre,
> Þoru preyʒere or mede
> Man of detʒ sulde be fre. (118)

Unpretentious as they are, the English lines not merely preserve the repeated phrase *prece vel precio* (though without the wordplay) but add, in the rhyme-words of lines 2 and 4, an antithesis of subjugation *versus* freedom which is not verbally present in the distich. I add two more examples which similarly show the virtues of Grimestone's art of translation:

> O quam cara, caro, racioni consona raro!
> Dum tibi tanta paro fercula, litus aro.

(O how dear you are, flesh, seldom at one with reason: While I prepare so many dishes for you, I plow sand.)

> Þu faire fles þat art me dere,
> Nou art þu fo, nou artu fere.
> Wan I þe fede as king of lond,
> I lese my time, I ere þe sond. (234)

The first and last half-lines of the Latin distich are rendered fairly closely, but for the intervening material Grimestone has abandoned his source and replaced its expressions with vernacular idioms. These include the commonplace "now this—now that" formula, here with alliteration, and the substitution of "feeding like a king" for the foreign idiom of "preparing dishes." As each Latin half-verse leads to a four-stress line, he has enough space left to add a phrase ("I waste my time") which explains the image of plowing sand and thereby links the quatrain firmly with the theme of the article in which it appears, *De tempore*. The Latin wordplay is lost, but the rendition has produced a verse that is not unappealing in its simplicity, directness, clarity, and vernacular idiom. The same observations can be made about another quatrain on the same theme, which adds a pleasing metric pattern of lines alternating between four and three stresses. One might even claim that the accelerated rhythm of lines 3-4 very effectively underscores their meaning:

> Dampna fleo rerum, sed plus fleo dampna dierum.
> Quis poterit rebus succurrere, nemo diebus.

(I weep for the loss of things, but I weep more for the loss of days. One can make up for things; nobody for days.)

> For lore of godes I wepe sore,
>> But more for lore of day.
> Þou godes ben lorn, I may han more;
>> Time lorn aȝen-comen ne may. (235)

It would seem then that, apart from his desire to formulate messages in a fluent verse form, Grimestone's major artistic concern was to be clear and simple and to say things in the popular idiom. In the case of translations, the result, to be sure, is at times insipid. But where Grimestone is successful, the opaque syntactic structure of a Latin hexameter becomes lucid and easy to grasp. A moment's reflection will tell us why this should have been so: his verses were made for the ear, for recitation within a longer oral discourse. They are preachers' verses in their very shape and texture. This does of course not mean that English poets of the fourteenth century were incapable of writing more sophisticated and densely woven lines. Some of the religious lyrics collected in MS. Harley 2253, for example, draw heavily on the devices of a more artistic literary expression, such as a complex stanza form, stanza linking, and especially alliteration, whose execution often leads to semantic obscurity. But these poems were evidently not meant for inclusion in sermons, as the anthology itself appears to have no connection with preaching and with sermon handbooks. The difference is palpable in that famous quatrain of Harley 2253:

> Erþe toc of erþe erþe wyþ woh.
> Erþe oþer erþe to þe erþe droh.
> Erþe leyde erþe in erþene þroh.
> Þo heuede erþe of erþe erþe ynoh.[63]

---

[63] A close parallel to such punning in English is the quatrain *De cupiditate*, which versifies a miser's words: "I think all day, I think of nought," printed in *RL XIV*, No. 39, lines 13-16. In the manuscript they occur separately, without sermon context, and no Latin source is given.

This poem is replete with the kind of wordplay we observed in several of Grimestone's Latin sources, here a play with the several meanings of the single noun *earth,* and it is an equal in sophistication to such hexameters. The punning Earth-upon-Earth poem evidently was a favorite with preachers for, as we noted earlier, various versions of it occur in extant sermons and sermon materials.[64] Grimestone himself wrote one version in four quatrains, of which the last two may now be quoted for stylistic comparison:

> Wan herde hat herde
> Wonnen with wo,
> An herde hat herde
> Loken in his clo,
>
> An herde hat of herde
> Joyʒe rith inow,
> Þan sal herde bewepen
> Þat he eer below.[65] (130)   earlier rejoiced at

The crucial difference between the two versions is that Grimestone consistently reduces the triple use of *erþe* per line to a twofold one, by replacing the third occurrence with a synonymous expression: *toc erþe* is rendered as *hat wonnen, to the erþe droh* as *hat . . . loken in his clo,* and *erþe ynoh* as *joyʒe rith inow.* This reduction leads to lines which, while still preserving the poem's essential pun, have become immediately accessible to a listener's ear and mind. The artistry of Grimestone's poems, as we have examined them so far, is thus clearly determined by their function in preaching.

[64] See above, pp. 125-26.
[65] Wilson's emendation of the last line (''þat he *is* eer below'') is unnecessary; *below* is the past tense of *bi-laugh.*

5

Grimestone

the

Lyricist

O ur discussion of Grimestone's English poems has so far ex-
cluded items that are longer and of far greater lyric power;
these are in fact frequently anthologized with the best Middle English po-
etry. They not only deserve but demand separate treatment, with a two-
fold view toward their poetic quality and to their appearance in a collec-
tion of preaching material. A fine example comes from the section on
Christ's Passion:

Lu[u]eli ter of loueli ey3e, qui dostu me so wo?
Sorful ter of sorful ey3e, þu brekst myn herte a-to.

    Þu sikest sore,   1
    Þi sorwe is more
        Þan mannis muth may telle;
    Þu singest of sorwe,
    Manken to borwe   5
        Out of þe pit of helle.

Luueli.

    I prud an kene,
    Þu meke an clene,
        With-outen wo or wile;
    Þu art ded for me,   10
    And I liue þoru þe,
        So blissed be þat wile.

Luueli.

    Þi moder seet
    Hou wo þe beet,
        An þerfore 3erne sche 3epte;   15

To hire þu speke,
Hire sorwe to sleke—
Suet sute wan þin herte.

Luueli.

Þin herte is rent,
Þi bodi is bent,   20
Vp-on þe rode tre;
Þe weder is went,
Þe deuel is schent,
Crist, þoru þe mith of þe.

Luueli.[1]

The verbal means here employed are of the simplest possible: very short sentences, all but two (lines 3 and 14) coordinated with a minimum of linking devices; native English diction made up of common, everyday words; no metaphoric language except for the third line from the end; a very simple stanza form; and only the barest hint of alliteration. Yet with its evocation of the speaker's compassion for the suffering Christ this poem surely represents one of the peaks of achievement in the Middle English religious lyric. It is based on an alternation between a brief series of descriptive statements concerning Christ's suffering in the four stanzas, and two expressions (one a question, the other a statement) of the speaker's reaction of sorrow and compassion in the burden. In stanza 2, two further statements about the speaker occur, both placing him in strong antithesis to Christ (lines 7 and 11); they give the reason for his emotion: through the death of the sinless Christ this unworthy sinful being is brought to eternal life. Only at the end (lines 21-24) are the sufferer and the scene of his suffering fully identified (*Þe rode tre, Crist*), and here the note of triumph fully breaks through the mood of sorrowing in the memorable phrase of lines 22-23, though the triumph has already been sounded consistently at the end of each of the preceding stanzas. Most importantly, the entire lyric is put in the form of an address to Christ; even the statement of the speaker's emotion in the burden forms part of an address to Christ's tear. Thus the entire poem, from beginning to end, speaks forth the speaker's emotion; it does so in a string of short,

---

[1] Grimestone 201; taken from *RL XIV* 69.

breathless sentences, whose formal suggestion of sobbing reinforces the poem's theme and mood in a most remarkable way.

In its concentration on religious emotion, its brilliant control of form and detail, and its great verbal and metrical simplicity that reaches the point of artlessness, *Þu sikest sore* is very reminiscent of *Nv Yh she* and, beyond that, the medieval hymn tradition. What is different here, however, is the absence of the element of petition. In contrast to earlier hymns and sequences with their prayer-like structure of invocation, praise, and petition, *Þu sikest sore* is pure outpouring of emotion. On the other hand, it equally lacks those elements that directly appeal to reason and will which we found so extensively present in Grimestone's shorter poems; it does not teach, or state a general truth, or exhort and warn. Here, Grimestone reveals himself as a pure lyricist.

In regard to these lyrical qualities, *Þu sikest sore* does not stand alone but forms part of a larger group comprising over twenty poems in Grimestone's collection. These all deal, thematically, with Christ's suffering and are put in the form of either addresses (in which a speaker addresses an audience of one or many) or dialogues (poems with at least two speakers who address each other). Nearly all appear in the section on *Passio Christi*, to which must be added four poems from the beginning of the manuscript which stand outside the alphabetical topics (5-8), and one poem (34) from the section *De Beata Virgine*. In several of them, in addition to their overall structure of address or dialogue, Grimestone makes further use of other poetic forms and devices, such as the lullaby, the narrative frame with a *chanson d'aventure* opening, and the carol.

What characterizes all these lyrics is their imaginative re-creation of a (biblical) scene and its main participants, whose interpersonal relations and feelings are concentrated upon. This is particularly noteworthy in the formally more complex poems of the group. Number 5, for example, with its 37 quatrains that are evidently intended to be followed by a burden, is first of all a post-Nativity scene witnessed by the speaker whose only characterization is his unspecified longing:

> Als I lay vpon a nith
> Alone in my longging.

The poem closes with practically the same lines, except that now *vpon a nith* becomes *Þis ȝolis-day* (line 147). The scene witnessed is a dialogue between the Infant Christ and his mother. Like a very human baby,

Christ will not fall asleep unless his mother sings him a lullaby as *don modres alle* (12), and Mary responds by protesting her limited experience (22, 57-60) and then recalling what little she knows: the Annunciation (21-48) and the Nativity (49-56). At that point Jesus takes over and teaches her what else to sing (62). He does so by foretelling his future, in a chronological order that is specified and emphasized and ranges from his Circumcision to the Ascension, Mary's Assumption, and the Last Judgment. This account of Christ's life and the history of salvation is twice interrupted by Mary. First she exclaims in joy at the (mistaken) possibility of his being made a king (105-8), and a little later she exclaims in anticipated grief at his Passion:

> Worto sal I biden þat day
> To beren þe to þis wo?   (127-28)

In both cases Jesus corrects her limited understanding by pointing to the larger perspective of his redemptive work. The poem thus re-creates a specific historical moment between the Nativity and the Circumcision and has Christ's life narrated from the particular viewpoint of its two speakers. In addition, it creates a genuine tension between the two speakers, in terms of request and response, lack of knowledge and information, and misapprehension and clarification. The beholding narrator of the scene and dialogue remains totally unobtrusive and emotionally outside the scene—truly alone but hardly longing; what tension there is in that relation remains unresolved, at least on the surface of things.[2]

With respect to the last-mentioned tension between beholder and the scene he witnesses, Verse 7 differs from Verse 5 significantly, even though otherwise it shares many of the earlier poem's features. In 7 the speaker is puzzled by the seeming paradox between the virginal beauty he sees in Mary and the fact that she is a mother:

> I wondrede of þat suete with,
> An to myself I sayde:
> "Sche hadde don mankindde vnrith   human nature
> But ȝif sche were a mayde."   (9-12)

His wonderment is solved by a longer speech by Joseph who tells him of the mystery of the Annunciation. This poem, thus, is a narrative address

---

[2] For a different analysis and appraisal of the poem, particularly its structure, see Sarah Appleton Weber, *Theology and Poetry in the Middle English Lyric* (Columbus, Ohio, 1969), pp. 69-86.

of the speaker and set within the narrative frame of a vision. The inner narrative comes from Joseph's point of view and is located at a specific point in history established in the first five stanzas. A very different poem dealing with the Nativity, Number 8, is likewise cast in the form of a lullaby and apparently intended as a carol, but here the speaker is Adam ("Aзenis my fadris wille I ches / An appel with a reuful res," 9-10), whose emotions of remorse and compassion at Christ's cradle form and infuse this poem. In contrast to 5 and 7, it has no narrative or dramatic elements at all but consists entirely of an address by the penitent Adam (or mankind) to the Christ Child. Besides the Nativity re-created in these poems, Christ's suffering on the cross furnishes the other major scene for a number of Grimestone's lyrics. Some of them are, again, cast in the form of addresses that express the speaker's pain or compassion, spoken by Christ (174, 184, 199, 206, 214) or the Virgin (34, 178) or an unspecified penitent (201, 210). Others achieve the same effect in the form of dialogues between Christ and Mary (181, 183, 185, 187) or Christ and a sinner (186).

The lyrics under discussion contrast with the preaching verses discussed in the previous chapter not only by their imaginative re-creation of a scene and emphasis on emotion, but also by their length. Length in itself, however, is not absolutely necessary to achieve the poetic effects we are here considering. Even a short poem such as:

> Allas, Iesu, þi loue is lorn.
> Allas, Iesu, þi det is suorn. death
> Allas, Iesu, þi bane is born   (168)

expresses compassion with the suffering Christ, although it says very little and is apparently intended as no more than a plain sermon division. In addition, it can be shown that many of the longer addresses and dialogues have directly grown out of shorter verses. In fact, several address poems have a distinct basis in a Scriptural or patristic text which they quote and expand. An example is Christ's prayer to his Father in Gethsemane (174) quoted in the previous chapter. Mary's address to the Jews at the cross (34), "Wy haue зe no reuthe on my child?" similarly expands a text attributed to Bernard, which is actually cited before the English poem and rendered in its two opening lines. Furthermore, a number of Passion lyrics that invite the person addressed to "behold" or "see" (181, 185, 195, 196, 204, 206) clearly derive from one or another shorter Latin commonplace, such as *O vos omnes* (211) or *Aspice mortalis* (216) or *Vide homo quid pro te patior* (202), which they develop in various forms. In her study of the Middle English religious lyric, Rosemary Woolf has traced in detail this development of meditative common-places, a process for which Grimestone's work is an important witness. One could in fact argue that his entire group of longer address poems represents a development of what I have classified as message verses.

The same applies to Grimestone's dialogue poems. The term "dialogue," however, may suggest more than these poems, especially those dealing with Christ's Passion, yield, for while they contain speeches from two different figures addressing each other, they lack the give-and-take of a genuine exchange or conversation. It is indeed more accurate to think of them as built on the pattern of an address followed by a response. The following item (186) illustrates this pattern very clearly:

> Vndo þi dore, my spuse dere,
> Allas! wy stond I loken out here?
> Fre am I, þi make.
> Loke mi lokkes and ek myn heued
> And al my bodi with blod be-weued
> For þi sake.

> Allas! allas! heuel haue I sped,
> For senne Iesu is fro me fled,
> Mi trewe fere.
> With-outen my gate he stant alone,
> Sorfuliche he maket his mone
> On his manere.

> Idco. þerfore:
> Lord, for senne I sike sore,
> Forȝef and I ne wil no more.[3]

. . . .

[3] The first two stanzas are also preserved in an earlier form in Lambeth Palace Library MS. 557, but in reversed order (i.e., lines 7-12, 1-6). Woolf thought the Lambeth version "preferable" (*RES* 13 [1962], 9), though in her later book her view is less definite (*Religious Lyric*, p. 51, n. 2). There are in fact further differences between the two versions than those mentioned by Woolf which suggest that Grimestone took up an earlier poem and changed it to meet his purpose. Of particular importance is the word *þerfore* which leads from the sinner's sorrowful response (lines 7-12) to his prayer (13ff.). The word was not noticed by Brown or Woolf. This linking surely indicates intelligent work on Grimestone's part, and verse 186 would therefore be another case like 213/215 and 180 discussed below.

The poem begins with an address and plea from Christ the Lover-Knight, based on two biblical phrases which it incorporates in English.[4] This is followed by a sorrowful response from the sinful soul thus addressed, who then continues with a prayer (in different meter) for forgiveness and the promise to let Christ into her heart. That the sinful soul's speech is more appropriately considered a response rather than part of a dialogue is underlined by Grimestone himself, who has labeled the second stanza *responsio peccatoris*. This pattern of invitation and response, as well as the particular texts used here, were both commonplace in medieval spirituality and were current long before Saint Bernard and the meditative impulse of the eleventh and twelfth centuries. In his much-read "Letter to Eustochium" (*Epistula 22*), Jerome gives the following instructions for the bride of Christ:

> Do you for your part stay within with the Bridegroom. If you shut your door, and according to the Gospel precept pray to your Father in secret, He will come and knock, and He will say: "Behold I stand at the door and knock; if any man open, I will come in to him and will sup with him, and he with me." And you forthwith will eagerly make reply: "It is the voice of my beloved that knocketh, saying 'Open to me, my sister, my nearest, my dove, my undefiled.' "[5]

This pattern of address and response is, moreover, carried into Passion scenes that include only Christ and the Virgin. Verse 181, for instance, begins with Christ's address:

> Behold, womman, a dolful sith:
> Þis is þ[i] sone þat hanget here.

In the third stanza Mary responds with the outcry of lament:

> Allas, mi sone, nou I dey3e
> For þi pines an for þi wo.
> Myn herte ne may no lengere drey3e
> For þi blod þat rennet þe fro.

---

[4] *Caput meum plenum est rore* (Canticles 5.2) and *Ecce, sto ad hostium et pulso* (Revelation 3.20).

[5] "Tu intrinsecus esto cum sponso, quia, si ostium cluseris et secundum evangelii praeceptum in occulto oraveris patrem tuum, veniet et pulsabit et dicet: 'Ecce ego sto ante ianuam et pulso. Si quis mihi aperuerit, intrabo et cenabo cum eo et ipse mecum.' Et tu statim sollicita respondebis: 'Vox fratruelis mei pulsantis: aperi mihi, soror mea, proxima mea,

The dialogue between the Crucified and his Sorrowful Mother is here reduced to an expression of sheer emotion, and such intellectual elements as the concept of Mary's motherhood of sorrow which we found in *Stabat juxta Christi crucem* have completely disappeared. The same is true of other dialogue poems on the Passion, such as 183 (which seems to be a companion piece to 181) and 187. The latter is based on a Scriptural verse, one of Christ's Words from the Cross (John 19.26), followed by Mary's response in which she laments the loss of her son:

> Womman, Jon I take to þe
> In stede of me þi sone to be.

> Allas, wo sal myn herte slaken?
> To Jon I am towarde taken,
> Mi blisful sone me hat forsaken
>   And I haue nomo.
> Wel may I mone an murning maken,
> An wepen til myn eyne aken,
> For wane of wel my wo is waken,
>   Was neuere wif so wo.

I have repeatedly stressed how much the expression or evocation of emotion predominates in Grimestone's longer lyrics, to the exclusion of other rhetorical purposes such as teaching or direct exhortation. Not all address and dialogue poems share this characteristic, of course. Poem 199, which deals with the topos of Christ's wounds set against the seven deadly sins, is put in the form of an address by Christ from the cross. It dwells a good deal on details of his Passion, yet its general tenor is not an expression of emotion but one of instruction and appeal to man's will (of course by pleading for his compassion). The third stanza, on covetousness, provides a good illustration:

> 3if þi lift hand helde or take
>   Any þing with wrong,
> Lo, my lift hand for þi sake
>   Is drawen out olong.

---

columba mea, perfecta mea.' '' Jerome, *Epistula 22*, 26; text and translation by F. A. Wright, *Select Letters of St. Jerome*, Loeb Library (Cambridge, Mass., 1933), pp. 112-13.

Þe nail went in, þe blod span out,
Þe fles was wonded sore;
Bare I heng, withouten clut—
Coueyte þu no more![6]

Though the topos is placed into Christ's mouth, it has much more of a sermonizing quality, a preacher's stance, about it than the dialogue lyrics discussed earlier. The same preacher's stance appears in a very different poem which makes a number of statements about Christ, from his Incarnation to his appearance at the Last Judgment. Each statement is here followed by a remark that points out the redemptive effect or importance of the historical event for mankind, such as:

Iesu to Marie cam—
Iesu for to deliuere man.
Iesu of Marie was born—
Iesu to sauen þat was forlorn.
. . . .
Iesu sal comen to demen vs—
Beseke we merci to suete Iesus.   (175, lines 3-6, 19-20)

With respect to such ongoing moralizing it is instructive to compare the vision lyric 5, analyzed earlier, with a thematically similar poem, *In Bedlem is a child iborn* (6). Like 5, the latter poem is a long narrative of Christ's life (80 lines), but unlike 5 it constantly points out the significance of events that Christ's life has "for us." Thus, with regard to Christ's becoming man in lowness and poverty, it says:

Þis ensample he hat vs brouth
To liuen in lounesse
An pride to putten out of oure þouth,
Þat brout vs in bitternesse.[7]

---

[6] Concerning stanzas like this, Woolf made the surprising comment: "There was . . . no reason why the wound of the right hand should be opposed to wrath and that of the left to avarice (or indeed why either sin should be opposed to a wounded hand at all)" (p. 224). Suffice it to say that murder and hoarding are usually carried out with one's hands, and that Christ's injunction not to let the left hand know what the right hand does (Matthew 6.3) appears to have some relevance to avarice.

[7] Lines 25-28. Similar passages occur in lines 5-8, 67-68, 70, 77-80.

It is not surprising that in a preacher's hand verses on Christ's life should insist on such explicit moralizing, since "Christ's every action is for our instruction."[8] What is surprising is that in a poem on the same theme (5) the same preacher should, in a process of genuine lyric invention, have achieved an imaginative re-creation of the Christ Child and his mother looking at his life in stanzas that are entirely free of moralizing comments, a quality they share with many address and dialogue poems on Christ's Passion.

This absence of a moralizing preacher's stance, and conversely the presence of a genuine lyricism with its expression of feeling and imaginative re-creation of an emotionally powerful scene make Grimestone a genuine lyric poet. Yet at the same time these qualities raise questions about the exact purposes for which such poems were created, their *Sitz im Leben*. Their lyricism as well as their sheer length place them in sharp contrast to the preaching verses discussed in the previous chapter, and on either of these counts or both together one finds it difficult to imagine how they could have been used in actual sermons—just as one hesitates to imagine Hallmark Greeting Cards reaching for a volume of poems published by the Graywolf Press. Lyricism itself is of course not a clear-cut criterion to set off one group from the other. The following poem,

> A, Iesu, so fair an fre,
> Suettest of alle þinge,
> Þat ful art of pite,
> Of heuene an herde kingge,
> Þe loue þat is in þe
> Noman may rede ne singge.
> Bliþe may þat herte be
> Þat hat of þe meni[n]gge,   (210)

a simple address, has all the lyrical qualities examined in the foregoing pages except that it does not re-create a historical scene, yet it is a simplifying rendition of these Latin verses:

> *O* amor vehemens, ita *dulcissime*
> Torcular exprimens liquorem *venie.*
> Mihi cor penitens da, fons clemencie,
> *Qui rex* et presidens *es trine machine.*

---

[8] "Omnis Christi actio est nostra instructio"; repeatedly quoted in Ludolf of Saxony, *Vita Christi*, ed. A.-C. Bolard, L.-M. Rigollot, and J. Carnandet (Paris, 1865).

Nullus exprimere quanta suauitas
Est in te sufficit, o summa caritas!
Beatum dixerim cuius sedulitas
Te querit iugiter, supprema veritas.[9]

Here the Latin model itself is a lyrical poem, and Grimestone's lines do no more than render an "authority" in English rhymes, very probably to be quoted as a proof text or message verse.[10] It is therefore length, or length combined with lyricism, that on the surface militates against the useability of Grimestone's address and dialogue poems in sermons; for we are here face to face with items that comprise more than a couple of stanzas and range from a dozen to nearly two hundred lines. Were these poems used in preaching?

From the group of about twenty-three poems that pose this problem I exclude the items which in Grimestone's manuscript have been written on pages before the alphabetical collection of commonplaces itself. These comprise the long narrative-frame poems discussed above (5-7) as well as a lullaby (8) and a rendition of the Hours of the Cross (4). While some of these, notably 4 and 8, could certainly have been used in sermons, the same cannot be said as readily of the others; and their being entered on pages outside the alphabetical section will serve me as a handy excuse not to be too concerned about their function in preaching.[11] Regarding the other eighteen long poems in the preaching tool,[12] however, there is sufficient evidence to demonstrate how such longer lyrics *might* have been used, and in a number of cases how indeed they *were* used, in actual sermons.

The best hint about their *Sitz im Leben* comes from Grimestone him-

[9] "O vehement love, wine press most sweetly squeezing out the juice of grace. Give me a penitent heart, fountain of mercy, who are king and ruler of the threefold universe. No one is capable of expressing how great a gentleness is in you, o highest love! I would call him blessed who seeks you with constant zeal, supreme truth." The Latin verses are quoted before English verse 210. I have italicized material on which Grimestone's poem is based.

[10] A similar case is 189, *But I me bethouthte*. I suspect that it, too, translates a Latin passage, though I have been unable to identify one. Beside it, in the manuscript, appears the abbreviation for *Augustinus*.

[11] I am of course aware that their position in the manuscript is no argument against their use in sermons. Grimestone seems to have added material, especially English verses, in blank spaces after he had written out a section; see my comment on the sample article on *Adulacio* in chapter 4.

[12] They are Nos. 34, 175, 178, 180, 181, 183-87, 198, 199, 201, 205, 206, 213 and 215 (counted as one), 214, and 218. All will be commented on in the following pages.

self, for all but two of the poems concerned appear in his section *De pas-sione Christi* (comprising verses 154-216).[13] Late medieval preaching on Christ's Passion and especially sermons for Good Friday present several features that set them apart from the routine Sunday pulpit oratory. For one thing, the Church singled out Good Friday as the only day on which a proper Mass was not celebrated. Its liturgy, though called "Mass of the Presanctified," consisted, as it still does, of a variety of commemorative devotions including the reading of the Gospel account of Christ's Passion according to John and a homily. In addition, late medieval preaching on Christ's Passion[14] is characterized—and thus is distinct from preaching on different themes and occasions—by its re-creation of a historical scene: primarily that of Christ hanging on the cross, with Mary at his feet, but also such other scenes as the Last Supper, or Peter's cutting off the soldier's ear, or Christ's being clothed with the purple coat. In narrating these scenes, the preacher would utilize a number of realistic details, taken from the gospels or from apocryphal literature:[15] Christ's wounds and their specific number, or the name of the soldier whose ear was cut off and then healed again, or Mary's covering her son's naked body with her veil. A most powerful and popular device to make these scenes come further alive was the use of speeches and dialogues. Beyond those reported in the gospels, especially Christ's Words on the Cross, the preacher might use one or more of the addresses spoken by Christ from the cross, or the laments voiced by Mary, or the dialogues between the two that had sprung up, in prose and verse, in medieval literature. The purpose of thus "painting the Passion" was of course to make as strong and vivid an appeal to the audience's emotions of compassion, sorrow, and repentance as possible, and for this purpose preachers spared neither emotion-charged words and details nor sharp antitheses, such as that between the joys of fondling the Infant and the grim horror of beholding his tortured and bleeding body.[16]

---

[13] The two exceptions, 34 and 218, however, also deal with Christ's Passion.

[14] Though dealing with Continental preachers, a relevant longer presentation of preaching on Christ's Passion can be found in Rudolf Cruel, *Geschichte der deutschen Predigt im Mittelalter* (Detmold, 1879; repr. Darmstadt, 1966), pp. 577-94. Cruel's somewhat unsympathetic views were rectified by P. W. von Keppler, "Zur Passionspredigt des Mittelalters," *Historisches Jahrbuch* 3 (1882), 285-315.

[15] For a recent survey of details of Christ's Passion, their literary sources, and their use in paintings, see James H. Marrow, *Passion Iconography in Northern European Art of the Late Middle Ages and Early Renaissance* (Kortrijk, Belgium, 1979).

[16] Representative examples in English can be found in G. R. Owst, *Literature and Pulpit in Medieval England*, second revised edition (Oxford, 1961), pp. 508-9 and 541; and

There is, however, another significant aspect of Good Friday sermons that is not as well known as these features of affective oratory. Preaching on Good Friday evidently posed the challenge or need to retell the events of Christ's Passion, from his Last Supper and betrayal to his burial, as fully and as coherently as possible. At the simplest level, the preacher could go through the Gospel account straightforwardly. But this impulse to give a linear chronological account brought Good Friday sermons into sharp conflict with the characteristic structure of the scholastic sermon with, as we noted in chapter 3, its network of logical and verbal relations based upon a short text and initiated by the three- or fourfold division of the theme. The conflict between the two patterns was resolved in various ways. On the one hand, a preacher could strictly adhere to a scholastic scheme and scatter a few details of the Passion here and there. Creating a distributive pattern of this sort must have challenged the ingenuity and inventiveness of many a preacher. One solution, a fairly elegant one, comes from the anonymous English preacher who wrote the sermon on *Amore langueo*.[17] Its main *partitio* speaks of seven aspects of love-longing, which then form the sermon's main parts. Each part develops a different aspect of Christ's Passion which it divides in turn into seven items. Thus, the following structure emerges:

Seven signs of love-longing:
1. Loss of strength: seven painful torments that Christ suffered.
2. Sighing: seven taunts to which Christ was subjected.
3. Loneliness: seven kinds of people who persecuted Christ.
4. Thinking of one's beloved: seven portents at Christ's Passion.
5. Sweet speech: seven words on the cross.
6. Suffering hardships for one's beloved: Christ's seven wounds (only listed).
7. Making gifts to one's beloved: seven sacraments (not developed).[18]

D. M. Grisdale (ed.), *Three Middle English Sermons from the Worcester Chapter Manuscript F.10* (Leeds, 1939), pp. 11-12.

[17] "*Amore langueo*. Canticorum 2. Prolative potest dici sic . . ." The full sermon with much English is extant in : Cambridge, University Library MS. Kk.4.24, fols. 143v-150; Dublin, Trinity College MS. 277, pp. 185-198; Oxford, Balliol College MS. 149, fols. 31-38v; Magdalen College MS. 93, fols. 152-157. A shorter version without the English appears in Bodleian Library MS. 649, fols. 159-164.

[18] In addition, each part includes a biblical *figura*, such as Daniel in the den of seven lions prefiguring Christ's torments. The sermon also has a fairly long antetheme and an introductory narrative before the *partitio*, as well as a résumé of the *materia sermonis* at its very beginning.

In part 1, the preacher goes through the main events of the Passion, from Christ's sweating blood in Gethsemane to the crucifixion, in fairly straight chronological order, as the following subdivision of the seven painful torments (given in English) reveals:

Blode swetyng	(Gethsemane)
hard byndyng	(capture)
gret trauaylyng	(being led to Annas, Caiaphas, Pilate, Calvary)
smert betyng	(scourging)
longe wakyng	(waking from his capture to his death)
þe crosberyng	(bearing the cross)
scharp / prykkyng	(being nailed to the cross).[19]

The subsequent parts of the sermon (2-7), however, mention further details of the Passion, which now appɤar outside their chronological order and are scattered as the topics of these parts require. Thus, Christ's being clothed in a purple cloak and crowned with thorns forms one of the taunts (part 2); Judas's betrayal and Pilate's condemnation appear in part 3; the tearing of the veil in the temple forms one of the portents (part 4); and details of Christ's suffering on the cross are related or at least listed in parts 5 and 6.

A network of divisions and relations may be elegant, but it loses much of the emotional impact which, in contrast, the straightforward chronological re-creation of the Passion could have. There is evidence that medieval preachers were quite aware of this shortcoming and did not hesitate to overcome it. For that they returned to the linear chronological narrative. A Good Friday sermon on *Percussa est tercia pars solis* ("The third part of the sun was smitten," Revelation 8.12), for example, first sets up a scholastic *divisio* in three parts based on the theme and dealing with Christ's divinity, human nature, and suffering:

> Hec verba signant:
> quomodo Christus wyrchit in hijs godhede, sicut *sol*;
> hou he wonitȝ in hijs manhede, quia in *tercia parte*;
> and wat he suffrid for houre mysdede, quia *percussa est tercia pars solis*.[20]

---

[19] Fol. 145r-v.

[20] Bodleian Library MS. 859, fol. 317. The sermon appears on fols. 314v-319v, 322-325v, and ends incomplete. The *partitio* of the theme cited above is increased by a set of adjectives included in the sermon division proper.

The preacher then launches into developing the announced parts in due order. When he comes to the third part, he adopts a subdivision attributed to "Bonaventure": "The Son of God suffered a Passion most universal, most painful, most shameful, and deadly,"[21] and he develops this in a manner that is more rational than affective. But as he gets into Christ's "most shameful Passion," he suddenly changes direction:

> So that all these previously mentioned things relating to the circum-stances of Christ's Passion may become even clearer to you, let the sequence of the Passion of the Son of God present itself, as blessed John describes it in today's Gospel.[22]

He divides the Passion according to John into four parts, but these do in-deed contain all the historical events, from the Last Supper and betrayal to the crucifixion (the sermon ends incomplete with Christ's being of-fered a drink of vinegar). And the development now includes at least some pious exclamations attributed to various Church Fathers that ex-press an emotional response, such as "O sweetest Mother, how these words pierced the innermost part of your heart."

This curious shift from thematic structure to chronological sequence can be found in many places and forms. In his French sermon on the Pas-sion, Gerson at one point declares: "I will therefore leave what I have been saying so far . . . and begin the story of the blessed Passion where Holy Church begins it today. And I shall take the meaning of the four evangelists together. . . . And I shall try above all to move your hearts to devotion and sorrow."[23] Other sermon collections actually call such a sermon *historia passionis*. The development of this *sermo historialis*[24] is

---

[21] "Dei filius passus est passione generalissima, passione acerbissima, passione igno-miniosissima, passione interemptoria." The division is derived from Hugh of Strassburg, *Compendium theologicae veritatis*, IV.19 (in Albertus Magnus, *Opera omnia*, ed. A. Borgnet, vol. 34 [Paris, 1895], p. 142).

[22] "Ut autem hec omnia predicta quantum ad circumstanciam [*sic*] passionis Christi vobis clarius innotescant, occurrat ordo passionis Filii Dei secundum quod eam discribit beatus Iohannes in ewangelio hodierno," fol. 322v.

[23] Jean Gerson, *Oeuvres complètes*, ed. Palémon Glorieux, vol. VII.2 (Paris, 1968), pp. 452-53.

[24] An interesting case from Italy is the Good Friday sermon on *Amore langueo* by the Franciscan Saint Matthew of Agrigent (who flourished in the 1430s and 1440s), which sud-denly changes into a long *Hystoria dominice passionis extracta ex quatuor evangelistis*. The entire sermon has been edited by Agostino Amore, O.F.M., *Beati Matthaei Agrigen-tini O. F. M. Sermones varii*. Studi e testi francescani 15 (Rome, 1960), pp. 191-234. This sermon is highly important for the use of vernacular *laude* in sermons and for the devel-

an interesting feature of late medieval preaching, not least so because formally it marks a return to preaching patterns of the pre-scholastic homily. Though primarily a chapter in the history of preaching, it bears directly on the development of preachers' verses because the *sermo historialis* furnishes the literary and rhetorical milieu in which more extensive lyrics would find their place.

An important feature of the *sermo historialis* is its dividing the long Gospel narrative into shorter sections. In the passage quoted a few lines earlier, Gerson continues: "And I shall always take one section of the text [i.e., the Gospel]. . . . And I divide the text into 24 parts, after the 24 hours that are in a day and a night—12 for this sermon and 12 for the [following] collation."[25] Other preachers divided the Passion story into as many sections as served their purpose.[26] Whatever the number of sections, however, the result is a segmented narrative: the lengthy historical report is cut up into segments each of which retells or quotes a part of the Gospel story and then develops it in some fashion before it moves on to the next segment, often with such a transitional device as *sequitur in evangelio*.[27] The development may vary in nature. Some preachers present no more than a chain of patristic quotations which, like a commentary, elucidate the meaning of the passage; others raise a question or *dubitatio* and answer it;[28] others again offer a devotional or moral reflection

---

opment of vernacular drama; see Vincenzo De Bartholomaeis, *Origini della poesia drammatica italiana*, second edition (Torino, 1952), pp. 325-34; and his edition of *Il Teatro Abruzzese del Medio Evo* (Bologna, 1924), pp. 313-17. An example from a French Dominican, Jacobus de Lausanne, is the sermon entitled *Hystoria passionis dominice* on *Mortuus est Abimelech* (Ruth 1.3), in Vatican Library, MS. Vat. Lat. 1250, fols. 100v-108.

[25] Gerson, *Oeuvres complètes*, p. 453.

[26] I have found examples of four sections in *Percussa est tercia pars solis* (Bodleian Library MS. 859); six in Jacobus de Lausanne (*Morior propter gloriam* and *Mortuus est Abimelech*); seven in Bonaventure (*Venite ad me*); eight in *Dilexit nos et lavit nos* (Lambeth Palace MS. 352); nine in Franciscus de Mayronis (*Expedit ut unus homo moriatur*) and Jacobus de Voragine (*Quo abit*, actually six parts plus three preliminary ones); fifteen in Guibert de Tournay (*Occisus est*). Undoubtedly further patterns can be found. Notice that in meditational treatises the Passion story is divided into seven sections, after the canonical hours; thus in Pseudo-Bede, *De meditatione passionis Christi per septem diei horas libellus* (PL 94:561-68; twelfth century), and Ludolf of Saxony, *Vita Christi*, pp. 605-86. Grimestone's verse 4 of course follows the latter pattern.

[27] Thus in Bodleian Library MS. 859, fol. 323.

[28] Thus the quoted sermon in MS. Bodl. 859 asks and answers such questions as, why did Jesus go into the garden? why did he address his mother as "woman"?, and so forth.

on the narrated event, leading to an emotional appeal to the audience and evoking its response in the form of a prayer.[29] This entire procedure— segmented narrative with commentary or reflection—comes directly out of the practice and the literature on meditating on Christ's life or his Passion, as it was summarized and "fixed" in such works as the *Meditationes vitae Christi* by Pseudo-Bonaventure or the *Vita Christi* by Ludolf of Saxony. In fact, much of the actual verbal material used in one Passion sermon after another can be found in these treatises as well.

A good example of the *sermo historialis* is a lengthy Good Friday sermon on *Dilexit nos et lavit nos a peccatis nostris in sanguine suo* ("He has loved us and washed us from our sins in his own blood," Revelation 1.5).[30] Here the story of Christ's life and Passion is divided into twelve sections, which are summarized in the following quatrains:

> Love did him fra heuen comen,
> Love did him man be-comen,
> Love did him wit man to wo[n]yn,
> And so of trauayl and wo to conin.

> For love he tok for man a fy3t,
> He favth wit al is my3t,
> He was wel fuly dy3t,
> And aftyr dampnid wyt-ovtin ri3t.

> Love did hym ys armes spredin,
> Love did hym wel lovd to gredin,
> Love did ys hert bledin,
> An wit ys bloud vr saules fedin.[31]

The individual lines of this division are then repeated in the development of the sermon, at the beginning and end of the respective parts. Grimestone's book contains three verses that could easily have been used in the same way. Two are unquestionably sermon divisions: *Loue made Crist in Oure Lady to lith* (25) and *Reuthe made God on mayden to lithte* (167). Both are of four lines only. The third, however, is a longer poem in three stanzas, of which the first may be quoted:

[29] As does the sermon on *Amore langueo* discussed above, pp. 147-48.

[30] Lambeth Palace MS. 352, fols. 216-224v, perhaps of the late fourteenth century; see my discussion in *N&Q* 228 (1983), 108.

[31] Fol. 218, not listed in *IMEV*.

> Loue me brouthte,
> An loue me wrouthte,
>   Man, to be þi fere.
> Loue me fedde,
> An loue me ledde,
>   An loue me lettet here. (184)

Though here the same thought is cast in the form of an address spoken by Christ, the events in his life which were caused by love appear in chronological order, much as they do in the long sermon division quoted above. A very similar structure together with anaphora appears in 175, where eleven couplets list aspects of Christ's life and death, from the Incarnation to his rule in heaven:

> Iesu God is becomen man—
>   Iesu mi loue an my lemman.
> Iesu to Marie cam—
>   Iesu for to deliuere man.[32]

Miss Woolf took this poem to be a meditation on the Holy Name. This is not impossible, but I believe it is also evident how this and similar poems could serve in sermons, for which purpose they were included in Grimestone's preaching tool.

A very different listing of the events of Christ's Passion, though again in chronological order, occurs in the ABC poem (198). Together with several introductory and concluding stanzas, 24 six-line stanzas, each beginning successively with a letter of the alphabet, narrate the Passion from Christ's capture to his resurrection. The underlying comparison of Christ's suffering or his body on the cross to a book[33] was a medieval commonplace, and several English ABC poems of this kind have been preserved. Their actual use can be witnessed in a fifteenth-century sermon in which the ABC poem forms its second principal and allows the preacher to retell the Passion chronologically.[34]

The same sermon illustrates how another poem of several stanzas was

---

[32] Printed by Woolf, p. 178.

[33] See Woolf, p. 253, n. 2; and Mary Caroline Spalding, *The Middle English Charters of Christ* (Bryn Mawr, Pa., 1914), pp. xlii-li.

[34] The sermon on *Ve michi, mater mea*, in Bodleian Library MS. Lat. theol. d.1, edited by Andrew G. Little, *Franciscan Papers, Lists, and Documents* (Manchester, 1943), pp. 251-55.

employed in preaching, the *Improperia*.³⁵ Christ's reproaches, "O my people, what have I done to you or in what have I molested you? Answer me" (Micah 6.3), followed by a listing of God's favors to the people of Israel which are contrasted with the torments inflicted on him, were sung during the Adoration of the Cross as part of the Good Friday liturgy. The Latin text was several times translated into Middle English, including a version in Grimestone (205).³⁶ These English verses actually appear in another Good Friday sermon, on *Quid fecit, quare morietur?* ("What has he done, why shall he die?" 1 Samuel 20.32), where they develop the first principal part, that Christ has died "for to destruyyn þe deuelys my3th":

> The Church remembers today, in her office and in Holy Scripture, that God conferred ten solemn good deeds on the Jews, for which they re- turned evil deeds to him on this day. . . . Mother Church rightly re- proaches this ingratitude today in the person of Christ, when she sings as follows: "My people, what have I done to you," etc.
>
> My folk, now ansuere me,
> Qwat haue I to the gylt?
> Qwat my3th I more a doon for te
> Þan I haue ful-fylt?
>   Owht of Egypti I browht the
>   Ther þou were in woo—
>   Thow dy3thest a cros now for my deth,
>   Os I were thy foo.
>
> This, then, was great ingratitude. Such ingratitude, and an even greater one, show Christians nowadays and sinners who crucify Christ.³⁷

The preacher thus recites these ten stanzas³⁸ with little else between them than a prose paraphrase that contains comments on the Old Testament event and its parallel in Christ's Passion.

---

³⁵ Ibid., p. 256.   ³⁶ See Woolf, pp. 40-41, and *RL XIV*, p. 268.

³⁷ "Recordatur enim Ecclesia hodierna die in officio ac sacra scriptura quod Deus decem solempnia beneficia contulit Iudeis, contra que hodierna die maleficia ei reddebant . . . Quam ingratitudinem iure reprehendit hodie Mater Ecclesia in persona Christi cantans in hunc modum: Popule meus, quid feci tibi, etc. My folk now ansuere me . . . Ista ergo fuit magna ingratitudo. Hanc ingratitudinem et maiorem ostendunt Christiani viventes et pec- catores qui Christum crucifigunt." Cambridge, Jesus College MS. 13, part vi, fol. 85. The English verses are *IMEV* 2240.

³⁸ Brown speaks of eleven (*RL XIV*, p. 268), counting the refrain "My folk . . . ful-fylt"

In another set of speeches from the cross, in six quatrains, Christ lists the sufferings he bore "for þe" (214). Grimestone's manuscript labels these stanzas as three songs (*cantus*) of Christ. These verses, too, could easily have been used in a segmented narrative of the Passion, for the metaphor of Christ's singing from the cross appears in several sermons[39] and is developed in at least one with some English verses. In it, Christ is likened to a nightingale that has been pierced by a thorn and dies from ecstatic singing. His song extended from midnight until the ninth hour. The following passage illustrates how the image is applied and developed with English rhymes:

> At the sixth hour, when Christ was nailed to the cross with the two thieves and was given gall and vinegar to drink, he called out with even greater voice, saying to mankind: "My soul faints after your salvation" [Psalm 118.81],
>> For thy sawle-sauyng
>> My sawle makyt hys endyng.[40]

Grimestone's verses under discussion end with a stanza which Carleton Brown printed as follows:

> Þe nailes, þe scourges, an þe spere,
> Þe galle, an þe þornes sarpe—
> Alle þese moun witnesse bere
> Þat I þe haue wonnen with myn harte.

That Christ won man's salvation with his *heart* is not an improbable statement, especially since a few lines earlier he had said:

---

as a separate verse. In the sermon from which I am quoting the refrain is quoted (in abbreviation) together with verses 8-10.

[39] In Lambeth Palace MS. 352, fol. 216v, Christ's entire Passion is called a "song," which was sung for the first time by Christ on the cross and is sung again by his preacher on Good Friday: "Revera, karissimi, sic videtur mihi quod est de cantu passionis Christi quem predicator cantat in Parasceve. Cantus et sermo in seipso est intime motivus et magne virtutis, et hoc apparet per primam vicem qua unquam fuit cantatus, quando Iesus Christus cantavit ipsemet super crucem."

[40] "Hora sexta, quando Christus fuit cum latronibus conclavatus, cum felle et aceto saturatus, tunc clamavit adhuc voce alciori sic dicens generi humano: 'Deficit in salutare tuum anima mea, For thy . . .' " Jesus College MS. 13, part vi, fol. 89. The songs occur at five canonical hours and are scriptural passages; only the last two are rendered in English rhymes. The last, at None, translates *Mirabilia testimonia tua* (Psalm 118.129): "Thy wondyrful wil and wytnesse / My sowle hath sowht in bitturnesse." Neither couplet is listed in *IMEV*.

Min herte is for-smite a-to,
Al, mankinde, for loue of þe.   (214:13-14)

However, the rhyme scheme requires *harpe*, and in fact that seems to be the manuscript's intended reading.[41] By using the image of a harp or harp playing[42] this poem shares one more feature with several of the sermons already cited, for the comparison of Christ's body on the cross to a harp, and of Christ himself to such famous harpers as Orpheus or Amphion, was a commonplace in sermons on the Passion.[43] Grimestone's poem 214, therefore, combines and versifies several commonplaces that are frequently found in Passion sermons, where its three parts could readily have functioned as message verses.

Another topic of some frequency in Good Friday sermons which could be used either to develop a section on Christ's Passion or to serve as a subdivision for a longer development is the listing of Christ's sufferings and putting them in relation to the seven deadly sins. Grimestone offers two poems of this type, both in seven stanzas, one simply spoken by "we" and translating Latin hexameters (218), the other spoken by Christ (199). A third poem (206), similarly spoken by Christ (*Behold þe þornes myn heued han þrongen*), lists the same sufferings in seven long couplets, though it does not mention the seven sins. And elsewhere Grimestone once more relates Christ's sufferings to the sins briefly in Latin: "These seven vices are healed by Christ's Passion."[44] What is thus a favorite topic in Grimestone's commonplace book can be found used in two Good Friday sermons by Bonaventure.[45] Further, the sermon in Je-

---

[41] The letter in question looks much like the upper part of a *p*. Grimestone consistently contracts *herte* to *hte* with either a horizontal line or a loop for *er*; but on one occasion the word rhymes with uncontracted *smerte* (No. 159, fol. 118v), which would make the form *harte* phonetically unlikely.

[42] *Harpe* could mean "harp playing, harp music"; see *Middle English Dictionary*, s. v. *harpe*, 2(a).

[43] Bodleian Library, MS. Lat.theol. d.1, ed. Little, pp. 255-56 (Christ's harp playing forms the third principal part); Grisdale, *Worcester Sermons*, p. 70 (part of the development of the first principal); Jesus College MS. 13, part vi, fol. 90 (a shorter passage, after the songs of the nightingale).

[44] "Ista septem vicia passione Christi curantur: Capitis in cruce inclinacio curat superbiam . . . ," fol. 159, in the section *De viciis*. There are some minor discrepancies, among the three forms, in the correlation of sufferings to sins: in place of the piercing of Christ's hands, in two stanzas (199), 214 gives his prayer for his enemies, for one hand, and the Latin passage the same prayer and the promise to the Good Thief, for both hands.

[45] Bonaventure, *Opera omnia*, ed. Patres Collegii a S. Bonaventura (Quaracchi, 1882-

sus College Cambridge MS. 13, which has already been quoted several
times, actually recites an entire English poem much like Grimestone
199, at the beginning of its second principal part:

For the second principal I said that Christ has died so that he might
strengthen us in battle. As I mentioned earlier, before Christ's death
the devil fought against man with a sevenfold host, namely the seven
sins, against which Christ sustained suffering in seven places, in order
to strengthen man. Therefore, a devout person, speaking to mankind
in the person of Christ, says as follows:
> Wyth the garlond of thornes kene
> Myn heed was bowonden, that was wyl sene.
> The streem of blod ran to my cheke—
> Thou proud man, ther-fore be meke!
Against wrath he suffered the nail in his right hand and therefore says
as follows . . .[46]

A different sequence of addresses spoken at the crucifixion is the bib-
lical Seven Words on the Cross. Grimestone has not given us a verse ren-
dering of all seven in a neat series labeled as such, but a versification of
several of them may appear in a poem where it has not been recognized
so far. Item 185 consists of three parts, which in the manuscript are as-
signed to different speakers. Part 1 is addressed to the Virgin, bidding
her to "cum an se" her child nailed "to a tre." Part 2 is her address to
Christ, asking why he is there and what she is to do. In part 3, then,
Christ says:

> Ion, þis womman for my sake,   15
> Womman, to Ion I þe be-take.
> Alone I am with-oten make,
> On rode I hange for mannis sake.

1902), 8:261b and 264-65. Similarly in the long sermon on *Vidi, et ecce in medio throni*,
9:261.

[46] "Secundo et principaliter dixi quod Christus mortuus est ut nos fortificaret in bello.
Ut enim tetigi prius, dyabolus ante mortem Christi hominem impugnabat septemplici
hoste, scilicet a peccatis, contra que ad roborandum hominem Christus sustinuit peniten-
ciam in septem locis. Et ideo quidam devotus loquens humano generi in persona Christi sic
dicit: 'Wyth the garlond . . .' Contra iram sustinuit clavum in manu dextera, et ideo sic
dicit . . .'' Cambridge, Jesus College MS. 13, part vi, fol. 86v. The English poem is *IMEV*
4185. Several different versions of the poem are printed in Henry A. Person (ed.), *Cam-
bridge Middle English Lyrics*, rev. edition (Seattle, 1962), Nos. 7-8 and pp. 68-69.

Þis gamen alone me must pley3e,
For mannis soule þis det to dey3e.   20
Mi blod is sched, my fles is falle,
Me þristet sore, for drink I calle.
Þei 3euen me eysil medlid with galle.
For mannis senne in wo I walle.
3ef þei weren kende to louen me outh,   25
Of al my peine me ne routh.
Fader, my soule I þe be-take!
Mi bodi dey3et for mannis sake;
Senful soules in helle lake,
To hem I go, awey to take.   30
Mannis soule, þu art my make:
Loue me wel, I þe nouth for-sake,
An my moder herteliche,
For sche helpet þe stedfas[t]liche.
An þu salt comen þat blisse to,   35
Per my fader is for euermo.   Amen.

(185; lines numbered as in *RL XIV*, 67)

These lines do not constitute Christ's response to Mary's question; in
fact, they are not a dialogue response at all, since in them Christ does not
address a single person or homogeneous group, but successively John,
Mary, his Father, and man's soul. It makes good sense to see in them an
adaptive translation of at least four Words on the Cross: *Mulier, ecce fi-
lius tuus* and *Ecce hic mater tua*, in reversed order, in lines 15-16; an al-
lusion to *Deus meus, Deus meus, ut quid me dereliquisti?* in 17-20; an
expansion of *Sitio* in 21-26; and a similar expansion of *Pater, in manus
tuas commendo spiritum meum* in 27-30, which is then followed by a
plea to mankind.[47] The Words are not simply translated but expanded
along the lines of standard biblical exegesis; thus, Christ's thirst is ex-
plained as his desire to save souls, frustrated by the vinegar and gall of
man's unkindness and obduracy; and commending his soul into his Fa-
ther's hands indicates that after this moment Christ's "soul descended to
hell" from where "the souls of the saints rise up into the hands of
God."[48] This process of quotation with exegetical comment is quite

[47] One could, further, find an echo of the Word to the Penitent Thief, *Hodie mecum eris
in paradiso*, in line 35, but that places this Word very much out of its biblical sequence.
[48] "Spiritus ille descendit ad infernos," Arnaud of Bonneval, *De septem verbis Domini*

characteristic of the great meditative treatises and appears likewise in Good Friday sermons. In one example, the Seven Words are employed to develop the section on how love made Christ cry out loud;[49] in another, the preacher selects five Words to develop the song of Christ the harp-player on the cross.[50]

The entire item 185 has caused readers some difficulty because, in Woolf's words, "the ascription of the first speech to *Ihesus* is undoubtedly a mistake." But *pace* the poem's first editor, there is no mistake in the manuscript, because Grimestone's text ascribes the speech to "Ihōes," a curious but unequivocal contraction of "Iohannes."[51] Whether or not it may be appropriate to call the entire item "an embryonic drama"[52]—in which John brings Mary the news of the crucifixion, Mary responds with a sorrowful address to her son, and Jesus in return responds with several Words from the Cross, which however together with the final promise of salvation are directed to mankind at large—the entire structure patently corresponds to the similar section in segmented narratives of the Passion.[53]

Among Christ's Seven Words on the Cross, the phrase addressed to his mother, *Mulier, ecce filius tuus,* takes a very special place, for the particular scene of Christ giving his mother to John and of addressing her not as "Mother" but as "Woman" formed a moment of great emotional intensity in Christ's Passion—a moment that invariably caused medieval preachers to linger and develop it with the devices of affective preaching, including verses. Grimestone's poem 187 does precisely that. Here Christ's words,

> Womman, Ion I take to þe,
> Instede of me þi sone to be,

---

in cruce, 6-7 (PL 189:1711); "per quod voluit nobis declarare, quod sanctorum animae ex tunc in manus Dei ascendunt," Ludolf of Saxony, *Vita Christi,* II.64.

[49] Lambeth Palace MS. 352, fols. 223-24v.

[50] Little, pp. 255-56. The combination of different topics can be seen in another occurrence of the Seven Words where they are set against the seven deadly sins: Jesus College MS. 13, part vi, fol. 133r-v. Further examples in Morton W. Bloomfield, *The Seven Deadly Sins* (East Lansing, Mich., 1952), pp. 126, 189, 224 (Audelay), 368, n. 162.

[51] The error stems from Brown, *RL XIV,* pp. 85 and 266, and is repeated by Woolf, p. 251. Wilson (p. 39) and R. L. Greene, in *EEC,* p. 106, independently misread the contraction.

[52] Woolf, p. 250.

[53] For a pattern in which Mary responds to five Words on the Cross, see the sermon edited by Little, pp. 255-56.

are followed by two stanzas of Mary's response and lament, beginning
"Allas! wo sal myn herte slaken?"[54] Such a response, either in the form
of a lament spoken by the Virgin as here, or a compassionate exclama-
tion addressed to her by the beholder as found elsewhere ("O sweetest
Mother, how these words pierced the innermost part of your soul when
you heard that instead of the Son of God the son of Zebedee was given
to you, instead of the master the disciple, instead of the Lord the ser-
vant!"[55]), is ubiquitous in Good Friday sermons that retell the events of
the Passion; and sermons whose tone is in general rather rational, such
as the one from which I have just quoted, will give this scene a more af-
fective development. Another topic often brought in at this point is the
contrast between the joys Mary experienced in Christ's infancy and the
horrors she witnessed beneath the cross. In the words of a sermon on
"Christ has died for our sins" (1 Corinthians 15.3): "Once, at his Nativ-
ity, she sang a song of love, but now she can sing a song of sadness and
pain. Note well her changed song."[56] Unfortunately, this preacher does
not tell us more about the *cantus alienus*; but it could be the one found in
the following passage from the Good Friday sermon on "Christ has suf-
fered for us leaving you an example that you should follow" (1 Peter
2.21). In talking about the great strength Mary showed by standing alone
under the cross, the preacher quotes Proverbs 31.10, "Who shall find a
valiant woman?" and then answers:

> One may reply that this valiant woman was found under the cross on
> which Christ died, namely the Blessed Virgin, his mother, whom he
> handed over to the protection of John when he said: "Woman, behold
> your son."
>
> A, blyssedful mayden and modyr, þis is a wonderful change:
> Þe angyll be-hette þe þat Kryst walde be þi sonne and dwel wyt
> þe,
> And now he takys þe a new son and gosse fro þe.

---

[54] Ed. R. H. Robbins, *MLN* 53 (1938), 244. Robbins considers the poem a carol, but the
two introductory lines quoted need not be a burden. Greene excludes the item from his col-
lection of carols.

[55] "O dulcissima mater, quomodo penetraverunt anime tue viscera verba ista quando au-
diebas tibi committi pro Filio Dei filium Zebedei, pro magistro discipulum, pro domino
servum." Bodleian Library MS. 859, fol. 325v.

[56] "Quondam in eius nativitate cantavit canticum amoris, sed iam cantare potest canti-
cum mesticie et doloris; et nota bene canticum alienum." Bodleian Library, MS. Barlow
24, fol. 163v. See also Grisdale, *Worcester Sermons*, p. 12, lines 96-101.

Þe angell sayde to þe þat þe fruyt off þi body sulde be blyssyde,
Ande now in þe dome of þe Iewys it es a-cursede.[57]

The contrast is developed at some length, including the couplet:

Some tyme þou hadest cause for to synge lullay,
Bot now þi songh ys all off wylaway.

Upon these antitheses follow three couplets in which the Virgin addresses Christ, "A, son, tak hede to me whas son þou was," which translate a passage attributed to Chrysostom. Mary's lament in turn leads to a response from her son, "Stynt now, modur, and wepe nomore," in four couplets, in which Jesus speaks of the necessity of his suffering and finally comforts her with these words:

Þow salt nogth now kare what þow salt done.
Lo, Jone þi kosyne sal be þi sone.

This long passage in English verses, which includes an address of the Virgin by the preacher or a meditator as well as the dialogue between Jesus and Mary, appears at the end of a narrative from 3 Esdras 3-4 in which the question "Who is the strongest?" is answered by different speakers who claim that it may be wine, or a king, or a woman. The story's moralization then leads to the quoted eulogy of the Virgin Mary beneath the cross. Both story and moralization apparently enjoyed some popularity in Good Friday sermons from England. They may also have furnished the context of another Grimestone verse, the two stanzas entitled "Christ's Prayer in Gethsemane" which begin with the somewhat unusual image of

A sory beuerech it is an sore it is a-bouth.
Nou in þis sarpe time þis brewing hat me brouth. (174)

For the "wine" of 3 Esdras is often interpreted as Christ's Passion, as in these lines from a macaronic sermon:

That was the wine in that chalice of which Christ spoke when he knelt before the Father and asked him to take the chalice from him. For he

---

[57] From the sermon "*Christus passus est pro nobis, vobis relinquens exemplum ut sequamini. 1 Petri 2.* Anglice: Crist . . . ," which has been preserved in London, British Library, MS. Harley 331, fols. 80-99; Oxford, Balliol College MS. 149, fols. 1-15v; and Worcester Cathedral MS. F.10, fols. 18-26v. The quoted text is from the Worcester MS; it has been printed with errors by Owst, *Literature*, pp. 541-42.

tasted only a little of it and smelled it and found it so strong that it made him sweat blood in his whole body.[58]

At this point a gifted preacher could easily have continued with "And thus Christ might have said" and quoted Grimestone's stanzas on the "painful beverage."

It is, therefore, points like these within fourteenth- and fifteenth-century sermons on Christ's Passion, especially *sermones historiales*, which called for vernacular poems, and in the preceding pages I have quoted specific sermons made in England which at such points employ exact parallels to Grimestone's longer lyrics. This applies equally to the few remaining Passion lyrics in Grimestone's collection, which include Mary's lament to the Jews (34), another lament to her son (178), and two dialogues between Jesus and Mary which are perhaps companion pieces (181 and 183). It applies further to poem 186, in which Christ addresses the sinful soul, who then responds with a lament and a prayer.[59] The scene here visualized, of Christ standing at the door of his "spuse dere" and knocking, is well known from an *exemplum* about Christ the Lover-Knight and its moralization in *Fasciculus morum*,[60] from where it was appropriated for a fifteenth-century sermon.[61] In this *exemplum* the soul's response is merely prescribed by the preacher.[62] But a different *exemplum* on the same theme formulates the soul's response in a first-person singular speech very similar to that in Grimestone's poem 186:

> While I haue in mynde
> The blode of hym that was so kynde [. . .],
> How shuld I hym forsake
> That the dethe for me wolde take?

[58] "Et ideo istud fuit vinum illius cifi, de quo loquebatur quando genuflexit Patri et rogavit eum quod transferret calicem ab eo, quia probavit nisi modicum de illo et odoravit ad illud et invenit illud ita forte quod fecit eum sudare sanguinem per totum corpus suum." Lambeth Palace MS. 352, fol. 224. The narrative and moralization also occur in British Library, MS. Harley 331, fol. 95v.

[59] Discussed above, pp. 140-41.

[60] Discussed by Woolf, *RES* 13 (1962), 7-10, and in *Religious Lyric*, p. 50.

[61] Cambridge, Corpus Christi College MS. 392, fol. 255.

[62] "O human soul, blush then and, according to the Psalm, 'Open the doors of justice,' that is, the affections of your soul towards God and his blessings . . ." ("O ergo, anima humana, erubesce et iuxta Psalmum, 'Aperite portas iusticie,' idest anime affecciones erga Deum et eius beneficia"), *Fasciculus morum*, Bodleian Library, MS. Rawlinson C.670, fol. 43.

> Nay, for sothe, I shall not so,
> For he brought me from mekill woo.[63]

There remains one lyric dealing with Christ's Passion that may put my contention that these poems found their place in actual sermons to a more severe test: *þu sikest sore* (201). As we saw earlier, it is formally a carol whose burden presents the speaker's (a penitent) address to Christ's tear. Could it, too, have been used in a sermon? I cannot, unfortunately, quote any sermon which, in Latin or the vernacular, contains such an address. But the topic of Christ's tears as well as the form of the speaker's address to the suffering Christ were, as we have seen, common in Good Friday preaching. Moreover, the use of a poem with refrain is certainly attested by the recitation of the *Improperia* in at least one sermon discussed earlier. There is, thus, no formal reason that would argue against the sermon use of this lyric. Perhaps one might say that 201 marks the point at which Grimestone's oeuvre tangibly goes beyond what is usual in preachers' verses. Such transcendence can be claimed for other Grimestone poems whose use in sermons can be proven beyond doubt. The shorter poem:

> But I me bethouthte
> Inderliche and ofte
>   Wat Crist drey for me,
> Withinnen an withouten
> And al awone buten
>   Wan he was on þe tre,
> Wol sore I may me drede
> At my moste nede
>   He wil for-saken me   (189)

has the same outpouring of emotion (though here a quiet reflection on the need for compassion with the suffering Christ) and absence of the preacher's stance we noticed in the best, most lyrical of Grimestone's longer poems. These lines are not accompanied by a Latin source.[64] But the initial couplet is more than reminiscent of the beginning of a similar poem that versifies the admonition to think of one's death:

---

[63] *The Early English Versions of the Gesta Romanorum*, ed. Sidney J. H. Herrtage, EETS, es, 33 (London, 1879), p. 26. *IMEV* 4074.5.

[64] Beside lines 2-3, however, an abbreviation appears that could mean either *Augustinus* or (less likely) the exclamation *A* (followed by *Iesu Merci*, further down).

If man him biþocte
Inderlike and ofte
Wu arde is te fore   to travel
Fro bedde te flore,
Wu reuful is to flitte
Fro flore te pitte,
Fro pitte te pine
Þat neure sal fine,   end
I wene non sinne   think
Sulde his herte winnen.[65]

These lines on death have been preserved in different forms and in several manuscripts from the thirteenth century on.[66] In none of them are they accompanied by a close Latin model, and in fact their textual variation as well as their structure of "If . . . then" or "Who . . . he" suggest strongly that they derive from an oral and native tradition.[67] This suggests that in 189 Grimestone has taken up a native verse on death and changed it into a fairly sophisticated lyric on Christ's Passion, retaining however its overall structure, short meter, and opening couplet. The earlier poem on death was definitely used in sermons;[68] it is therefore plausible that Grimestone's *But I me bethouthte* was intended for the same purpose.

A similar process of transformation can be observed in the two final poems that belong to Grimestone's longer lyrics. They do not deal with Christ on the cross but with the Infant in his cradle or on his mother's lap. Yet despite their different setting they, too, speak essentially of Christ's

---

[65] *EL* 13.

[66] The form quoted (*IMEV* 1422) is preserved in two manuscripts. Another version beginning *Who-so him biþou3te* (*IMEV* 4129) has been listed in nine manuscripts, to which must be added British Library, MS. Harley 3221, fol. 3v. For discussion of these versions and the poem's background, see *EL*, pp. 173-75. The two Latin hexameters quoted by Brown lack the descent images altogether.

[67] See further ch. 6, pp. 198-200.

[68] In British Library, MS. Harley 3221, fol. 3v, a late thirteenth-century manuscript, a sermon on *Ductus est Iesus in desertum* contains this series of proof texts: "Unde Ieronimus: 'Facile contempnit omnia qui se semper cogitat mori.' Ubi de inperatore qui statim post eleccionem deberet eligere materiam sepulcri, etc. Anglice: Hwo þe wel bithoste / Inworliche an ofte / Hwoche were þe uore / From bedde to þe flore, etc." The poem further occurs with sermon notes in Aberdeen, University Library MS. 154 and British Library, MS. Harley 7322.

suffering, and as such they would *a priori* fit into the context of Good Friday sermons. We have already seen how preachers heightened the horrors of the crucifixion by a comparison with the joys of Christ's infancy. In addition, the notion that "Christ's whole life can be called suffering"[69] might lead to a glance at the Incarnation before the preacher would begin to develop his Passion proper.[70] But there is also direct evidence that these two Infancy poems, or at least poems very similar to Grimestone's, were in fact used in actual sermons.

The first of them, poem 180, consists of five stanzas, each containing six lines with seven stresses. Four stanzas begin with "Lullay, lullay," and the fifth line in all stanzas repeats "Lullay, lullay, litel child," much like a refrain. Thus the poem's opening stanza reads:

> Lullay, lullay, litel child, child reste þe a þrowe,   space of time
> Fro heyȝe hider art þu sent with us to wone lowe;
> Pore an litel art þu mad, vnkut and vnknowe,   unknown
> Pine an wo to suffren her for þing þat was þin owe.
> Lullay, lullay, litel child, sorwe mauth þu make;
> Þu art sent in-to þis werd, as tu were for-sake.

The whole poem is in this way addressed to the Infant Christ (cf. line 2), whose sufferings in life and death on the cross are compassionately foretold. Nothing in it identifies the speaker specifically as Mary; instead, references to "oure owen gilt" (line 26) and the like suggest that it is spoken by a general representative of sinful mankind.

Grimestone's poem is identical in its metrical structure with a lullaby in six stanzas preserved in a manuscript written half a century earlier and containing various preaching materials: *Lollai, lollai, litil child, whi wepistou so sore?*[71] Most noticeable is the repeated "Lollai, lollai, litil child" in line 5 of each stanza. However, here the stanzas do not address the Infant Christ but any baby confronting a grim existence in an unredeemed world:

---

[69] "Tota vita Christi potest dici passio sive passiones, sic quod non solum in fine paciebatur set in principio vite sue et in medio et in fine." British Library, MS. Harley 331, fol. 81.

[70] Thus in the Good Friday sermon in Lambeth Palace MS. 352.

[71] *RL XIV* 28; from British Library, MS. Harley 913, the Kildare MS., studied by W. Heuser, *Die Kildare-Gedichte*, Bonner Beiträge zur Anglistik XIV (Bonn, 1904; repr. Darmstadt, 1965).

Child, þou nert a pilgrim bot an vncuþe gist,
Þi dawes beþ itold, þi iurneis beþ icast,
Whoder þou salt wend norþ oþer est,
Deþ þe sal be-tide wiþ bitter bale in brest.
   Lolla[i], lollai, litil chil[d], þis wo Adam þe wroȝt,
   Whan he of þe appil ete, and Eue hit him betacht.

It would seem, therefore, that in 180 Grimestone has taken up a poem on Everyman's wretched condition which was addressed to a weeping infant, and turned it into an address to the Christ Child, retaining its ancient seven-stress line, stanza form, and some verbal material. The earlier poem, from the Kildare manuscript, is the oldest English lullaby that has been preserved. One may momentarily wonder if it is folk poetry, a native cradle song such as medieval English nurses would hum when lulling their babies to sleep. But the Kildare poem is far too learned: it not only smacks of Innocent III's *De miseria humanae conditionis* throughout but reveals its derived nature plainly in stanza 4, which incorporates a rhymed proverbial quatrain on Lady Fortune that is normally preserved by itself.[72] But whatever the background of this lullaby may have been, it was certainly used in preaching. The fifteenth century collection in Worcester Cathedral MS. F.10 contains a sermon on *Est vita eterna ut cognoscant te* ("This is eternal life, that they may know You," John 17.3), apparently made for the Vigil of Ascension. The sermon, somewhat scrappy because of frequent referrals "to look up" an *exemplum* and its moralization elsewhere, deals at some length with self-knowledge. In a passage heavily indebted to "Hugh of St. Victor" and "Bernard," the preacher expands:

> Blessed Bernard admonishes us to recognize our wretchedness, as quoted earlier, in chapter 3:[73] "Consider, o man, what you were before your birth, and what you are from birth to death, and what you will be after this life." He says in the same place that "you were made out of vile matter"; and before that, beginning with "Why," he says: "I come from parents who made me a person condemned before I was born, because sinners begot a sinner in their sin, wretches brought a

---

[72] See *Verses*, pp. 173-75. Notice also that stanza 3 of the Kildare poem is an expansion of the three questions attributed to "Blessed Bernard" in the text quoted in the following.

[73] Pseudo-Bernard, *Meditationes piissimae de cognitione humanae conditionis*, III.8 (PL 184:490).

wretch into this wretched light.''[74] And well may he be called wretched if he reflects on the vileness of his origin and the weakness of his human condition, since the newborn is neither capable nor does he know how to help himself, just like a being that is weak, ignorant, and ill. On his weakness there used to be a popular song as follows:

Þer nys no best olyue, made of bon and blod,

Þat hwen he comet3 into world ne kan dun himself sum god,

But a barn unbliþe, a brol of Adam blod.

And that he is joyless is evident in his song, which is either "woe" or "weylawey." If [the speaker] is a woman, it is no wonder, for she comes to the sorrow of this life[75] and, unless she does well, to eternal sorrow. Therefore, the quoted song begins as follows:

Lullay, lullay, litil schild, hwu wepust þou so sore?—

Nede mot Y wepe, hyt was me 3arkud 3ore.

For to liuen in sorwe and kare, now and ewermore,

Als myen eldres han don þat warn me beforne.

Behold, there is great wretchedness in man's coming into this world.[76]

The lines quoted in this sermon are part of stanzas 2 and 1 of the Kildare poem. It should be noted that in the sermon citation the poem appears as a dialogue: the initial question why he is weeping is answered by the child, whereas in the Kildare version it is answered by the speaker himself ("Nedis mostou wepe . . ."").

The other Infancy poem among Grimestone's longer lyrics under discussion consists of two parts (215/213). The first is a six-line stanza, *Ler to louen as I loue þe* (215), spoken by Christ who is "quaking" with cold

---

[74] Ibid., II.4 (PL 184:487).

[75] Perhaps an allusion to Genesis 3.16.

[76] "Nostram miseriam cognoscere ammonet beatus Bernardus ubi supra, capitulo iii: 'Attende, o homo, quid fuisti ante ortum et quid es ab ortu usque ad occasum, atque quid eris post hanc vitam.' Ubi dicit quod 'de vili materia factus es' et prius cur dicit: 'De parentibus venio qui prius fecerunt dampnatum quam natum, quia peccatores in peccato suo peccatorem genuerunt, miseri miserum in hanc lucis miseriam induxerunt.' Et bene miserum si consideretur vilitas originis et dibilitas humane condicionis, cum natus nec potest nec scit seipsum adiuvare, utpote debilis, inscius, et infirmus. De cuius dibilitate cantabatur vulgariter sic: 'þer nys no best . . .' Et quod sit iniocundus patet per cantum eius, quoniam vel est cantus eius wal vel we. Si mulier, nec mirum, quoniam ad dolorem huius vite venit et nisi bene faciat ad dolorem sempiternum. Unde et predictus cantus sic incipit: 'Lullay . . .' Ecce quod [in] ingressu magna miseria est." Worcester Cathedral MS. F.10, fol. 100v. I am grateful to Dr. Joseph Goering for rechecking the manuscript for me.

(line 3) and addressed to an unspecified "thee." In the second part (213) Mary addresses "Iesu" in four stanzas of the same meter, laments his poverty and cold, speaks of his necessary suffering "for loue of man," and asks him not to leave her in this life for too long after his death. If read in this sequence, the two parts form a dialogue poem or address-and-response, much like 181, 183, 185, or 187, but now re-creating a post-Nativity scene. The two parts were indeed printed in this order by their first editor; but more recently, Woolf has called attention to the fact that they appear in reverse order in the manuscript (i.e., 213—215) and, since a line of red dots indicates someone's intention to place 215 before 213, has speculated that a reviser combined into one lyric what had been intended as two separate poems.[77] Woolf's argument, however, rests on an important error,[78] and the arrangement of its two parts on the page is in fact not sufficient reason to separate and order them as she suggested.

There is additional evidence to show that the order 215—213 was originally intended and derives in all probability from Grimestone. The two parts, in the sequence 215—213, are quoted in a roughly contemporary macaronic sermon for Saint Martin, on *Ecce venio cito* ("Behold I come quickly," Revelation 3.11). The preacher divides his theme into four parts that speak of different characteristics of Christ (little, fearful, young, and poor) and of different aspects under which he comes to man (knight, lawyer, teacher, and emperor); but he concentrates on the first of these, that Christ was little and yet powerful, coming as a knight to fight for us. This leads to three parts, Christ's battles against the flesh, the world, and the devil, which he overcame with his virtues of chastity, poverty, and humility:

> In the second place he came as a knight to do battle against our second enemy, namely the world and worldly prosperity, which he overcame through his poverty. For he who was king and lord of the whole earth and creator of all things came into the world absolutely poor and naked. / . . . For a chamber he had the crib, for a hall the stable, for linen and precious clothes a little hay. Yet the season was very cold, and he was just like any other newborn, and I strongly believe that in

[77] Woolf, pp. 156-57.

[78] *Ler to louen* is not preceded by *Aspice mortalis* but rather followed by it. See Wilson, p. 55. Woolf also repeats Furnivall's mistaken reading of *reuera* as *Regina* in the Latin sentence that connects the two parts in Harley 7322 (see below), which one can hardly call "a scrap of Latin narrative" (p. 156).

his human nature he suffered from the cold. Now behold how lying in his cradle he said:

Leorne to loue as Ich loue þe.
On alle my lymes þou mith seo
Hou sore Ich quake for colde.
For þe Ich soffre muche colde and wo.
Loue me wel and nomo,
To þe I take and holde.

And indeed his mother had nothing whereby she might clothe him. Therefore she said to him:

Iesu, swete sone dere . . .[79]

The first (that is, Christ's) speech quoted by the preacher appears elsewhere in the same manuscript in a different context. This is a version of the popular *exemplum* "Elopement of Princess,"[80] in which an emperor's daughter repents of her escapade, is rescued and then honorably married, and receives a number of gifts, including four rings from a *Mediator*. All the gifts bear inscriptions, which in this version are rendered in English verses. The lengthy moralization applies all this to the common notion of Christ as the soul's chivalric lover who fights and dies for her, and the gifts, seven in all (clothes, crown, four rings, and a seal), are all related to aspects of Christ's Passion including his wounds. What concerns us here especially is the first ring, because it bears the following inscription:

Sicut te dilexi disce me diligere,
Nam in toto corpore poteris illud cernere.
Lere to loue as Ic loue þe,

[79] "Secundo venit ut miles ad pungnandum contra secundum inimicum nostrum, scilicet mundum et mundanam prosperitatem, quam devicit per suam paupertatem, quia iste qui erat rex et dominus universe terre et omnium conditor ut pauperimus et nudus mundum intravit . . . / Pro camera habuit presepe, pro aula stabulum, pro linthiaminibus et pannis preciosis modicum fenum cum tamen tempus erat multum frigidum, et ipse ut puer alius natus; et firmiter credo quod secundum naturam humanam ipse defecisset pro frigore. Set nunc videatis qualiter iacens in presepio dixit: 'Leorne to loue . . .' Et revera mater sua nichil habuit unde posset eum induere. Ideo dixit sibi: 'Iesu swete sone . . .' " British Library, MS. Harley 7322, fol. 135r-v.

[80] Tubach, No. 1888; and Pfander, pp. 63 and 65. The oldest version apparently dates from the thirteenth century. The story appears in Holcot, *Moralitates*, VII. In addition to the manuscripts cited by Pfander, the *exemplum* with some English verses is also found in Cambridge, Corpus Christi College MS. 423, p. 265.

On al my lemes þou mait it se.
For þe I suffrede mikel wo.
Þou loue treuli and no mo.   (fol. 152)

Part of this inscription is later repeated in the moralization:

> The last word[81] is obvious because we Christians have all offered him
> our faith for ever in baptism. Therefore he continuously calls to us in
> English:
> Lere to loue as I loue þe,
> For on al mi lemes þou mait it se.[82]

It appears that the *exemplum* quatrain *Lere to loue* is either a translation
of the two Latin lines quoted before it or at least an expanded translation
of the first Latin line. Since the inscription *Sicut [te] dilexi disce [me]
diligere* occurs in earlier versions of the story without English verses,
and since in one version of the *exemplum* it is rendered in English verses
that differ substantially from the lines in Harley 7322,[83] the Latin inscrip-
tion and not the English verses must be the original. In any case, to the
English quatrain as it is found in this *exemplum* the preacher who used
Ler to loue in the quoted sermon as well as Grimestone 215 have added
the detail of "shivering with cold" (line 3) and a sixth line. This surely
means that here an older message verse has been metrically and themat-
ically adapted to become part of an Infancy dialogue. And further: of the
two occurrences of *Ler to loue* followed by the Virgin's response
(Grimestone and Harley 7322), Grimestone's version is textually better:
besides being longer and having a more satisfying closure, it is free of
what is obviously a scribal corruption in the second stanza of the Harley
version.[84] One cannot, I think, escape the conclusion that Grimestone's
version is closer to the original or in fact the original itself; and this proc-
ess of adaptation was, therefore, not as Woolf suggested a chance asso-
ciation due to "a reviser" of Grimestone's manuscript, but rather a de-
liberate fusing and reworking of existing material by a poet who was very

[81] Referring to the last line of a love song spoken by Christ, *Loue þou art of mikel mit*;
see EETS 15:262.

[82] "Ultimum verbum patet quia nos omnes Christiani in baptismo fidem perpetuo sibi
optulimus. Anglice ergo quare [?] continuo sic nobis clamat: 'Lere . . . ,' " fol. 154.

[83] "Y haue þe louyd as þu mayst se, / Lern þou aȝen to loue me." Oxford, Magdalen
College MS. 93, fol. 191v. Printed in Pfander, p. 63, n. 79.

[84] See EETS 15:255; line 10 virtually repeats line 9, giving a seven-line stanza.

fond of dialogue poems. Line 3 of verse 215, "Hou sore þei quaken for colde," puts this conclusion beyond doubt.

This minute examination of the two Infancy poems and comparison with related material show us that Grimestone took up older verse material, such as the Kildare lullaby or the inscription verse *Ler to loue*, and made it into poems which re-create a scene from the life of Christ by means of address or dialogue. Such a process, I believe, lies behind most if not all of the longer poems examined in this chapter, whose building blocks come from a variety of traditions, whether learned Latin verse and prose, or more specifically meditative traditions, or native folk poetry. Grimestone does not seem to have invented any major lyric forms. The dialogue structure, which clearly was a favorite with him, originated in the Latin hymn tradition, as we saw in an earlier chapter. And the device of introducing or framing a longer religious narrative poem or dialogue with a report spoken by a first-person narrator who supposedly witnessed a scene (as in poems 5 and 7) has its model in the *chanson d'aventure* originating in secular French poetry and used in English religious lyrics long before the 1370s.[85] In drawing on material from such diverse traditions and utilizing it for specific functions in preaching, Grimestone shared a trend common among popular preachers, especially Franciscans, which can be seen equally in areas other than preaching verses, as for instance the use of *exempla* and of "classical" tales.[86] The tendency to adapt learned or native traditions for religious purposes would soon after Grimestone's life cause a veritable explosion in the production of religious carols. Again, Grimestone holds a place in the history of the carol because his work contains at least three poems that definitely belong to this genre.[87] But even though these are among the earliest carols that have been preserved, there is some evidence that the form existed before 1372.[88]

If Grimestone's work moves within the wide current of popular preaching, it yet sails before a wind that pushes it beyond the common

[85] See the study by Helen E. Sandison, *The "Chanson d'aventure" in Middle English* (Bryn Mawr, Pa., 1913).

[86] See Beryl Smalley, *English Friars and Antiquity in the Early Fourteenth Century* (Oxford, 1960), esp. pp. 306-7.

[87] Nos. 5, 8, and 201. Robbins and Woolf have argued that additional Grimestone lyrics are carols or at least "in carol style"; see Woolf, p. 150, n. 1, and pp. 383-88, with references to Robbins's articles.

[88] The oldest preserved Nativity carol in English dates from ca. 1350, and the carol form itself may be even older. See *EEC*, pp. cliv and 345-46.

channels, for Grimestone certainly is a genuine lyricist. Medievalists have become a little shy in avoiding Romantic and post-Romantic views on lyrical poetry. Ruskin's famous definition, "Lyric Poetry is the expression by the poet of his own feelings," is of course meaningless for medieval poetry as long as the emphasis lies on "his own." But if we think of lyric poetry as dealing essentially with feelings or emotions which it expresses artistically with the help of all sorts of linguistic means available to the artist, then the best of Grimestone's poems qualify to stand next to verses by Wordsworth, T.S. Eliot, or Robert Frost. The difference lies in the nature of the emotions he expressed, which in contrast to the more recent poetry are not personal or private but form part of a shared culture. But in calling a poem successful or a lyric, we are not—or at least should not be—primarily concerned with the nature of these emotions but rather with the quality of their verbal expression. Rosemary Woolf has described the effect of lyric poetry in these terms:

> We gain the greatest pleasure from a poem when familiarity with a mode of thought and expression provides the framework within which variations delightfully occur, both astonishing and fulfilling expectation.[89]

The remark was made with respect to seventeenth-century poets and their individuality, the diversity of their "personal manner of thought." I think the remark can be equally applied to medieval lyrics if one understands that their "mode of thought" is not that of an individual consciousness but of a common culture. In the case of Grimestone's lyrics and indeed elsewhere in medieval poetry, the common mode of thought is compassion with the suffering Christ, love of the good, fear of damnation, and sorrow for one's failures or insufficiency. These modes of thought or emotions may be commonplace, even tedious; but they provide the matter that gets formed into individual works of verbal art, whose appreciation and evaluation as verbal structures is the literary critic's first and exclusive business.

Earlier in this chapter I have tried to show that a number of Grimestone's longer poems concentrate on expressing an emotion, and that they do so with an almost incredible simplicity of language, a simplicity that is of course totally appropriate to their subject matter. One might indeed speak of them as poetry dressed in the habit of the *Poverello*. Their

---

[89] Woolf, p. 5.

concentration on the fictional speaker's emotion to the point of excluding
the preacher's stance altogether surely gives them full citizenship in the
realm of lyric poetry. I would now add a further consideration to under-
score Grimestone's position as a lyric poet. In discussing the Infancy
poems, notably 215/213, we noticed a predilection in Grimestone's
oeuvre for address and dialogue forms. I have argued that his dialogue
poems are not so much genuine dialogues as addresses followed by a re-
sponse, the latter then exploring the speaker's emotions. In addition, we
have noticed that in some cases where the preservation of older English
material allows us to see the changes Grimestone has made, the result is
an address-and-response poem. To those cases can be added verse 186,
explicitly labeled *responsio*, in which Grimestone apparently reversed
the order of previous material to have Christ's address followed by the
soul's response and prayer. Similarly, older message verses on a depic-
tion of *Pietas* are followed in Grimestone by a four-line response, a
prayer for mercy (107).[90] This susceptibility to, perhaps even fascination
with, the pattern of address and response can be interpreted as revealing
a deep sensitivity in Grimestone to the very essence of lyrical poetry. For
all lyric poetry, from the simplest nature introduction to the most sophis-
ticated Romantic song, springs from the poet's or a persona's affective
response to a given situation, whatever the latter may be. Thus, the set-
ting stars at midnight evoke the female speaker's lonesomeness in this
poem from the Greek Anthology:

> The moon has set and the Pleiades,
> It is the middle of the night.
> The hour is passing,
> and I lie down alone.[91]

And in a quite similar pattern, Goethe's *Wandrers Nachtlied* has the im-
ages of a calm evening evoke the thought of coming death:

> Über allen Gipfeln
> Ist Ruh,
> In allen Wipfeln
> Spürest du
> Kaum einen Hauch;

---

[90] See above, ch. 4, p. 121.
[91] *Greek Lyric*, ed. David A. Campbell. Loeb Library, vol. I (Cambridge, Mass., 1982),
p. 172.

Die Vöglein schweigen im Walde.
Warte nur, balde
Ruhest du auch.

I do not think it far-fetched to see the same lyrical impulse and pattern at work in such poems as *Ler to louen* or *Þu sikest sore*.

Yet the impact of preaching on such poems is undeniable. Their simple language, native diction, straightforward syntax, scarcity of imagery, and relative lack of wordplay and poetic wit not only conform with the style of shorter preaching verses but are best explained by reference to the oral nature of the concrete situation for which they were created. Even the best of Grimestone's lyrics share the language he and his fellow preachers employed in their sermon verses, including such everyday rhyme-words as right/might/fight or sped/fled or take/make/forsake or verb forms in *-ing* which are ubiquitous in the rhymed divisions and message verses of fourteenth- and fifteenth-century sermons. What is surprising and wonderfully gratifying is that in spite of the paucity of his means Grimestone has succeeded in producing a number of poems that are deeply moving in the emotions they express and ''within which variations delightfully occur, both astonishing and fulfilling expectation.''

6

Complaint
Verses and Oral
Traditions

The preceding discussion of Grimestone's preaching verses has paid no attention to a class of verses that may be referred to as "complaint verses" or "political poems" or, less accurately, "historical poems." Grimestone's collection includes at least three items of this kind. One of them (60) translates four Latin lines beginning *Multis annis iam transactis*:

> Manie ȝeres ben iwent
> Siþen treuthe outȝ of londe is lent.
> Faire wordis and wikke dede
> Begilen man in al is nede.

Another states that "now" (*modo*) the seven deadly sins have become acceptable or have even gained the status of virtues:

> Gula is samel[es];
> Luxuria is laweles;
> Ira is rithfulness[e];
> Invidia is holiness[e];
> Accidia is feblesse;
> Superbia in pris;
> Cupiditas is holden wys.   (219)

And the third conversely lists four virtues which have become vices: *Frenchipe is felounie*, etc. (26) Part of a very fertile production in both Latin and vernacular languages, such verses frequently appear in sermons—and often have been preserved because of their use by preachers—and hence deserve closer examination. But I will no longer be concerned with demonstrating their presence and function in sermons; suffice it to say that *Multis annis iam transactis*, for instance, is quoted in a handbook for preachers,[1] and that further illustration of their precise

---

[1] *Fasciculus morum*, III.5; Oxford, Bodleian Library, MS. Rawlinson C.670, fol. 35v.

174

context and sermon use can be found in several examples quoted in the course of the following pages. Instead, this chapter will examine the shape of such verses and the "life" they led in the literary milieu that has preserved them.

All poems in the genre I have called "complaint verses" speak of the moral degeneracy of contemporary society, but instead of criticizing or satirizing specific failings—such as oppression of peasants or clipping of coins or an immoderate interest in clothing and cosmetics—they talk about general aspects of human behavior including the vices and virtues, as we have already seen in the three Grimestone verses. Another example is the following couplet which appears in one of the Latin sermons collected by John Sheppey in the 1330s:

> Ri3tful dom is ouercast and trouþe is fer agon,
> Soþnesse is ileyd adoun and ri3t nis þer non.[2]

The statement that justice and truth have been turned upside down and are no longer present translates a biblical verse, Isaiah 59.14, which is quoted in Latin before the couplet: "Conqueritur Ieremias: 'Conversum est, inquit, retrorsum iudicium, et iustitia longe stetit: corruit in platea veritas, et equitas non potuerit ingredi.' " The medieval preacher identified his source wrongly ("Jeremiah"), but his mistake is a happy one for it shows that he evidently conceived of this verse, in Latin and in English, as a jeremiad. He thereby unwittingly authenticated the generic term "complaint" that was applied to this kind of poem over six centuries later by John Peter.[3]

Several scholars have attempted to bring some order to this large genre by classifying its members with the help of various titles and generic labels. Thus, the *Index to Middle English Verse* and its *Supplement*, in their respective indices, speak of "Evils of the Time" (38 separate entries) and of "Abuses of the Age" (another 24 entries).[4] These two la-

---

[2] *IMEV* 2829, printed in *HP*, p. 327. My text and the Latin quotation are taken directly from Oxford, Merton College MS. 248, fol. 146v.

[3] John Peter, *Complaint and Satire in Early English Literature* (Oxford, 1956), esp. chs. 1-3. Complaint verses have recently attracted the attention of several scholars, among whom J. R. Keller, "The Triumph of Vice. A Formal Approach to the Medieval Complaint Against the Times," *AnM* 10 (1969), 120-37, and R. H. Nicholson, "The State of the Nation: Some Complaint Topics in Late Medieval English Literature," *Parergon* [Canberra] 23 (1979), 9-28, are particularly concerned with the form of these poems.

[4] Several items appear in both categories; the total is 55 separate entries. Many other items could be added, especially 1857, 1934, 2729, 3650, and 3943.

bels, however, which have become fixed through the work of Carleton Brown and R. H. Robbins, have not proven wholly satisfactory, since further labels, such as "The Wicked Age" or "Songs of the Decadence of Virtue," have been added to them. Moreover, a critical perusal and comparison of the poems that have been thus labeled and grouped together reveals a great deal of confusion and even inaccuracy, most of it caused by the indiscriminate use and extension of the term "abuses," which as a result has penetrated into several entries of *IMEV*. I therefore offer a new classification of these poems[5] that is primarily based on their linguistic forms, with some attention given to their background and genesis. This analysis derives from all items listed in *IMEV* under "Evils of the Times" and "Abuses of the Age," with the exception of a few very late and complex poems[6] and some clearly irrelevant items.[7]

Versified laments at the decay or disappearance or perversion of virtues can be divided into two major types. Type A comprises poems that consist of a series of phrases made up of a noun or noun phrase and an adjective or modifying phrase, in which the modifier establishes a contradiction or paradox to the idea contained in the noun. Thus, in the phrases "a prelate negligent," "an old man witless," "a scholar without learning," the modifiers *negligent, witless,* and *without learning,* in plain juxtaposition, declare that a positive quality that should naturally be in certain human types, such as care and industry, wisdom, or erudition, is in fact not present. The subjects about which such statements are made are characteristically social types, such as a prelate, an old man, and so forth, although in some later adaptations of this type their place can be taken by abstractions (marriage without love).

Such lists or catalogues, commonly referred to as "The Twelve Abuses," derive from a very popular Latin treatise entitled *De duodecim abusivis,* which went under the names of Cyprian and other Church Fathers but has been shown to have originated in Ireland in the seventh cen-

---

[5] On the surface the following discussion may appear similar to the account given by R. H. Robbins in *A Manual of the Writings in Middle English 1050-1500,* ed. Albert E. Hartung, vol. 5 (New Haven, Conn., 1975), pp. 1432-35. But Robbins's account of the relations between *De duodecim abusivis* and its "two main versions"—one of which is *De duodecim abusivis* itself, which is then claimed to be "the immediate source" of *Might is right*—is very confused, as is the similar discussion in *HP,* pp. 324-28.

[6] Items attributed to Dunbar (*IMEV* 3866.5; 4116.5) and Skelton (1810.5; 3168.2), and further 1982 (elements of Type B), 3113, 4144.

[7] *IMEV* 1138, 1320 (misprint for 1320.5?), 2025, 3306, 3778, 3987, 1602.5, *2685.5, and probably 4128.4.

tury.[8] It is a little treatise on Christian ethics that teaches morality not on the usual scheme of the seven deadly sins but by discussing twelve human types (wise man, old man, rich man, poor man, woman, king, etc.) whose essential moral characteristics are concentrated in a single virtue that is expressed by its opposite: *sapiens sine operibus, dives sine elemosina, Christianus contentiosus* (meaning "worldly-ambitious"), *rex iniquus*, and so on. The treatise may have been seminal for later *sermones ad status* and medieval estate satire. It not only became very popular in its Latin form throughout the Middle Ages but also generated translations and imitations of its twelve *contradictiones* in various vernacular languages.[9] An English prose version of the abuses appears as early as Aelfric's homilies: "3if þe wisa mon biþ butan gode wercan . . . and þe richen butan elmesdedan . . . and 3if þe cristene mon biþ sacful . . . and 3if þe king biþ unrihtwis," etc.[10] The topos was likewise rendered in vernacular verse, in various forms that preserve the same syntactic pattern even though they may differ in the number, sequence, and kinds of abuses they list. The most widespread is a series of five, extant from the thirteenth century on:

> Bissop lorles,
> Kyng redeles,
> 3ung man rechles,
> Old man witles,
> Womman ssamles—
> I swer bi heuen kyng
> Þos beþ fiue liþer þing.[11]

These verses occur in more than a dozen manuscripts, including a copy of *Ancrene Wisse*. Of special interest for our discussion is the fact that the order of the five abuses varies, so that other occurrences of the same list begin with "King conseilles," "Hold man wytles," or another line

---

[8] Siegmund Hellmann, *Pseudo-Cyprianus De XII abusivis saeculi*, Texte und Untersuchungen zur Geschichte der altchristlichen Literatur, third series, vol. IV, fasc. 1 (Leipzig, 1909).

[9] Ibid., pp. 23-25.

[10] Richard Morris (ed.), *Old English Homilies*, EETS 29 and 34 (London, 1868), p. 107; see also p. 299. The homily is entitled *De octo uiciis et de duodecim abusiuis huius seculi*. For Aelfric and later English renderings of the Twelve Abuses see also Carleton Brown, "The 'Pride of Life' and the 'Twelve abuses'," *Archiv* 128 (1912), 72-78.

[11] *IMEV* 1820; *HP* 56.

177

instead.[12] The poem was also quoted by preachers. Not hitherto noticed has been its appearance in a late thirteenth-century sermon, whose preacher says of the Blessed Virgin:

> [She was] full of modesty, namely when [the Gospel says of her] "she was troubled" [Luke 1.29]. Jerome: "It is characteristic of virgins to be troubled whenever a man enters." Notice that English [saying]: "Old man witles."[13]

Since the context suggests that the preacher was thinking of the line "Womman ssamles," his quoting "Old man witles," evidently as the poem's first line, indicates that he was familiar with a form of this poem that began with "Old man."

The quoted poem is formally a priamel, in which a list of individual instances, the *abusiva*, leads to a "particular point of interest or importance,"[14] the "evil things" of the last line. Since this verse explicitly mentions "five," it also shares in the tradition of the "numerical saying" (*Zahlenspruch*),[15] so well known from the Old Testament sapiential books. Elsewhere the "Abuses" appear combined with yet another form, the prophecy, as in the following item:

Hwan þu sixst on leode	among the people
King þat is wilful,	
And domesman nymynde,	judge; taking
Preost þat is wilde,	
Biscop slouh,	
Old mon lechur,	
Yong mon lyere,	
Wymmon schomeles,	

---

[12] In some versions the lines are also slightly expanded: "A yong man rewler (*or* chiftane) recheles," etc. One such version appears as a graffito in a thirteenth-century church: see V. Pritchard, *English Medieval Graffiti* (Cambridge, 1967), p. 75.

[13] "Pudorata, ibi: 'Turbata est.' Ieronimus: 'Proprium est virginum turbari ad omnem ingressum viri.' Nota illud Anglicum: 'Old man witles.' " Oxford, New College MS. 88, fol. 321.

[14] William H. Race, *The Classical Priamel from Homer to Boethius*. Mnemosyne, Supp. 74 (Leiden, 1982), p. x.

[15] See Walter Kröhling, *Die Priamel (Beispielreihung) als Stilmittel in der griechischrömischen Dichtung*. Greifswalder Beiträge 10 (Greifswald, 1935), p. 11, distinguishing *Zahlenspruch* from priamel.

Child vnþewed,	without manners
Þral vnbuhsum,	without obedience
Aþelyng bryþeling,	nobleman; worthless *or* poor
Lond wiþ-vten lawe—	
Al-so seyde Bede:	
Wo þere þeode![16]	nation

The quoted saying, which has been attributed to Bede, has no end-rhyme and can at best be called free verse. Richard Morris, who first printed the lines, entitled them "Ten Abuses," a label that has firmly stuck even though in both manuscripts that preserve the lines there are clearly eleven evils listed.[17]

The basic formula of the Latin "Twelve Abuses," which is thus combined with different poetic forms, was also applied to failings in religious people alone, in Latin[18] as well as in an English translation.[19] Finally, several early fourteenth-century poems used the same traditional topos with other formal variations. One appears in the sermon collection by John Sheppey:

> Wis man wranglere,
> Riche man robbere,
> Nedi man gadererre,
> Liþer man ledere,
> Lered man lyere,
> Pouere man pinchere.[20]

Another is a mutation of the "Twelve Abuses" in which the original social types are replaced with abstractions. A series of sermon notes contains the following lines, whose structure as well as the introductory note clearly establish their membership in Type A:

> Tres abusiones seculi—
>   Weddyng withoutyn luffe,

[16] *IMEV* 4051; taken from Morris (see following note).

[17] R. Morris (ed.), *An Old English Miscellany*, EETS 49 (London, 1872), pp. 184-85. Apparently Morris counted "Preost þat is wilde. Biscop slouh" as one abuse of the clergy, as is shown in his marginal notes.

[18] Hugh of Folieto, *De claustro animae*, PL 176:1058. The text is reproduced by Brown, "The 'Pride of Life'," p. 73, n. 1.

[19] *IMEV* 86.8.

[20] *IMEV* 4180; taken from Oxford, Merton College MS. 248, fol. 120, col. b (not a).

> Deth withoutyn sorow,
> Synn withoutynn schame.[21]

It is evident that all these English complaint poems of Type A are closely related to *De duodecim abusivis saeculi*. But this relationship differs significantly from the relation that other preaching verses have to a Latin literary source. Instead of merely translating their source and at best expanding it with necessary verbal material, they shorten or increase the original number of twelve; they create new categories or types of abuses; and they become combined with different formulas or structures, such as the priamel, numerical saying, or prophecy. In this, the English complaint verses reveal a remarkable vitality. In contrast to the couplet translating Isaiah 59.14, which is strictly dependent on a fixed literary text, these Type A verses in English adopt an underlying pattern or structural formula and continually generate new versions.[22]

This vitality is further shown in the following verses reported in a chronicle for the early years of Edward III:

> And þe Scottes comen þider vnto þe kyng forto make pees and accorde, but þe accordement bituene hem laste but a litel while. And at þat tyme þe Englisshe-men were cloþe alle in cotes and hodes, peyntede wiþ lettres and wiþ floures ful sembli [*var.* semely], wiþ longe berdes; and þerfore þe Scotes made a bille þat was fastenede oppon þe cherche dores of Seint Peres toward Stangate. And þus saide þe Scripture in despite of the Englisshe-men:
> > Longe berde hertles,
> > Peyntede hode witles,
> > Gay cote graceles,
> > Makeþ Engl[i]ssheman þriftless.[23]

Here the abstract human types of the ''Twelve Abuses'' have been replaced by three external attributes of ''thriftless'' contemporary Englishmen, and general moral lament has turned into particular invective. The *Longe berde hertles* verse itself was apparently quite popular, and once it became dissociated from its historical occasion, it too was expanded

---

[21] British Library, MS. Additional 6716, fol. 126; in a series of unrelated notes for preachers.

[22] The following items not yet mentioned show the continuing influence of Type A: *IMEV* 920, 4131, 2056, 2335, 2805.

[23] *IMEV* 1934: the text is from *The Brut, or The Chronicles of England*, ed. Friedrich W. D. Brie, EETS 131 (London, 1906), p. 249.

and its reference made more general, as is shown in the following as yet
unpublished version:

Longe berdes hertles,
Streyte cotes graceles,
Peyntet hodes wytles,
Longe tepetes redles,
Partie hosen þryfles,
Makeþt þis world laweles.
In auenture witles,
Mariage laweles,
Eritage riþthles,
Febleye penyles, [*or* Nobleye?]
Makeþt þis worl þrifles.[24]

The quoted chronicle report yields a further important insight into the
life of such complaint poems. It is not likely that in composing this short
invective the Scottish rhymesters had recourse to a learned Latin tradi-
tion; instead, they must have relied on verses that were orally transmitted
and in all probability also orally composed.[25] This suggests that a good
many complaint verses of Type A are not only variants of certain struc-
tural formulas but derive from a native and oral tradition.

Further proof for the oral background of such verses comes from the
way in which they are inserted and quoted in Latin sermon texts. Where
such an English verse is not preceded or accompanied by a Latin equiv-
alent, there is a strong probability of an oral and vernacular background,
although it must of course be realized that often enough a verse thus
quoted without a source may still be the result of translation, and that on

---

[24] *IMEV* 1934, revised in *Supplement*. Text from Worcester Cathedral MS. Q.46, fol.
238 (not F.10 as stated in *Supplement*); the verse occurs with later additions, perhaps sec-
ond half of the fourteenth century. Lines 7-10 of this poem have been preserved separately,
as an acrostic for AMEN. See Klaus Bitterling, "Mittelenglische Verse aus lateinischen und
anglonormannischen Handschriften," *Archiv* 220 (1983), 356-60, item 4.

[25] For the difficulties in defining "oral traditions" and "oral poetry" see Ruth Finnegan,
Oral Poetry: Its Nature, Significance, and Social Context (Cambridge, 1977). I use the
term "oral" to distinguish these poems from other preaching verses that derive from a lit-
erary, written text, usually in Latin. Their oralness, therefore, rests primarily on their trans-
mission, on the way in which they came to the individual preacher or sermon writer, to use
Finnegan's distinctions. For an interesting study of the use of Latin as well as vernacular
materials in Old English preaching, see M. R. Godden, "An Old English Penitential Mo-
tif," *ASE* 2 (1973), 221-39.

181

the other hand occasionally the Latin quoted with the English is second-ary, a translation of the English lines. A less equivocal hint of the poem's vernacular origin is given by such introductory formulas as *vulgariter, sicut vulgariter dicitur*, or *sicut quidam dixit in Anglico*. Where such contextual indications are lacking, as often happens in Grimestone's book or on the flyleaves of other manuscripts, a poem's native back-ground may still be inferred by analyzing its form and comparing it with similar structures elsewhere.

The Latin *De duodecim abusivis* which continues to live in *Biscop lorles* and its variants seems itself not to have been entirely a product of a learned and literary enterprise. Siegmund Hellmann has pointed out that while the list of twelve probably imitates the twelve steps of humility in the Rule of Saint Benedict, and the phrase *pauper superbus* is bor-rowed from Ecclesiasticus 25.4,[26] the other items in the list may derive from vernacular Irish laws.[27] However this may be, it is a fact that in their manuscript contexts the variegated members of the Latin treatise's off-spring are as a rule not preceded by Latin source texts. Hence it is plau-sible to think that *Bissop lorles* and *Longe berde hertles* and the other poems we have perused are the tip of an iceberg of popular rhymes and sayings which, together with proverbs and charms, stem from a prima-rily native and oral culture.

Quite different in form from the "Twelve Abuses" (Type A) is the second major type of complaint verses (Type B). Their basic syntactic structure is not a noun or noun phrase plus modifier but a complete pred-ication with verb. Instead of listing a series of static, timeless conditions ("a bishop without learning") they speak of change, of a development through time, usually from good to bad: the old virtues have passed away, vices are now triumphant, what used to be prized highly is nowa-days scorned, and the like. They are all, as it were, utterances of the pro-verbial *laudator temporis acti* for whom the past was paradise while the contemporary world is a moral morass. The idea of degeneracy through time is essential to this type, and it is expressed in various ways. Some verses state that vice is, or has become, or appears as, a virtue. A good

---

[26] Notice however that the syntactic pattern of the "Abuses" occurs in all three items listed in Ecclesiasticus: *Tres species odivit anima mea, et aggravor valde animae illorum: Pauperem superbum, divitem mendacem, senem fatuum et insensatum* ("Three sorts my soul hates, and I am greatly grieved at their life: A poor man that is proud, a rich man that is a liar, an old man that is a fool and doting," Ecclesiasticus 25.3-4).

[27] Hellmann, *Pseudo-Cyprianus*, p. 15.

example, which especially in lines 3-4 neatly illustrates the contrast to
Type A, is the poem which begins,

> Now pride ys yn pris,
> Now couetyse ys wyse,
> Now lechery ys schameles,
> Now glotenye ys lawles,[28]

a poem much like Grimestone's verse 219 quoted at the beginning of this
chapter. Conversely, other poems of this type declare that virtues are, or
have become, vices. Again it is Grimestone who furnishes a good ex-
ample:

> Frenchipe is felounie;
> Manchipe is vileynie;
> Clergie is tresorie;
> And borwing is roberie.[29]

Some poems may mix these two patterns, as in the following example:

> Charite, chaste, pite arn waxin al colde,
> Couetise, lust, and maistrie arn be-comin al bolde.[30]

For their predication these verses frequently use the simple copula *to be*
or verbs of appearing or becoming. An example of the latter appears in a
sermon on *Quomodo stabit regnum?* (''How shall the kingdom stand?''
Matthew 12.26), hitherto unnoticed:

> But surely, mischief is now growing more than ever before, which is
> to be lamented. Whence throughout all England four most evil
> changes are taking place, namely:
>> Pouerte ys tornd in-to coueytynge,
>> Trevthe in-to trecherie.
>> Pays is y-tornd in-to flaterynge,
>> Richesse into roberye.
>> Myght is y-torned into ry3t,
>> Godnesse in-to symonie.
>> Þe world is y-tornd for tho vy3te,
>> Þe del is is [*sic*] redy to aspeye.[31]   devil

---

[28] *IMEV* 2356; *HP*, p. xlii. Further discussed below.
[29] *IMEV* 873; Grimestone No. 26, without Latin model.
[30] *IMEV* 592; taken from Furnivall, EETS 15:264.
[31] ''Set certe, quod dolendum est, plus nunc crescit malicia quam unquam ante. Unde

But just as often the change is expressed with verbs of action or movement:

> Now is loue and lewte shet vndir lok,   shut
> Falshode and flateryng berith the bell in euery flok.
> Rightuysnes is rauysshid and doluyn wondir depe.   buried
> Pees now and speke softe, for truth is a-slepe![32]

Elsewhere, love has left this country (*IMEV* 2008), manhood and mercy have been chased out (2085), truth is dead and falsehood lives (2146), and so forth.[33] Given these syntactic and semantic differences, one could separate poems of Type B into a number of distinct sub-types; but such a classification would at once become unrealistic because there is much overlap among these sub-types, whose elements tend to cross over and form new combinations, as we shall see later in analyzing some specific examples.

The essential message of Type B poems is much the same as that of "The Twelve Abuses" (i.e., Type A): things are not what they should be. But in their form poems of Type B are so different from Type A that they must not be labeled "Abuses of the Age." It seems that the unfortunate equivocation, current in modern classifications, of applying the term "abuses" to both types is due to Carleton Brown, who translated the medieval title *De duodecim abusivis huius saeculi* as "Twelve Abuses of the Age."[34] But *huius saeculi* here means "of this world," not "of this [contemporary] age," as Aelfric and his successors well realized when they translated: "twelf unþeawas syndon on þyssere *worulde*."[35] Part of the confusion of course stems from the fact that later Middle English complaint poems frequently mix the two basic types. The prime case is *Gifte is domesman* (see below), which lists several evils in the form of Type B: "wyth is trechery . . . , pley turnyt to vylanye," but next to them it gives others in the form of Type A: "Lordes ben lawles and children ben awles." Unfortunately, *Gifte is domesman* was chosen by Rob-

---

secundum (?) et per totam Angliam quatuor fiunt conversiones pessimas, videlicet: Pouerte. . . ." Worcester Cathedral MS. F.126, fol. 112.

[32] Bodleian Library, MS. Tanner 201, fol. 2. *IMEV* lists this as part of 2500, but the preceding six lines deal with a totally different topic.

[33] Further items belonging to Type B are: *IMEV* 884, 1020, 1655, 1871, 2364, 2787, 3282, 3851, 3852, 1088.5, 2536.5.

[34] Brown, "The 'Pride of Life'," pp. 72 and 75.

[35] Morris, *Old English Homilies*, Appendix II, p. 299; compare ibid., p. 107.

bins to set off one major type or "version" of complaint verses from the other, with the natural result of blotting out formal distinctions between them and confusing two very different entities.[36] I should add that Type B must not be seen as in any way deriving from Type A, either logically or historically. The couplet quoted earlier: *Riȝtful dom is ouercast*, which belongs to Type B, translates a verse that was composed perhaps as much as a millennium before *De duodecim abusivis*.

Among Middle English complaint verses of Type B, four demand special attention because of their great popularity with medieval preachers, writers, and audiences, as well as the light they shed on the backgrounds and the "life" of certain structural formulas. The first poem has been given the title "Sayings of the Four Philosophers." It consists of four short triplets which are set in a story told in either Latin or English about a king who is worried about various disasters that have befallen his realm.[37] At his request, four philosophers speak or write down three somewhat cryptic lines each, which are then explained. The first triplet, for example, runs:

> Myȝte is ryȝte,
> Lyȝte is nyȝte,
> Fyȝt is flyȝt.[38]

The story with the verses appears in a collection of preaching materials in MS. Harley 7322 and in the *Speculum Christiani*. In both, the English lines are set into the Latin text without Latin equivalents,[39] which would strongly suggest that the English phrases are of native origin, not translated.[40] This suggestion is strengthened by the form in which the story appears without the English verses in a third text, the *Gesta Romanorum*. Here the "message" of the missing English lines is given in a Latin that is so clumsy and devoid of the customary rhymed endings that one is

---

[36] See the references to Robbins above, n. 5. The confusion there noted apparently stems from a remark made by Brown, in which he called *Gifte* and its Latin source "one of these metrical variations of the Twelve Abuses of the Age" ("The 'Pride of Life'," p. 75).

[37] Tubach No. 3753.

[38] *IMEV* 2167; taken from Gustaf Holmstedt (ed.), *Speculum Christiani*, EETS 182 (London, 1933), p. 125.

[39] "Primus philosophus dixit: Myȝte is ryȝte," etc.; ibid., pp. 125ff. and 333ff.

[40] Holmstedt, *Speculum*, p. clxxxix, and Scattergood, "Political Context" (see note 51), p. 162, claim that "the sayings" derive from a Latin original but offer no evidence. I suspect that both were led to this claim by the confusion that relates *Might is right* to *Munus fit judex*.

compelled to consider the Latin sayings as derived from the vernacular; compare for example the Latin equivalents of the three lines already quoted:

> Potentia est justitia,
> dies est nox,
> fuga est pugna.[41]

The prose exposition which interprets the brief sayings is quite different in the three versions of the *exemplum*. In Harley 7322[42] the four philosophers explain the phrases discursively by consistently comparing the present age and its degeneracy with the virtues and standards of the *antiquum tempus*. Very often explicit references to England are made, and criticism is directed against such specific evils as oppression of the poor, pride of clothing, and the like. The rhetorical development is fleshed out with several *exempla* and at least two proverbs, one of them quoted in English. The general drift of this exposition reappears, even if in a more rambling style, in the Latin *Gesta Romanorum* (*GR* 144): former virtues are contrasted with present evils in a number of social or professional classes. But in contrast to Harley 7322, here the social evils are given an additional spiritual interpretation—a procedure typical of *Gesta Romanorum*—and there are no references to England whatsoever.[43] It is also worth noting that in *GR* the sayings of the philosophers were found inscribed on the four gates of the city. The traditional sayings—here reported only in Latin—are expanded as follows:

> Potentia est justitia, ideo terra sine lege;
> dies est nox, ideo terra sine via;
> fuga est pugna, ideo regnum sine honore.

The syntactic form of these expansions is very reminiscent of Type A: *terra sine lege* echoes *populus sine lege* and *lond wiþ-vten lawe*.[44] While this may suggest some influence from Type A, it should be noted that the subject of all twelve expansions in *GR* is uniformly "the land" (*terra*,

---

[41] *GR* 144, p. 500.

[42] Printed with several transcription errors by Holmstedt, *Speculum*, pp. 331-36.

[43] The origin and date of *GR* are still matters of great uncertainty. The earliest surviving manuscript, used by Oesterley, is of German provenance, and the *exemplum* under discussion actually contains a German proverb (p. 502).

[44] The second phrase is from *De duodecim abusivis* (see note 8); the third, from *IMEV* 4051, line 12.

regnum, patria),[45] in stark contrast to Type A poems whose character-istic it is to catalogue social types, not abstractions like "the nation," and to list a number of them, not speak of one and the same.

In the third form of the *exemplum*, which appears in *Speculum Chris-tiani*,[46] the development differs radically from that of both Harley 7322 and *GR*. Here each English phrase is "proven" or authenticated with several quotations from the Bible, the Church Fathers (including Lincolniensis, that is, Grosseteste), and Seneca. It is difficult to establish a relative chronology for the three versions, but it would appear that on formal grounds the version in Harley 7322 represents an earlier state than that of *GR*, which I believe to be the case for other reasons also.[47]

The twelve English lines of *Might is right* with their frame story en-joyed some popularity outside the three works mentioned. They can be found in a fifteenth-century collection of sermons[48] and in another col-lection of stories for devotional reading made by the Canterbury monk William Chartham in 1448.[49] More interesting is their appearance in the Auchinleck MS. composed ca. 1330-40. Here they occur as "vn sar-moun / Of iiij wise men þat þer were, / Whi Engelond is brouht adoun,"[50] incorporated into a poem made up of two distinct parts. The first part (lines 1-16) consists of two macaronic stanzas evidently dealing with political events of 1311.[51] After a four-line macaronic transition, lines 21-98 then continue in English and give the "Sayings of the Four Philosophers." This part is written in six-line stanzas reminiscent of *The Proverbs of Hending*. The stanzas report what each philosopher said and end with more general reflections and exhortations. After each of the four stanzas that give the philosophers' sayings, the corresponding triplet from *Might is right* is inserted, in the same form as in *Speculum Chris-*

[45] The expanded version of *Might is right* appears in English in the Auchinleck MS. dis-cussed below. There all twelve lines are predicated uniformly of "þe lond" (*HP* 54).
[46] Holmstedt, *Speculum*, pp. 125-31.
[47] *Speculum Christiani* is conventionally thought to have been composed ca. 1330-40.
[48] Bodleian Library, MS. Lat. theol. d. 1, fols. 41v-42. Fol. 41 is mutilated and the sur-viving text is partially illegible.
[49] Lambeth Palace Library MS. 78, fol. 245r-v.
[50] *IMEV* 1857 (but only in MS. 2); *HP* 54.
[51] The unity and date of the poem have been challenged by Isabel S. T. Aspin (ed.), *An-glo-Norman Political Songs*, Anglo-Norman Text Society 11 (Oxford, 1953), pp. 56-61, but defended by V. J. Scattergood, "Political Context, Date, and Composition of The Say-ings of The Four Philosophers," *MAe* 37 (1968), 157-65.

187

tiani.[52] But here the reader is struck by two curious facts. First, the philosophers' sayings in the *stanzas* are quite different in substance from *Might is right*, and two of them use sea imagery that goes poorly with the simple triplets. Second, the triplets are cited twice, the second time in a form that is a fairly exact translation of the expanded Latin sayings we found in *GR* 144. It seems inescapable to conclude that in this second part the unkown poet has made a potpourri from three different though related things: his own verses and two forms of *Might is right*. Notwithstanding his thematic announcement ("why England has been brought down"), the entire second part of the poem has no references to England, in sharp contrast to the exposition of the *exemplum* found in Harley 7322. The whole tenor of part 2 of the poem is thus sapiential-proverbial rather than "political."[53]

The syntactic pattern of *Might is right*, together with its message that virtues have become vices, is also imitated in a verse of different metrical form. A collection of sermons and sermon notes of ca. 1400 declares:

> For now—
> Worst is best,
> Strengthe is akaste,
> An prou is pyne. profit
> Ly3t is ny3t,
> And fly3t is fy3t,
> And ded is aslawe [*read* aslayne?]. death

First I say that "worst is best," for among all things sin is the worst, and yet nowadays it is believed to be the best, for people . . . place it before the joy of heaven. . . . In the fourth place I say that "light is night," because the knowledge which the holy fathers had [has been turned] into ignorance by modern people.[54]

---

[52] Except that the sequence of two lines is reversed and that the triplets are introduced by such words as *For* and *Nu*.

[53] My point is strengthened by the fact that the second and fourth speeches in stanzas (i.e., lines 31-36 and 57-62) evidently use material from *The Proverbs of Alfred*, sts. 8 and 11; see O. Arngart (ed.), *The Proverbs of Alfred. II. The Texts* . . . (Lund, 1955), pp. 84-87 and 90-93.

[54] "Nunc enim: Worst . . . Primo dico quod worst is best, quia inter omnia peccatum est pessimum, et tamen hiis diebus optimum esse creditur, quia celesti gaudio non [*sic*] anteponunt . . . Quarto dico quod lux est nox, quia cognicio quam sancti patres habuerunt a modernis in ignoranciam [*sic*]." Cambridge University Library, MS. Ii.3.8, fol. 62. See Erb, p. 76. Quoted with error by Robbins, *Manual* 5:1433. The "another list of evils" referred to occurs in a different sermon (Erb, p. 77).

Beyond its three occurrences discussed earlier, the story of "The Say-
ings of the Four Philosophers" appears also in an English translation of
the *Gesta Romanorum*, in a single fifteenth-century manuscript.[55] But
here the English verses take a quite different form. Each philosopher
speaks not three but four lines, and these are very different in substance
from *Might is right*; thus the first quatrain runs:

> Gifte is domesman,
> And gile is chapman;
> The grete holde no lawe,
> And seruauntes have none awe.[56]

The following lines continue this pattern; they speak not only of the evil
that is being done to human types ("wise men are but scorned") and of
human types that lack their expected virtue ("kinsmen are unkind") but
also lament that virtues have become vices ("wit is turned into treach-
ery"), thus mixing the characteristic forms of Types A and B. *Gifte is
domesman* therefore contains not the "Twelve Abuses" but sixteen
evils. This poem has been preserved—outside the English version of
Gesta Romanorum—in nearly twenty manuscripts, often without the
framing *exemplum* and sometimes only in part.[57] Judged by the number
of different *works* that preserve it, it was considerably more popular than
Might is right. A fine illustration of how parts of this poem were used in
the pulpit comes from a sermon on *Convertimini ad Dominum* ("Return
to the Lord," Hosea 14.3). The preacher proves his point that "when
someone for some worldly love abandons God, everything that God has
ordained for his help and comfort abandons the sinner" with two Scrip-
tural passages and then continues:

[55] Sidney J. H. Herrtage (ed.), *The Early English Versions of the Gesta Romanorum*,
EETS, es, 33 (London, 1879), p. 360. This version of the *exemplum* has no exposition of
the sayings.

[56] *IMEV* 906; taken from the edition cited in the preceding note. Another version has
been printed by Robbins, *HP* 55, lines 1-16, who combines it with a different poem and its
Latin source, two *versus rapportati* (lines 17-23).

[57] The entry in *Index* as revised in *Supplement* has several errors: MS. 4 (Merton 248)
contains not *IMEV* 906 but 4180; MSS. 16 (Digby 53) and 20 (Rylands Latin 201) contain
a translation of an unrelated Latin poem ("Ve populo cuius puer rex, censor agrestis . . .";
Walther, *Prov* 32836); and MS. 18 (Douce 107) is *Speculum Christiani* with *Might is right*.
Evidently influenced by *IMEV* 906 are lines used in epitaphs (e.g., *IMEV* 1206.8 and
2818.2).

To prove this, Marco Polo tells about a city whose princes, who once were most noble and wealthy, suddenly became miserable beggars. As they consulted their gods about the cause of such ruin and want that had befallen them, the latter answered in the following verses:

Ingenium dolus est, amor omnis ceca voluntas,
Ludus rusticitas, et gula festa dies.

In English:

Trewþe ys turnyd into trecherye,
Chast loue into lecherye,
Pleye and solas to velenye,
And holy-day to glotonye.[58]

The four lines are then used further to structure the subsequent development, which deals with "witty" lawyers in contemporary society (*modo*), with seduction, and with leisure activities at the tavern where people will hear nothing of God, but—

if there is someone with a tipped staff, or someone else who can tell dirty jokes dealing with lechery and the like and swear great oaths, he will be called a king of fellows . . . and will be more eagerly listened to than the best preacher of the world.[59]

Gifte is domesman definitely translates four Latin distichs beginning:

Munus fit judex, fraus est mercator in urbe,
Non lex est dominis, nec timor est pueris.

The Latin verses themselves are richly attested, in manuscripts from England as well as the Continent.[60] They frequently precede the English lines, but are also found without the translation, even in one sermon manuscript that contains much English verse.[61] It would appear that in

---

[58] "Ad confirmacionem hoc narrat Marcus Paulus de quadam civitate cuius principes quondam nobilissimi et ditissimi facti sunt quasi subito miseri et mendici. Qui consuluerunt deos suos de causa tante ruine et inopie irruentis. Qui responderunt per istos versus: Ingenium . . . Anglice: Trewþe . . ." Cambridge University Library, MS. Kk.4.24, fol. 187v. The English lines were printed in "Unrecorded," No. 76.

[59] "Set si sit ibi unus wyth a typped stykke vel aliquis alius qui sciverit recitare viles et turpes historias de luxuria et huiusmodi, et iurare magna iuramenta, ipse vocabitur a kyng of felawys, quia ipse est a cronny felaw, et magis solicite audietur quam melior predicator mundi." Ibid., fol. 189. I do not know what to make of *cronny*.

[60] Walther, *Prov* 15730 and *In* 11487; a variant is *Nummus est judex*, *Prov* 19178 and *In* 12405.

the late English *Gesta Romanorum*, *Gifte is domesman*—by then a well established complaint poem—simply replaced *Might is right*. The two poems are of course very similar in their messages, and they even share a verbal link: in the form of MS. Harley 7322, line 8 of *Might is right* reads "Gift is reeve," which is nearly identical with "Gifte is domesman."[62] Nonetheless, they are certainly separate and distinct sub-types of Type B, with quite different backgrounds and traditions. *Gifte is domesman* translates a popular Latin complaint poem, whereas *Might is right* is of vernacular origin.

A third very popular poem that belongs to Type B also derives from a Latin source. The two hexameters:

> Heu, plebs conqueritur, quia raro fides reperitur,
> Lex viris [*var.* iuris] moritur, fraus vincit, amor sepelitur[63]

lament (*conqueritur*) the disappearance of faithfulness, law, and love, and the triumph of fraud. The English rendition of these lines, a quatrain, has been preserved in at least six manuscripts, all connected with preaching. Though in *IMEV* the six versions appear under three different entries (2145, 2146, and 3650), they are clearly variants of one and the same poem; the differences between 2145 and the other two entries are certainly not greater than those among the four versions listed under 2145. A glance at their specific differences will be instructive for our discussion of variations that appear within several occurrences of the same translation. The following text is taken from John Sheppey's sermon collection, to which I add substantive variants from the other versions.

> Hallas, men planys of litel trwthe,
> Hit ys dede and tat is rwthe.
> Falsedam regnis and es abowe,
> And byrid es trwloue.

Text: Merton 248, fol. 166v. Collated with: Harley 2316, fol. 26 (H); Balliol 227, fol. 258 (B), all three listed as *IMEV* 2145; Hatton 107, fol. 1v (Ht), listed as *IMEV* 2146; and Cambridge, Pembroke College MS. 258, fol. 136 (P), listed as *IMEV* 3650.

---

[61] British Library, MS. Harley 7322, fol. 212v.

[62] *Speculum Christiani* and *IMEV* 1857, however, have "Thef is refe," and *GR* 144 similarly reads *fur est propositus*. Harley's *ʒift* thus may be a scribal form for *þift/þeft* or an error.

[63] Walther, *Prov* 10757-58 and others.

Hallas] *om all others*.
men] þis world P.
planys] hem bimenin H; hem pleynit B; ⟨hem com⟩pleynes Ht;
      hymn pleyneʒ P.
litel trwthe] mikil vntrewthe BP; vntrewyth Ht.
Hit] Ryt BP; la⟨we⟩ Ht.
Falsedam] lesing H; trecherye BHt; falsnesse P.
regnis] liuet HB; *om* Ht.
and es] es al Ht.
and] and now H; nouthe B; nou P.
byried es] grauen he as Ht.
trwloue] trewthe and loue H.

In British Library, MS. Egerton 2788, fol. 53v (listed as *IMEV* 2145)
the poem appears as follows:

Ryght es deed and þat is rewþe,
And haþ be-beried pees and trewþe.
Falsne and pride regnen aboue,
And han be-beried trewe loue.[64]

At first glance it might indeed seem that the six occurrences represent
two or three different and independent translations of the Latin hexame-
ters. Variants like men:þis world (for *plebs*) or ryt:lawe (for *lex*) or
falsedam:lesing:trecherye (for *fraus*) are certainly not the result of sim-
ple scribal corruption and emendation. The degree of variation is even
greater in the Egerton MS., whose author starts with line 2 and then
makes up a new line anticipating the image of line 4. However, the six
occurrences have exactly the same syntactic structure throughout their
four lines, and more importantly they have exactly the same rhyme-
words. In this respect their variation is very different from that found in
multiple translations of a Latin source, as the following example will il-
lustrate. The two hexameters,

Si tibi copia, si sapiencia formaque detur,
Sola superbia destruit omnia si commitetur,

are translated in *Fasciculus morum* thus:

If þu be rych and wyse also
And of bewte fressh þerto,

---

[64] I owe a transcription of the English poem to Dr. Susan Cavanaugh.

Þes virtuse pride wyll sone vndo
If hit ones be knyt þerto.

But in Grimestone's collection, the translation (No. 223) appears in the following form:

ȝef þu be riche, and wys in lore,
    In tunge gracious,
Pride destruiȝet þis an more,
    For he is venimous.[65]

Differing not only in the Englishing of the Latin wording but also in their rhyme-words and their metrical pattern, the two quatrains are clearly independent translations of the same source. In contrast, the six occurrences of *Hallas, men planys*, including the Egerton form, appear to be variants of one and the same translation. Their variation can, I think, be explained by a process involving partial quotation from memory. I suggest that at the moment of writing them down, the writers had the poem's English metrical structure as well as its rhyme scheme present in their memories, and the Latin model before their eyes. Some of the latter's key terms (*plebs, lex, fraus*) were retranslated by the individual writers, but the basic shape set by the English translation's syntactic and metrical structure remained intact. The results of such a process can equally be seen in other preaching verses.[66] Yet this variation found within one and the same translation of a Latin source, while it reveals some influence of oral transmission, still differs significantly from the generation of new variants in poems that have grown out of genuinely native and oral traditions.

The fourth and final complaint poem of Type B is represented by a group of verses which, like members of a family, are diversified in their appearance but carry the same genetic makeup in their structure and other formal characteristics. For lack of a better label and in agreement with earlier scholars, I shall refer to them generically as "The Prophecy," even though not all members of this group appear as prophecies. Typical is the following item which has been preserved in at least seventeen manuscripts from about 1400 on:

---

[65] Texts taken from *Verses*, p. 142. Another example which neatly shows the differences among multiple translations is the "Three Sorrowful Things." See Thomas J. Heffernan, "Unpublished Middle English Verses on the 'Three Sorrowful Things'," *NM* 83 (1982), 31-33. Heffernan includes some irrelevant texts, though, and misses Alan J. Fletcher, *N&Q* 223 (1978), 108.

[66] For some examples in *Fasciculus morum*, see *Verses*, Nos. 24, 26, 34, 39, 41.

When feythe fayleth in prestys sawys,
And lordys wyll be londys lawys,
And lechery is preuy solas,
And robbery ys goode purchas,
Than shall the londe of Albeon
Be turned into confusion.[67]

The extant versions of this poem, *IMEV* 3943, show some variation in phrasing that may be illustrated in the following verse from the early fifteenth century:

Whenne lordis wol lose hare olde lawis,
And prestis buth varyynge in hare sawys,
And lecherye is holde solas,
And oppressyoun for purchas,
Þanne schal þe lond of Albyon
Be nyx to his confusyoun.[68]

Nonetheless, all extant versions agree in three major characteristics: they follow the same pattern in which a series of four evils[69] leads to a prophetic final couplet; they use the same rhyme words (sawys/lawys, solas/purchas, Albion/confusion); and they list the same four moral and social evils: faithlessness in priests, willfulness in lords, lechery, and robbery or oppression. Though the first two lines may be said to carry an echo from the "Twelve Abuses" tradition (our Type A), the whole poem essentially declares that vices have become virtues, thus establishing itself

---

[67] *IMEV* 3943, taken from *SL*, p. 241. The poem is called "Merlin's Prophecy," on the basis of its medieval title.

[68] *IMEV* 3943; taken from Manchester, John Rylands Library, MS. Lat. 201, fol. 130 (not 227a, as given in *Supplement*). See also E. C. and R. Fawtier, "From Merlin to Shakespeare. Adventures of an English Prophecy," *BJRL* 5 (1918-20), 388-92. Another version with a similar beginning is *HP* 47, originally *IMEV* 3986, now 3943 (see *Supplement*).

[69] If my view of the history of "The Prophecy" is correct, the list of four evils is one of its original constituent features. The appearance of the number four is a curious trait in English complaints at the time. Besides "The Prophecy" it appears in "The Sayings of the Four Philosophers" and the four initials of "The Roman Prophecy" (cf. below, note 101). Another verse in *Fasciculus morum* lists *quatuor contradictoria* that are very similar to complaint verses (*Verses*, No. 52). And the poem *Pouerte ys tornd in-to coueytynge*, quoted earlier, is said to speak of "four most evil changes" though it actually lists several more (cf. note 31). An entire sermon that deals with *quatuor principalia mala que regnant in hoc mundo* (pride, envy, greed, and lust) is *Christus passus est pro nobis* in MS. Harley 7322, fols. 139v-150.

unmistakably as Type B.[70] The stanza, and particularly its final couplet, enjoyed an unusual popularity: it was frequently attributed to Chaucer;[71] it was cast into rhyme royal and incorporated in Peter Idley's *Instructions to His Son* ("It hath be said before in olde langwage");[72] and it was finally parodied by the Fool in *King Lear*.[73]

The stanzas just cited (*IMEV* 3943) have a close parallel in a poem found in eleven manuscripts of *Fasciculus morum* (*IMEV* 3133):

> Sithyn law for wyll bygynnyt to slakyn,
> And falsehed for sleythe is i-takyn,   prudence
> Robbyng and reuyng ys holden purchas,
> And of vnthewes is made solas—
> Engelond may synge "alas, alas!"[74]

The similarities are striking. Both poems give not only the same number of evils but the same evils. Willfulness in place of law and the appearance of robbery as lawful acquisition are verbally the same in both. The vice of *vnthewes* in *Fasciculus morum*, though it could mean more than lechery (i.e., "vices" or "bad manners"), was in fact understood as "lust" by early readers of the work, as several scribes have made clear, and thus parallels line 3 of the former verse. And the *falsehed* of line 2 is conceptually not very far from the unreliability of priests' words lamented in *IMEV* 3943. In addition, the verse in *Fasciculus morum* follows the same pattern as *IMEV* 3943: a series of four evils, here set in a "since—therefore" frame instead of "when—then," leads to a reference to England. Finally, even one pair of rhyme-words is shared by the two poems. All this points to a clear genetic relation between them. Yet the verse in *Fasciculus morum* is at least a century older than *IMEV* 3943, since the handbook was composed shortly after 1300 and shows evidence of having contained English verses, including "The Prophecy," at the time of its composition.[75] The greater age of the *Fasciculus morum* verse is further revealed in such words as *sleythe* ("prudence") and *vnthewes* which, in the sense with which they are here employed, had become ar-

---

[70] The poem has nothing to do with "impossible situations," let alone the medieval version of "I gave my love a cherry," as claimed by Robbins, *SL*, p. 241.

[71] From Caxton on; see *Supplement* 3943 and Fawtier, "From Merlin."

[72] Ed. Charlotte d'Evelyn, MLA Monograph Series 6 (Boston, 1935), p. 144, lines 2264ff.

[73] *King Lear*, III.ii.81-94.   [74] *Verses*, pp. 178-79.

[75] *Verses*, pp. 26-41 and 108-10.

chaic by 1400 and were in fact replaced with more current synonyms in several manuscripts.[76] In addition to its earlier date, the English verse in *Fasciculus morum* also furnishes some indication of the poem's background: the lines are not preceded by a Latin source text but instead introduced with the remark *unde quidam dixit Anglice* ("whence someone has said in English"), which surely is clear proof of the poem's native origin. This would mean that the entire group of poems here discussed under the title of "The Prophecy" derives from native and oral traditions.

Yet another stanza, *IMEV* 4006, is curiously similar to the quoted verses:

> Whene pryde is moste in prys,
> Ande couetyse moste wys,
> Ande lucchery moste in vse,
> Þefe maade reue,
> Þenne schall Englonde mys-chewe.[77]

We meet again a list of four vices that have become socially and morally accepted, followed by a reference to England, all of it set in a "when—then" frame. The vices listed are substantively the same as in the two preceding poems. But here three of them are named by the more abstract, "learned" terms from the seven-deadly-sins scheme (or perhaps more accurately, the three major sins[78]), while the fourth member seems to have been borrowed from the *Might is right* verses of *Speculum Christiani*.[79] Despite these differences, the close relationship of *IMEV* 4006 with 3943 and 3133 is unmistakable. It is as if someone had poured different but equally stale wine into an old bottle.

And one further poem should be included in this family of complaint verses:

[76] See the variants given in *Verses*, p. 179, and the discussion of linguistic updating on pp. 111-14.

[77] F. J. Furnivall (ed.), Queene Elizabethes Achademye, *A Booke of Precedence* . . . , EETS, es, 8 (London, 1869), p. 85.

[78] Pride, avarice, and lust, corresponding to the sins of the world, the flesh, and the devil of 1 John 2.16; see Donald R. Howard, *The Three Temptations* (Princeton, 1966), esp. pp. 43-56; and Wenzel, "The Three Enemies of Man," *MS* 29 (1967), esp. pp. 57ff.

[79] See earlier comment, p. 191 and n. 62. *IMEV* 4006 appears further expanded and enriched with other traditions ("halie kirk awles and Iustise lawles") in *IMEV* 4005.5; similarly in *IMEV* 4008.

Now pride ys yn pris,
Now couetyse ys wyse,
Now lechery ys schameles,
Now gloteny ys lawles,
Now slewþe ys yn seson,
In envie and wreþe ys treson.
  Now haþ God enchesyn
  To dystrie þys worle by reson.[80]

This form, *IMEV* 2356, begins with the same couplet as the preceding poem (4006) and ends with a similar generalizing reflection. But here the "when—then" frame is replaced by "now—now" (not unlike *IMEV* 3133), and the prophecy has become a present-tense statement justifying God for taking vengeance. Nevertheless, the general structure of 2356 remains very similar to that of 4006, 3133, and 3943. It is more significant to note that the four evils we have so far encountered have here become six or seven[81]—in fact, they are the traditional seven deadly sins. In accordance with what is known about the genesis of literary works, it seems reasonable to think that *IMEV* 2356, with its full list of the seven deadly sins, is a secondary development, a learned imitation of the original form with four evils or of the intermediary mixture (*IMEV* 4006) of one evil and three deadly sins. The imitative character of 2356 is further shown in its rhyme-words *schameles* and *lawles*, evidently borrowed from Type A (*Bissop lorles*, *IMEV* 1820). *IMEV* 2356 itself seems to have led to further imitation in a stanza that has gained far greater renown:

Now raygneth pride in price,
Couetise is holden wise,
Lechery without shame,
Gluttonie without blame,
Enuye raygneth with reason [*var.* tresone],
And sloath is taken in great season.
  God doe boote, for nowe is time. Amen.[82]

---

[80] *HP*, p. xlii.

[81] In fourteenth-century English works, envy and wrath are frequently joined and even confused.

[82] *IMEV* 1791; *HP* 17.

This stanza is attributed to the notorious John Ball and preserved in Henry Knighton's *Chronicon* and the revised edition of Stow's *Annales*. Whether John Ball ever spoke or wrote these lines is of course anybody's guess, given the late date of the records that have preserved them. But of their derivative and learned nature there can hardly be any doubt; they utilize six of the seven deadly sins in a structure that is but the last off-spring of a family whose roots date back at least to the late thirteenth century.

Two family traits of "The Prophecy" call for some further remarks. We have noticed that the syntactic sequence of "when—then," varied as "since—therefore" or "now—now," recurs in these poems as one of their constituent features. But this pattern is in fact much more wide-spread in Middle English poetry. It belongs to a general structural formula which can be schematized as:

when/if/who, etc. . . . . list of items . . . *then/so/he*, etc.

This formula appears in a variety of short poems on diverse topics, all of them of early date and utilized in preaching. One instance is the following poem on death:

> If man him biþocte
> Inderlike and ofte:
> Wu arde is te fore   how. travel
> Fro bedde te flore,
> Wu reuful is te flitte
> Fro flore te pitte,
> Fro pitte te pine
> Þat neure sal fine—   end
>   I wene non sinne
>   Sulde his herte winnen.[83]

First written out in the late thirteenth century, these lines were to recur in many texts and various combinations.[84] Similarly, one form of the "Three Sorrowful Things" appears in the frame "Wanne ich þenche

---

[83] *IMEV* 1422; *EL* 13.

[84] Obviously *IMEV* 4129 is a variant, and 3201 and 3219 are part of 4129. See further "Unrecorded," No. 85, and Alan J. Fletcher, "A Death Lyric from the Summa predican-tium, MS. Oriel College 10," *N&Q* 222 (1977), 11-12.

þinges þre . . . I ne woth nevre wuder I sal fare.''[85] From the same time
also comes the much anthologized poem:

> Wen þe turuf is þi tuur,
> And þi put is þi bour,
> Þi wel and þi wite þrote   skin
> Ssullen wormes to note—   profit
>   Wat helpit þe þenne
>   Al þe worilde wnne?[86]

The structure likewise underlies several common poems on ''The Signs
of Death,'' as for instance: ''When þe hede quakyth . . . þe body ne tyt
but a clowte.''[87] In addition, it appears in a number of short meditations
on Christ's Passion beginning ''When I see (*or* think) on the cross'' or
''Whoso sees on the cross.''[88] A number of very similar poems also oc-
curs in the large corpus of medieval *Latin* verses, usually beginning with
Si. These include a very popular longer one which also was translated
into English:

> Si tibi pulcra domus, si splendida mensa, quid inde?[89]

But it is safe to assert that this structural formula does not derive from
learned Latin models but comes out of the vernacular, native tradition.
Many of the shorter English poems that have been quoted are not trans-
lations. What is more, those that do have a Latin model borrow their sub-
stance from the Latin but not their ''when—then'' structure. This can be
most readily seen in renderings of the ''Three Sorrowful Things.'' Here
the Latin model:

> Sunt tria ve que mestificant me nocte dieque:
> Hinc quia migro, nescio quando, deveniam quo[90]

[85] *IMEV* 3969; *EL* 12. Another occurrence of this poem has been noticed by Fletcher in *N&Q* 223 (1978), 108.

[86] *IMEV* 4044; *EL* 30.

[87] *IMEV* 4035. Printed and discussed in *Verses*, pp. 197-99. Very similar are *IMEV* 4031, 4033, 4047, and 4036.5.

[88] *IMEV* 3961, 3964-66, 4107, 4141; and 3968.

[89] Walther, *In* 18017: printed by A. G. Rigg, *A Glastonbury Miscellany of the Fifteenth Century* (Oxford, 1968), p. 92. The English translation in ''Unrecorded,'' No. 72.

[90] Walther, *Prov* 30850.

(There are three woes that make me sad by night and day: that I go away from here, I know not when nor where I shall get to)

is occasionally rendered in the same simple declarative pattern: "Thre thinges ben, in fay, / That makith me to sorowe all way."[91] But elsewhere the numerical saying is cast in the "when—[then]" formula, as quoted above, which has no base in the Latin hexameters. The same holds for the "When I see on the cross" verses:

> Wenne Hic soe on rode idon
>   Ihesus, mi leman,
> And bi him stonde
>   Maria and Iohan,
> His herte duepe i-stunge,
> His bodi þis scurge i-ssuenge,
>   For þe sunne of man,
> Hiþe Hi mai wepen   loudly
> And selte teres leten,
>   Ief Hic of luue chan.[92]

Latin meditative passages similarly list aspects of Christ's Passion, but they are cast in the imperative mood, commonly beginning *Respice in faciem Christi* (addressed either to God or to a meditating person). None of these possible models contains anything like the English "when— then" formula.[93]

The other family trait present in at least some members of "The Prophecy" is their vaticinal form, in which England's ruin or future lamentation is predicted.[94] Should the prophetic element be considered a constituent feature that sets these poems apart from others I have included in the same group? I think not, because these poems are not gen-

---

[91] *IMEV* 3711; ed. Herrtage, *Early English Versions*, p. 304. A rather garbled version of this English verse, so far not noticed, appears in New Haven, Yale University MS. 15, fol. 91r-v (sermons). Different translations of the two hexameters are *IMEV* 695, 1615, 3712, 3713, and 3969. For the Latin model, see *Verses*, pp. 123, n. 48; 90, n. 138; and 85.

[92] *IMEV* 3965; *EL* 35.

[93] The various versions of the poem and its relation to Latin models are discussed by Karl Reichl, *Religiöse Dichtung im englischen Hochmittelalter. Untersuchungen und Edition der Handschrift B.14.39 des Trinity College in Cambridge* (Munich, 1973), pp. 488-99 and 89-95; and by Woolf, pp. 33-34. For a hitherto unnoticed quotation of the poem in a sermon, see below, ch. 7, p. 236.

[94] Especially in *IMEV* 3943; see above, p. 194 and notes 67-68.

uine prophecy. True prophecies may be extremely cryptic, but they talk of specific things even when they are veiled under allegory, such as: "Thus says the Lord God: Behold I will lay a stone in the foundations of Sion, a tried stone, a corner stone . . . and hail shall overturn the hope of falsehood, and waters shall overflow its protection" (Isaiah 28.16-17); or: "When the hills smoke, the end of Babylon will have come";[95] or: "Woe to the red dragon, for his end is nearing fast; the white dragon will occupy his cave."[96] In contrast, the poems here considered speak of abstract qualities: the willfulness of lords becomes law, pride is most apprized, robbery is called lawful acquisition, and so forth. Moreover, these poems show none of the distinctive devices used in genuine political prophecies from medieval England, such as animal symbolism, arbitrary names, or etymology.[97] For these reasons I would not consider them genuine prophecies but Type B poems of complaint at the evil times *put in the form of a prophecy*. The vaticinal mode occurs in other forms of both Types A and B as well. One version of the "Twelve Abuses," already discussed, poses as a prophecy by Bede: "Hwan þu sixst on leode . . . (series of abuses) . . . Al-so seide Bede: Wo þere þeode."[98] Carleton Brown printed another, Latin version of the "Twelve Abuses" (here nine items) which begins with "Quando senes erunt sine sensu" and ends in "Aliqui dicunt quod appropinquabit finis mundi" and is in the manuscript introduced as "þe wordes of Ierome þe prophete."[99] On the other hand, the variant of the so-called "Merlin's Prophecy," which I believe to be older than *IMEV* 3943, that is, *IMEV* 3133, does not predict a future state of affairs but a corruption already present. It would therefore appear that genetically in all these cases the vaticinal form is a secondary development and formally less important than the "when—then" formula. As Scattergood has remarked, "the manuscript attribution to Merlin [of a version of *IMEV* 3943] and the prophecy form are used only to give its rather trite observations some sort of authority and interest."[100]

---

[95] Cf. "Unrecorded," No. 88. The Latin text occurs also in *Convertimini*, British Library, MS. Royal 7.C.i, fol. 108.

[96] From Merlin's prophecies in Book VII of the *Historia regum Britanniae* by Geoffrey of Monmouth, ed. Acton Griscom (London, 1929), p. 385.

[97] See Rupert Taylor, *The Political Prophecy in England* (New York, 1911), pp. 5-6.

[98] *IMEV* 4051: see above, pp. 178-79.

[99] Brown, "The 'Pride of Life'," p. 75. The Latin is connected with *IMEV* 502.5.

[100] Scattergood, *Politics*, p. 301.

This is not to deny the fascination that "political prophecies" of this vague sort had for medieval minds including preachers. A message verse on the fall of Rome which is often found in an *exemplum* is of some interest here. *Fasciculus morum* tells of a Roman senator who asked his god why Rome was plagued by so many wars, hunger, and diseases. In response he was sent to the city gate, where he found the letters SSS. PPP. RRR. FFF. inscribed. Not knowing what to make of them he asked for an explanation and learned:

> Seculum sapienciam sustulit.
> Pax patrie perditur.
> Regnum Rome ruet
> Ferro, fame, flamma.

The verse is then translated into English.[101] The entire story, which is evidently a near cousin to "The Sayings of the Four Philosophers,"[102] enjoyed great popularity among fourteenth- and fifteenth-century preachers. But the prophecy itself and particularly its alliterative form in Latin are much older, for lines with the same message that alliterate on *V, R, F, A*, and other initials have been found in eighth- and ninth-century manuscripts of the letters of Saint Boniface.[103] The use of alliteration in connection with magic and prophecy was of course deeply ingrained in medieval and earlier cultures, and the "Roman Prophecy," which is sometimes attributed to the Sibyl or to Bede, surely has its distant prototype in the famous handwriting Belshazzar saw on the wall and its interpretation by Daniel (Daniel 5.26-28).[104] What surprises is that this form should have continued to hold such a lively interest among late medieval preachers. I am here not thinking of the well attested popular thirst for political prophecy in the fourteenth and fifteenth centuries but more specifically of the utilization of alliterative formulas in general complaint verses. Thus, one scribe who copied the prediction of Rome's fall, with the usual lines on *S-P-R-F*, added a few folios later another story with a

---

[101] *IMEV* 2729; *Verses*, pp. 169-70.

[102] Tubach No. 1150. Notice that in the *GR* 144 version of "The Sayings" (Tubach No. 3753) the four philosophers write the causes of the realm's degeneracy on the gates of the city.

[103] For references see *Verses*, pp. 169-70.

[104] Daniel interprets the three mysterious words with the aid of similar consonant groups (in Hebrew). For the "Sibyllic" type of prophecy, which uses initial letters, see Taylor, *Political Prophecy*, pp. 3, 114-15.

similar oracular answer. This, too, involves play with five initial letters (*A-C-D-E-I*) in the following pattern:

$$\left.\begin{array}{l}\text{Avaricia}\\\text{Adulacio}\\\text{Astucia}\end{array}\right\} \text{sine} \left\{\begin{array}{l}\text{mensura}\\\text{amore}\\\text{fide}\end{array}\right\} \text{habundant.}$$

or more simply:

$$\left.\begin{array}{l}\text{Irreverencia iuniorum}\\\text{Insipiencia seniorum}\\\text{Inmundicia populorum}\end{array}\right\} \text{regnant.}$$

The fifteen Latin lines are then translated into six English couplets, of which five correspond closely to the five Latin triplets but do not manage completely to imitate the alliteration:

> 3issinge and glosinge and felsship beon riue.
>
> . . . .
>
> Vnkundenesse, vnkunninge, vnclannesse beon arerd,
> So þat harmes þei boden, as Ich am aferd.[105]

The compiler of Harley 7322[106] was still not satisfied with this much oracular wisdom and let loose another firework of alliterating complaints at the evil times:

> Caritas, castitas, compassio refrigescunt.
> Census, caro, crudelitas incalescunt.
> Concilium, concordia, coniugium evanescunt.

In English:

> Charite, chaste, pite arn waxin al colde.
> Couetise, lust, and maistrie arn becomin al bolde.
> Consel, god acord, and wedloc ben nou noþing of tolde.

This continues for three more stanzas which, in Latin, alliterate in *F, L,* and *V* respectively.[107]

Alliterative prophecies, the vaticinatory form, numerical sayings, and

---

[105] MS. Harley 7322, fols. 63v-64. The English verse is *IMEV* 4273, printed by Furnivall, EETS 15:251.

[106] A different hand from the earlier section, though.

[107] MS. Harley 7322, fol. 162. The English verse is *IMEV* 592, printed by Furnivall, EETS 15:264-65.

priamels and other catalogues[108] are so many structural patterns that apparently have their distant origins in folk poetry. They are also closely related to the vast field of proverbs and proverbial sayings. It would be tedious to quote once more examples of the latter that were used in sermons or preaching handbooks and often have been preserved for us only through that medium. But it is worth noting how important an element vernacular proverbs were in the early Middle English lyric itself. A particularly fine example is the poem that has been titled "Death's Wither-Clench," written about 1250, a five-stanza warning to consider the inescapability of death and hence to flee sin and the false attraction of the world. What makes the poem so interesting, apart from its early date and powerful English diction, is the fact that it is a song whose music has been preserved in the oldest manuscript.[109] At the same time, it has strong connections with preaching. Neither the oldest manuscript nor the two poetry anthologies that contain it (together with *The Owl and the Nightingale* and other English poems) can be definitely shown to have been compiled for use in preaching, but a fourth manuscript which contains the poem certainly was.[110] In addition, parts of the poem are quoted elsewhere in sermon contexts.[111] The poem begins with a generalization that at once sets its proverbial tone:

> Man mei longe him liues wene,
> Ac ofte him liyet þe wreinch[112]

(Man may think that he will live long, but the trick often deceives him),

and which is continued in "Fair weder ofte him went to rene" (line 3) and "Al sel valui þe grene" ("All the green will fade," line 6)[113] and

---

[108] For a wideranging analysis of the literary catalogue, see Stephen A. Barney, "Chaucer's Lists," in *The Wisdom of Poetry. Essays in Early English Literature in honor of Morton W. Bloomfield*, ed. Larry D. Benson and Siegfried Wenzel (Kalamazoo, Mich., 1982), pp. 189-223, 297-307.

[109] Dobson, pp. 122-30.

[110] Bodleian Library, MS. Laud Misc. 471. The part of the volume that contains the poem is filled with pious stories and miracles of the Blessed Virgin. The later part likewise contains *exempla*, French and English sermons, and similar preaching material.

[111] See Dobson, p. 123.

[112] *IMEV* 2070; *EL* 10. "The couplet is modelled on one in *The Proverbs of Alfred*, ll. 108-9" (Dobson, p. 125), which occurs in the same manuscript. Several other occurrences are listed in O. Arngart, *The Proverbs*, p. 161.

[113] On the two lines, cf. Bartlett Jere Whiting and Helen Wescott Whiting, *Proverbs,*

many other lines. Stanza 3 actually refers to the counsel of Solomon, and stanza 5 incorporates two lines from "The Proverbs of Hending":

> Þar-fore let lust ouer-gon,
> Man, and eft it sal þe liken.[114]

The same dense texture of proverbial material still appears in lyrics from the end of the Middle English period, in a literary form that is far removed from simple preaching verses:

> What is this worlde but oonly vanyte?
> Who trustith fortune sonnest hath a falle.
> Ech man tak heed of prodigalite,
> Welth that is past no man agayn may calle.
> The grenowst wounde þat euer man had or schalle
> Is to thynk on welth þat is gon and past,
> And in olde age in mysery to be cast.[115]

Homespun wisdom has yielded to Boethian "philosophy," yet the mentality of medieval preaching is still very much present.

Making use of proverbs and of other poetic forms current in folk poetry is of course not an exclusive privilege of preachers; many great poets and writers have done the same. But medieval preachers' interest in formulating a general truth effectively, their closeness to the illiterate masses coupled with the desire to prove a point with sayings that would be familiar to their audience, and above all the predominantly oral nature of preaching, made their work a broad channel through which these elements could readily enter lyric poetry. The fact that preaching—and by implication the production of preaching verses —is essentially an oral activity may explain a further aspect we have frequently noticed in the discussion of complaint verses, namely that verbal material that originally belonged to different and separate formulas or types, and occasionally entire formulas reappear mixed and fused in various new combinations. Thus in one version of the "Sayings of the Four Philosophers" the usual *Might is right* was replaced with *Gifte is domesman*, or one phrase from the "Twelve Abuses" turned up in *Gifte is domesman*, while an-

---

Sentences, and Proverbial Phrases from English Writings Mainly before 1500 (Cambridge, Mass., 1968), W.154 and L.145.

[114] Whiting, *Proverbs*, L.591.

[115] *IMEV* 3909; *RL XV* 168. *Grenowst* in line 5 should probably read *greuowst*, i.e., "most grievous."

other from *Might is right* had found its way into a variant of "The Prophecy." This freedom to borrow, mix, and recombine, not surprising in any aspect of oral culture, meets us in larger aspects of sermon-making as well. For instance, detailed analysis of almost any sermon *exemplum* that enjoyed a relatively long life can show that in the hands of preachers a given narrative was not only expanded or shortened, but also combined with motifs from one or several quite different stories[116]—a process that is well known to students of the folktale,[117] whose results meet us on practically every folio of late medieval sermon collections. Furthermore, medieval preachers felt quite at liberty to borrow not only small motifs or details but entire paragraph-length developments of a topic or *exempla* with their moralizations verbatim and reuse them in new contexts wherever they might fit. Occasionally we even find a preacher employing the same passage again and again. A good example occurs in the macaronic sermons of MS. Bodley 649: one of their most remarkable passages, developing the "ship of state" image and commenting on the political and moral situation of England in the 1420s, recurs in nearly identical form in at least three different sermons.[118] Another case of what might be called the free use of macro-formulas concerns prothemes, which apparently were readily available as detached units to be used in whatever sermon might be appropriate. Thus, a protheme on the decay of mankind from the Golden Age to the present time is used in an Easter sermon on *Viderunt revolutum lapidem* (which quotes the English song *Maiden in*

---

[116] A good illustration is the already mentioned fact that the sayings of the four philosophers appear inscribed on the city gates in *GR* 144, a motif perhaps borrowed from the "Roman Prophecy." For further illustrations, see *Verses*, pp. 29-34; or Brian S. Lee, " 'This is no fable': Historical Residues in Two Medieval *Exempla*," *Speculum* 56 (1981), 728-60.

[117] Students of Middle English literature will be particularly familiar with this process from discussions of the background of *St. Erkenwald*, *Sir Orfeo*, or some of the Canterbury Tales. See also the volumes of FF Communications (Academia Scientiarum Fennica, Helsinki); or Bruce A. Rosenberg, "The Three Tales of *Sir Degare*," *NM* 75 (1975), 39-51.

[118] Bodleian Library MS. 649, fols. 22, 97, and 129v. Roy M. Haines, "Church, Society and Politics in the Early Fifteenth Century as Viewed from an English Pulpit," in *Church, Society and Politics*, ed. Derek Baker (Oxford, 1975), pp. 143-57, mentions many similar cases from the same manuscript. One sermon with the ship-of-state image was edited by Haines, " 'Our Master Mariner, Our Sovereign Lord': A Contemporary Preacher's View of King Henry V," *MS* 38 (1976), 85-96. See also G. R. Owst, *Literature and Pulpit in Medieval England*, second revised edition (Oxford, 1961), pp. 72-73. For another case of repeating the same material, in *Fasciculus morum*, see below, ch. 7, pp. 232-33.

the mor lay).[119] The same passage with only minor verbal differences
(but without the English song) appears a second time in the same manu-
script,[120] in a sermon that seems to be identical with Holcot's sermon 50
on *Dic ut lapides isti panes fiant* (again without the English song).[121] In
all these cases, we are not dealing with small commonplaces, such as
biblical and other authoritative quotations, or similes, or short *exempla*,
but with large blocks of material that are reused in their entirety.

This generic freedom to use parts of one verbal structure in another
and thereby to create new combinations and mixtures was also a major
feature of English lyric poetry in the late fourteenth and fifteenth centu-
ries. It shows in the simple, unexpanded insertion of preaching common-
places into longer poems, such as the well-known stanza on Lady For-
tune in a lullaby contained in the Kildare manuscript of the early
fourteenth century.[122] Similarly, a poem attributed to "the school of
Richard Rolle" incorporates a straightforward translation of *Candet nu-
datum pectus*,[123] and another poem on Christ's Passion uses the last
stanza as well as, with some adjustment, the burden of *Þu sikest sore*
("Luueli ter of loueli eyʒe").[124] Going beyond these cases of what might
be considered simple quotation, a fifteenth-century extended complaint
poem demonstrates even better the process of combining various struc-
tural topoi. The poem entitled "A Series of Trials"[125] begins with three
"poyntis of myscheff," which are three of the age-old "Abuses": a poor
man proud, a rich man thief, and an old man lecher (sts. 1-3). Next it
turns to three "points" in which God should be worshipped: justice,
mercy, and purity; but these virtues have become vices, and the poem
now utilizes the format of Type B complaint verses: "Wrong is set þer
right schuld be," and so on (sts. 5-6). Another triad follows, the "three
degrees which the world keeps," namely priesthood, knighthood, and
laborers, and the duties as well as the failures of each estate are briefly
traced (sts. 8-10). The poem then closes with a *memento mori* ("Man,
tak hed what þu arte," st. 11) and a prayer to God and Christ for mercy

---

[119] Worcester Cathedral MS. F.126, fol. 145. Cf. Wenzel, "The Moor Maiden—A Con-
temporary View," *Speculum* 49 (1974), 69-74.

[120] Worcester Cathedral MS. F.126, fol. 106.

[121] Cambridge, Peterhouse MS. 210, fols. 64v-65.

[122] *IMEV* 2025; *RL XIV* 28. Cf. *Verses*, pp. 173-75.

[123] *IMEV* 1715; *RL XIV* 83, lines 37-40.

[124] *IMEV* 611; *RL XIV* 90, lines 15-18 and 31-32. *Þu sikest sore* is *IMEV* 3691 (Grime-
stone 201).

and grace (sts. 12-13). Even such a personal lyric as Skelton's "Lament of the Soul of Edward IV,"[126] which includes a catalogue of specific achievements of the king (lines 49-60), cannot do without utilizing such commonplace building blocks as the *Ubi sunt* formula (lines 61-72), the *Unde superbis?* attributed to Saint Bernard (lines 73-76), and a series of exemplary figures: great Alexander, strong Samson, and so on (lines 77-84). And finally, this "agglutinating" process has recently been shown to operate even in fifteenth-century love lyrics.[127]

Our study of the two major types of complaint verses, and of several unusually popular members of the second type, has thus led us into aspects of oral literature—oral by transmission, by origin, and probably by performance as well (certainly in the case of sermons and their verses). The influence that oral traditions had on the early English lyric and on some aspects of sermon making was evidently profound and continuous. In particular, certain basic structures or formulas underwent a wide range of formal variation and freely combined with different poetic forms, thus leading a remarkably vigorous life that is documented in the surviving sermon literature. To this life preachers made a fundamental contribution, for it was they who appropriated native oral material, formulated it, and transmitted it in varying shapes.

[125] *IMEV* 3522; *RL XV* 177.
[126] *IMEV* 2192; *RL XV* 159.
[127] R. H. Robbins, "The Structure of Longer Middle English Court Poems," in *Chaucerian Problems and Perspectives. Essays Presented to Paul E. Beichner, C.S.C.*, ed. Edward Vasta and Zacharias P. Thundy (Notre Dame, Ind., 1979), pp. 244-64.

7

Love

Sacred and

Profane

Like complaint verses, secular love poems found in sermons open another window on the backgrounds of the early English lyric and provide its historian with fascinating if fragmentary material. From the later thirteenth into the fifteenth century preachers were evidently quite willing to enliven their discourse with well-known songs or snatches of worldly love. Mostly quoted as single lines or at best as a short stanza, such snatches have been eagerly gathered as so many precious remnants from the otherwise lost literature of medieval England. Thus, popular sermons form an extensive quarry that has preserved some precious shards which testify, for instance, to the existence of vernacular lover's complaints and nature introductions before the first substantial body of worldly love songs in English, those contained in Harley MS. 2253, burst upon the literary scene "without warning."[1] And beyond these "courtly" tones, other snatches carry voices from perhaps even farther back in time, with their figures of maidens standing by wells or lying on the moor, dance songs, and women's songs—voices that may well sound the primitive song of the people long before wandering scholars or court poets created more sophisticated lyrics. The vexing questions of what influenced what—folksong or art poetry—and of the origins of medieval love song cannot concern us here, for in this respect the shards, while fascinating, remain intensely frustrating: they suggest round shapes but refuse to tell us whether these once were cosmetic vials or cooking pots. But collecting such shards will at least point to the richness and variety of secular love song in England that has otherwise been lost; and presenting them in their immediate context (which is usually neg-

[1] R. H. Robbins, in *SL*, p. lii. Robbins revised this view in his review of Theo Stemmler, *Die englischen Liebesgedichte des MS. Harley 2253* (Bonn, 1962), in *Anglia* 82 (1964), 507-8. Stemmler discusses some ten "fragments of Middle English love poems" predating Harley 2253 on pp. 14-25.

lected in modern anthologies) will further tell us something about the preachers' attitudes to secular song.

In addition, their quoting secular love songs can throw some light on a major problem regarding secular poetry of the Middle Ages. The assumption that all medieval literature of any consequence was written in order to teach *caritas* has led some critics to subject even the few outwardly secular lyrics predating MS. Harley 2253 to spiritual exegesis, with the result that to their ears *Foweles in þe frith* and *Maiden in the mor lay* no longer speak of sexual attraction to a girl and a real though mysterious woman in the woods, but rather of "the inadequacies of man's existence and . . . the spiritual burdens put on him by Christianity" and of the Blessed Virgin or Saint Mary Magdalene.[2] This problem of interpretation would apply also to the following poem:

1   At a sprynge-wel vnder a þorn,
      Þer was bote of bale, a lytel here a-forn;
      Þer by-syde stant a mayde,
      Fulle of loue y-bounde.
      Ho-so wol seche trwe loue,
      Yn hyr hyt schal be founde.[3]

The poem's central image of a love-bound maiden standing at a fountain beneath a tree or bush surely evokes a "mysterious resonance" of secular poetry.[4] Fountains are favored places for a lovers' tryst in medieval love poetry.[5] The hawthorn (*alba spina*), which "bloweth swotest / Of everykune tre," equally seems to have been a favorite motif with English and Continental love poets since at least William of Poitou.[6] And maid-

---

[2] For *Foweles in þe frith* see Edmund Reiss, *The Art of the Middle English Lyric* (Athens, Ga., 1972), especially p. 22. The various spiritual interpretations of *Maiden in the mor lay* are summarized in Wenzel, "The Moor Maiden—A Contemporary View," *Speculum* 49 (1974), 70.

[3] *IMEV* 420; *RL XIV*, 130. The poems discussed in this chapter are numbered consecutively in the margins for easier reference.

[4] R. T. Davies (ed.), *Medieval English Lyrics* (Evanston, Ill., 1964), p. 350.

[5] A collection of passages is given by Dimitri Scheludko, "Beiträge zur Entstehungsgeschichte der altprovenzalischen Lyrik. Die Volksliedertheorie," *ZFSL* 52 (1929), 205-11. See also Nos. 14 and 30 below.

[6] William IX of Poitou, *Ab la dolchor del temps novel*, 14. Other occurrences in Middle English lyrics: *Of euerykune tre* (*IMEV* 2622) and the quatrain *Vnder a law as I me lay* (*IMEV* 3820.5), which probably should read "Vnder a haw."

ens in love have been said to find solace in the woods from Origen[7] through the *dulcis amica* of the Cambridge Songs[8] to the famous Moor Maiden[9] and their less fortunate sister who eventually laments,

2   Weilawei þat Ich ne span
        Þo Ich into wude ran.[10]

But does *At a sprynge-wel* really speak of a secular maiden and her love? Could it not perhaps refer to a holy woman at a literal fountain, such as Mary who, in the apocryphal Gospel of Pseudo-Matthew, is greeted by the angel as she stands by a well to fetch water,[11] a scene known to Englishmen from the *Nativity of Mary and Christ*?[12] Since our poem does not seem to have anything to do with the Annunciation, it might perhaps be read as pointing to the Blessed Virgin standing beside a metaphorical wellspring of mercy, that is, her son crowned with thorns. Such is in fact the interpretation it received from the medieval preacher who quoted it, as we shall see further on. The critical question, however, is not whether such poems were *interpreted* spiritually; we know that they were, by medieval preachers and by their modern successors. Rather, we should like to know whether they were *originally made* and used for purposes other than religious and moral teaching. For an answer to this question medieval sermons do indeed provide some help, for in contrast to *Foweles in þe frith*, the quoted poem—*At a sprynge-wel*—and similar songs appear in contexts that bear directly on our problem.[13]

How then do we know whether a quoted song is secular, that is, not only speaks of worldly love but originated outside the religious context

---

[7] "Amoris enim vulnere percussa arborum solatia silvarumque sectatur." Origen, *In Canticum Canticorum*, 3 (PG 13:160).

[8] "Ego fui sola in silvis," st. 3; ed. Karl Strecker, *Die Cambridger Lieder*. Monumenta Germaniae historica (Berlin, 1926), p. 71.

[9] *IMEV* 2037.5; the variant printed in *Speculum* 49 (1974), 71, reads "be wode lay."

[10] *IMEV* 3900.5.

[11] Constantinus de Tischendorf (ed.), *Evangelia apocrypha*, second edition (Leipzig, 1876), pp. 70-71. The scene derives from the Greek *Protevangelium Jacobi*, 11; ibid., p. 21; it was frequently represented in Byzantine art.

[12] *The South English Nativity of Mary and Christ*, lines 221-25; ed. O. S. Pickering, Middle English Texts 1 (Heidelberg, 1975), p. 70.

[13] An illuminating attempt to overcome the problem of understanding medieval English verses preserved without context is J. A. Burrow, "Poems without Contexts," *EIC* 29 (1979), 6-32, reprinted in Burrow, *Essays on Medieval Literature* (Oxford, 1984).

in which it is quoted? The mere presence of themes and expressions that it may share with non-religious love poetry is obviously not sufficient, for these elements could be—and indeed were—employed by religious poets as well. For example, the following lines—

3   Me þingkit þou art so loueli,
        So fair and so swete,
        Þat sikerli it were mi det
        Þi companie to lete[14]

have elicited the comment that they "may originally have been secular."[15] The commentator does not tell us why he thinks so, but presumably his reason was that they sound like a lover's complaint, with their evocation of the sweetness found in the company of a lovely woman and the bitterness of separation—all this so common in love song and romance. But the four lines appear in a moralized *pictura* of Worldly Glory, where they translate a Latin verse that is written on the crown worn by, apparently, an ape engaged in fondly kissing and embracing Worldly Glory:

        Est mihi mors vere nunc te, sponsa, carere.

        (Truly, it is death for me to miss you, my spouse, now.)[16]

Other Latin inscriptions in this picture are similarly put into English verses,[17] though they do not share the same tone of romantic love, as they need not since they speak of matters other than foolish infatuation with worldly glory. It would appear, therefore, that *Me þingkit* does not represent an originally independent song once chanted by a real courtly lover to his lady, but was made up by a cleric on the verbal basis of a Latin verse. The case against secular origins is even more clear-cut in another example:

4   He Iesus is myth and waxit wan,
        He syket as a sorful man.
        A loue [*or* Alone] hem drawes fro compenye,
        And euer he herkenes one ys drurie.

[14] *IMEV* 2141; *SL*, 142.

[15] R. M. Wilson, *The Lost Literature of Medieval England*, second edition (London, 1970), p. 167.

[16] British Library, MS. Harley 7322, fol. 162v.

[17] Printed by F. J. Furnivall, EETS 15, second edition (London, 1903), pp. 265-66.

Louelyche he spekis to his herte,
For hym he suffrus peynis smert.
Þorow tokenes of ʒyftes ʒyuynge
He schewet in hert loue-mornyng.[18]

Their first editor considered these lines "a simple secular verse," pre-
sumably because they enumerate the signs of love-longing familiar
enough from courtly romance and lyrics. Though Rosemary Woolf rec-
ognized that these signs of love are then applied to Christ's Passion and
expounded in the course of the sermon, she was evidently not aware that
the quoted lines form the technical *divisio thematis*, a fact already sug-
gested by the wooden, list-like form of the lines. Rather than deriving
from a secular song, they were most probably created by the preacher for
this structural purpose.[19]

It may be objected that their function as sermon division is no argu-
ment against the secular, extra-homiletic origin of such lines, because a
late thirteenth-century sermon in Latin and English quotes the lines:

5   Atte wrastlinge my lemman I ches,
       And atte ston-kasting I him forles,

almost as if they were its theme, identifies the couplet as a popular dance,
and then moralizes its images of lover, wrestling, and casting the stone
in due order as referring to Christ, fighting against one's spiritual enemy,
and losing one's union with God through hard-heartedness.[20] Here, then,
a preacher quotes what is definitely a secular song and uses its elements,
duly moralized, to structure his subsequent discourse. This objection,

---

[18] I have reedited the lines from Oxford, Balliol College MS. 149, fols. 32v-33. The last
two lines read: "[þorow tokenes of ʒyftes ʒyuynge He schewet] wet in hert loue morn-
yng," with the bracketed words written in the margin and marked for insertion. Woolf (see
following note) overlooked the final couplet and introduced several errors. The lines also
occur in Cambridge University Library, MS. Kk.4.24, fol. 145; Dublin, Trinity College
MS. 277, p. 188 (fragmentary, in upper margin, marked for insertion); and Oxford, Mag-
dalen College MS. 93, fol. 153r-v.

[19] Woolf, p. 192. For a plan of the sermon, see above, ch. 5, pp. 147-48.

[20] *IMEV* 445. The entire "sermon" has been printed by Max Förster, "Kleinere mittel-
englische Texte," *Anglia* 42 (1918), 152-54; and by Carleton Brown, "Texts and the
Man," *Bulletin of the Modern Humanities Research Association* 2 (1928), 106-7. The song
is quoted with four lines in another sermon, where it is introduced thus: "Therefore God
can say of anyone who turned to him in Lent of the previous year and has now been over-
thrown by the devil through mortal sin, what once a maiden said of her lover at the stone-
throwing . . ." See Stemmler, No. 19.

213

though valid in principle, actually proves my case against *He Iesus is myth*. For one thing, *Atte wrastlinge* is not a formal *divisio thematis* of a scholastic sermon, as *He Iesus is myth* is. As it stands, the text following *Atte wrastlinge* leads to a prayer such as was normally said at the end of a protheme;[21] and the suggestion that *Atte wrastlinge* with its moralization is merely a protheme is further strengthened by the fact that in both theory and practice prothemes of scholastic sermons very often began with a proverb or popular saying.[22] More importantly for our purposes, in contrast to *He Iesus is myth*, the secular, extra-homiletic provenance of *Atte wrastlinge* is explicitly identified in its context: "Wild women and wanton men in my country," the preacher tells us, "when they dance in the ring, among many other songs they sing, which are worth little, say as follows . . ." Besides their technical sermon function it is therefore their relation to the accompanying Latin text and, further, remarks made about them in the context, particularly in introductory phrases or sentences, that can help us to discriminate and discern the background of such poems.[23]

Such context is, of course, not always present. Several of the snatches collected by R. M. Wilson[24] have been preserved on flyleaves or in the margins of manuscripts without any discernible relation to their context. But the majority of the collected items, to which I can add over a dozen hitherto unlisted ones, appear in contexts that yield some information about their background. Such information is quite varied in nature and explicitness. In several instances, the surrounding narrative leaves no doubt about the secular nature of the quoted song, as is the case with *Atte*

[21] I therefore disagree with Pfander's view (pp. 52-53) that the two English lines form the *thema* of a complete sermon. It is highly unlikely that secular songs would have been used as the formal *thema*; authors of *artes praedicandi* were very emphatic that the *thema* should be a biblical text: Robert Basevorn, *Forma praedicandi*, in Th.-M. Charland, *Artes praedicandi* (Paris, 1936), pp. 249-53, 264-68; and Thomas Waleys, *De modo componendi*, ibid., pp. 341-42.

[22] For the advice to begin a protheme or the *introductio thematis* with a vernacular *proverbium* (which could be a song), see *Verses*, p. 96.

[23] A very similar case to *Atte wrastlinge* is the moralization of *Bele Aliz matin leua* ascribed to Stephen Langton and in some manuscripts called a "sermon." Its eight lines are seriatim interpreted as referring to the Blessed Virgin. The secular nature of the French poem is established by the survival of several Bele-Aliz songs and the fact that it is called *tripudium*, "dance [song]." See Reichl, *Religiöse Dichtung*, pp. 379-88.

[24] Wilson, *Lost Literature*, ch. 9.

wrastlinge or with a glutton who customarily ate his breakfast while other people attended Mass and then went to the woods singing:

6   Jolyfte, jolyfte,

      Maket me to þe wode the.[25]   draw

A similar picture of a young gallant is drawn in a sermon on *Venit* ("He comes," Matthew 21.5), bearing the marginal remark: "Note well this sermon to move your audience." The jovial youth is described with a number of colorful details, including his song:

> For a little while you are strong and powerful, handsome and well shaped, elegantly dressed in fine red and good gray, and your shoes are tightly laced with many points. You have gotten for yourself a merry girl (?) and a bird's eye[26] to wash your head once or twice a week and to put on it a chaplet. To show off your curls, you wander about the city square. Thus you strut like a peacock, with a truncheon or a recorder in your hand, and you sing:
>
> 7   Ych haue so long, etc.
>
> And as you fondly look at your thighs and your large chest and reflect on how strong you are . . .[27]

What end this paragon of youthful pride may come to is reported in another sermon which includes a story about "someone who was so noble and powerful, handsome and strong, and totally given to the vanities, pleasures, and cheer of the world, that he rejected his own name and had himself called gay Gay." In his last sickness, the singing and dancing of

---

[25] *IMEV* 1799; printed by Thomas Wright (ed.), *A Selection of Latin Stories from Manuscripts of the Thirteenth and Fourteenth Centuries*, Percy Society 8 (London, 1842), p. 81.

[26] I am not certain of the accuracy of my translation of the English phrase. But *brydys ney* seems to be analogous to Chaucer's *piggesnye* (*MiT* I.3268) and denote a flower (see *OED* under *bird's-eye*).

[27] "Modico tempore tu es fortis et potens, pulcher et bene formatus, curiose apparatus in fyn reed and god gre, non parcis ligulis et calige tue stricte innodentur. Adquisivisti tibi a gay gyrl and a brydys ney ad lavandum caput tuum semel vel bis in septimana et ad ponendum super illud a chapylyt. For trumpyng off yt [*canceled ?*] þin lokkys circuis plateas. Adeo superbis sicut pavo cum warderer aut recordour in manu tua, et cantas: 'Ych haue so long, etc.' Et cum respicis tibias tuas et magnum pectus tuum et recogitas quam fortis tu es . . ." Worcester Cathedral, MS. F.10, fol. 194v. The quoted song is probably the same as *So long Ik aue, lefmon, stonden at þe yathe* discussed below, pp. 240-41 (*IMEV* 3167.3).

his household, with which he tries to cheer himself up, eventually leads to a gruesome parody in which devils dance around his bed and sing:

8 Gay, Gay, þou ert yhent,   <small>are caught</small>
    Gay, þou schalt deyn.[28]

The Latin account which precedes the English lines (six in all) makes it clear that, while not necessarily a secular song, this is formally a dance song performed alternately by the "leader" of the dance (*ductor coree*) and his companions.

Songs whose nature is thus established by their narrative context do not always deal with youthful pride or the merry life but occasionally descend into the world of the Wife of Bath. The following piece occurs in a late thirteenth-century manuscript which contains sermons and preaching material in a series of alphabetical articles. An article on dancing, *coree*, claims that women who dance (clearly singing songs at the same time) act against all the sacraments of the Church. The article is taken verbatim from Peraldus's *Summa de vitiis*, into which several vernacular verses have been inserted:

> They [act] contrary to the sacrament of marriage because they slander their husbands when they say,
> Pur mun barun, fi!
> Vn plus bel me at choisi.

(For my man, fy! one more handsome has chosen me.)

And in English they say:

9 Of my husband giu I noht,   <small>I do not care</small>
    Another hauet my luue ybohit,
    For tuo gloues wyht ynoht.   <small>for two white gloves</small>
    If Hic him luue, Y naue no woht.   <small>woe</small>

Many are also incited to act against marital fidelity; for the law of marriage is openly denied when one sings that a wife should not abstain from taking a friend in place of her ill-favored husband. Hence:

10 Lete þe cukewald syte at hom
    And chese þe anoþer lefmon.
    Lete þe chorl site at hom and pile, <small>scratch himself?</small>

---

[28] *IMEV* 900. The verse, its context, and analogues have been printed and discussed in Wenzel, "The 'Gay' Carol and Exemplum," *NM* 77 (1976), 85-91.

And þu salt don wat þu wile—
God hit wot hit nys no skile!

For according to divine law she may not even abandon her husband
when he is leprous, but must render him her debt in time and place if
he so wants it.[29]

The tone of the last stanza is echoed by another poem, which is worth
quoting even though it is not introduced or otherwise characterized as a
song. It forms the climax of an *exemplum*:

There is a story of someone who gathered much gold and in his old age
married a young girl. Soon she allowed others to sin with her. Then it
happened that the old man got sick and made his will, and he left none
of his gold and riches to his wife. And she cried and wailed before him
that he might leave her some thing, and swore under oath that she
would do much for his soul, in prayer, fasting, and almsgiving. And
the old man was seduced and willed her all his gold. After three days
he died. Then the neighbors came to carry the dead man to church. His
wife did not want to go to church with the body, but at her neighbors'
bidding she went with ill will. As soon as Mass was over she started
to go home. Then one of her neighbors said: "Wait, woman, and say
a prayer for your husband's soul, an Our Father or something else."
But she spoke the following for his soul:

11   Longe Y was a gygelot,
      Yyl þou was on lyue.
      Gode þe loke, sire [*blank, erasure*]
      Þat haues liuen dayes fyue.
      I wol with þi tresour
      Mak me glad and bliþe.
      Ly nou still þere, [*blank, erasure*],
      Wel euel mote þou thriue!
Well did this one win his goods![30]

[29] "Contra matrimonium [faciunt], quia maritis multum detrahitur quibus dicitur: 'Pur
mun . . .' Et Anglice dicitur: 'Of my . . .' Multi eciam incitantur ad faciendum contra ma-
trimonii fidem. Aperte vero contra legem matrimonii predicatur cum cantatur quod pro
pravo viro uxor dimittere non debeat quin amicum faciat. Unde: 'Lete . . .' Cum secundum
legem Dei eciam leprosum dimittere non debeat, quin loco et tempore debitum ei reddat si
ipse voluerit." Dublin, Trinity College MS. 347, fol. 199v. Cf. Peraldus, *Summa vitiorum*
III.iv.3; edition of Lyons 1668, p. 39.

[30] "Narratur de quodam qui multum aurum congregabat et senex fuit et iuvenculam in

A final instance in which the narrative context establishes the extra-homiletic provenance of the quoted song—or in this case perhaps a children's game—comes from a thirteenth-century collection of saints' lives and pious tales. This contains an expression that has not otherwise been recorded until much later in history. In admonishing grown-ups to teach their children while they are young, the collector of these tales gives the following charming story about "Master Walter of London":

> He was at the house of a citizen of London, ate and drank well, and
> 12 played "toldiri-toldiro" with a little boy. Then, half a year later, he
> came to the same house again; and as soon as the boy saw him, he
> called out and said: " 'Toldiri-toldiro' is here!" When Master Walter
> heard this, he said: "Alas, why didn't I teach him something useful!
> He would have understood it just as easily as this trifle."[31]

Unfortunately this manuscript tells us nothing about the nature of Master Walter's *ludus*; but it would appear that he sang—in English or conceivably in French—"a very ancient lyrical burden or refrain" which "long survived in English popular music in the form of . . . 'tol-de-rol'."[32]

Such narratives lead us to contexts in which a quoted poem is explicitly introduced with a term that places it within a specific non-homiletic literary genre. Thus, a fifteenth-century sermon for Pentecost, on the

---

sponsam accepit. Et ipsa cito post alios peccare permisit. Contigit quod senex ille infirmabatur et testimonium suum condebat et nihil de auro et thesauro suo legavit uxori. Et ipsa plorabat et ululabat coram ipso supplicans eum ut sibi aliquid legaret, et cum iuramento affirmavit quod multum pro eius anima faceret in oracione et ieiunio et elemosina. Et seductus senex totum aurum suum sibi legavit. Moriebatur senex triduo lapso. Veniebant vicini ut mortuum ad ecclesiam portarent. Set ipsa noluit cum corpore illius ad ecclesiam ire set invite ad rogatum vicinorum ad ecclesiam ibat. Set missa completa ipsa ad hospicium cepit iter arripere. Et tunc dixit unus de vicinis eius: 'O mulier, exspecta et pro anima sponsi aliquid ora dicendo unum Pater Noster vel aliquid aliud.' Set tunc ipsa dixit illud pro anima illius: 'Longe Y was . . .' Bene iste bona lucrabatur!" Worcester Cathedral, MS. F.126, fol. 116v, in a sermon on *Ut quid dereliquisti me* ("Why have you forsaken me," Matthew 27.46). I have been unable to recover the two erased words, evidently vituperative terms.

[31] "Fuit in domo cuiusdam civis Lond., commedit et bene potatus est, et ludit cum quodam parvulo toldiri-toldiro. Et post dimidium annum venit ad eandem domum et statim illo viso clamavit puer et dixit: 'Hic adest toldiri-toldiro.' Quo audito dixit Magister Walterus: 'Heu mihi quod non dixi ei aliquod bonum! Ideo facile intellexisset sicut hoc frivolum.' " Bodleian Library, MS. Laud Misc. 471, fol. 123.

[32] E.J.P., "Ture-lure," in *Grove's Dictionary of Music and Musicians*, fifth edition, ed. Eric Blom (New York, 1954), 8:602.

theme *Spiritus Domini repleti* ("Filled with the spirit of the Lord," cf. Acts 2.4), makes the homely observation that a cloud in the sky looks big, but when it has fallen to earth, "you could not gather a handful from it." The image is then applied to men of rank and wealth, for "all those things will pass away like a shadow" (cf. Wisdom 5.9):

> Et tunc de tali apparencia sicut et de nebula recte dici potest illa vulgaris proposicio anglicana qua dicitur:
> 13 Tintful, tantful,
>   Al is þis lond ful.
>   Yehc I go al dai,   *if*
>   Ne habbe Ich min hond ful.
> Hoc est dicere: Plena est tota terra nebula, sed licet tota die ad colligendum porrexero, plenum pungnum non habeo.

> (And of such an appearance, as of the fog, can then rightly be spoken that popular English riddle in which is said: "Tintful . . ." That is to say: The whole land is full of fog, but if I were to grab at it all day long to gather it, I don't have a handful.)[33]

The generic label *proposicio* which these lines have been given is unusual, but medieval commentaries on Psalm 48.5 (*Aperiam in psalterio propositionem meam*) or Psalm 77.2 (*Loquar propositiones ab initio*) leave no doubt that the word meant "riddle."[34] The quatrain therefore belongs to a genre of which very few representatives have been preserved from the Middle English period.

14 A similar case of generic labeling relates to the lyric *Maiden in the mor lay*, of which four stanzas have been preserved independently: in a fourteenth-century sermon it is called "karole."[35] Other poems are introduced as "love songs." Thus, a sermon on *Luna mutatur* ("The moon is changed," Ecclesiasticus 27.12) speaks of Christ's lament at human ingratitude and faithlessness:

> Thus the Lord, when he is abandoned by the soul as a cuckold is abandoned by his wife, could after Easter use this love song:

---

[33] British Library, MS. Arundel 231, fol. 29v.

[34] Gerhoch: "Propositio est aenigma, quod proponitur ad solvendum" (PL 193: 1589). Similarly Jerome (CC 78:65), *Glossa ordinaria* (PL 113:967), Peter Lombard (PL 191:724).

[35] Wenzel, "Moor Maiden," p. 71.

15   Ich aue a loue vntrewe,
    Þat [is] myn herte wo.
    Þat makeʒ me of reufol hewe
    Lat[e] to bedde go.
    Sore me may rewe
    Þat eure Hi louede hire so.[36]

This *amorosa cantilena*, with its signs of unrequited love-longing, may be contrasted to a *cantus* about foolish love, *fatuus amor*, cited more briefly in another sermon. Here the preacher laments that people can hardly speak or think of anything that is not tainted with lechery, "for all their songs and entertainments deal with the foolish love of paramours (*amasiarum*)," even the only one he has heard about "the good love that should be between husband and wife":

    Et est iste cantus Anglice:
16   Euerech kokewoldes dore stondeþ anyne, etc.[37]

Another item is more briefly introduced as *canticum vulgare*, a popular song, that used to be sung (see below, 33). A similar label—*communis cantus*—is attached to another, though not a love song, which is alluded to in a sermon that condemns various social vices:

17   Þer nys no God but gold alone,

for people "these days" are more intent upon acquiring gold than 18 God's grace.[38] Elsewhere, a four-line stanza is called "an old song" and attributed to women "who lull their child with their foot."[39] A different allusion is to a song of lament (*lamentabile carmen*). It is found in a sermon on *Dies mei transierunt quasi navis* ("My days have passed by

---

[36] "Ideo Dominus relictus ab anima sicut unus cokewold relictus ab uxore sua propria iam uti poterit post Pascha illa / amorosa cantilena . . ." Cambridge University Library, MS. Ii.3.8, fols. 83v-84. *IMEV* 1301. See Stemmler, No. 17.

[37] Worcester Cathedral, MS. F.126, fol. 27. Previously printed in "Unrecorded," No. 14. The condemnation of lecherous love songs is a common sermon topic; cf. *Fasciculus morum*, VII.12: "Quid ergo dicam de illis qui non tantum cogitant corde sed eciam exprimunt ore quam dulce sit peccatum luxurie, et tota die de illa materia feda loquuntur? Vix enim est aliquis popularis qui sciat loqui aut trufare [vel] cantus insolentes componere nisi de illa materia."

[38] "Et ideo communis cantus est hiis diebus: 'þer . . . ,' quia populus pro maiori parte est magis sollicitus ad adquirendum sibi aurum quam Deum." Worcester Cathedral MS. F.10, fol. 125.

[39] *IMEV* 3859.5; *SL*, p. xxxix.

as a ship,'' cf. Job 9.25-26), which develops the traditional images of the sea of this world and the ship of man's life. On the latter, the forecastle denotes youth:

He who sits in the forecastle of youth and sees the straits and perils through which he must sail, and the worries and tribulations he is to meet, can well sing this song of lament:

19   Myn hert is sore, I may not synge.[40]

A final poem, introduced apparently as a love song or perhaps rather a message inscribed on a ring or stone, appears in a lengthy sermon on *Hoc est signum federis* (''This is the sign of the covenant,'' Genesis 9.12). Here the astronomical sign of Gemini is said to symbolize Christ and, specifically, the Eucharist, in which he is present with his twofold nature, human and divine. This sacrament we should guard as a precious gift, for on its account Christ could say

the words of Gen. 9 [.12], ''This is the sign of the covenant which I have given between me and you and all flesh,'' that is, anyone who is bound to me in faith through firm love, as if Christ were speaking those English words of love in a token:

20   Wanne þo lokest in þis stone . . . ,
     Þonk on hur from wham it com . . . .
     A lef it hy gaf to his lemman . . . ,
     For his loue ne he gy sit [*read* gylit?] noman.

The first three lines of the quatrain are immediately interpreted with reference to the Eucharist.[41]

The last example leads us to quotations that introduce a poem with the bare words ''that (English) song'' or similar phrases without any further

[40] ''Antecastellum huius navis est iuventus, qui est principium humane vite et sicud antecastellum ponitur contra procellas et freta huius mundi, to hurle and to juste cum wele and wo and wordli tribulacion. Qui sederet in antecastello iuventutis et viderit freta et pericula que ipsum oportet transire, curas et tribulaciones quas ipse est toward, bene potest incipere hoc lamentabile carmen: 'Myn hert . . .' '' Bodleian Library, MS. 649, fol. 121.
[41] ''Quasi diceret illud Gen. 9: 'Hoc signum federis quod constitui inter me et te et omnem carnem,' mihi scilicet per amoris firmitatem fidei adherentem, tanquam diceret Christus illud amoris Anglicum [*or* Anglice] in signum: 'Wanne . . . ,' scilicet altaris sacramentum; 'þonk . . . ,' scilicet Christus qui dedit illum; 'a lef . . . ,' idest fideli anime; 'for . . .' '' The precise meaning of *in signum* is not entirely clear to me. Worcester Cathedral MS. F.126, fol. 247v.

221

qualification. The first of these is a quatrain whose beginning appears three times in the Red Book of Ossory. In a Good Friday sermon, the preacher puts the entire stanza in the mouth of the suffering Christ, who "could sing a song which I once heard":

21   Haue mercy of me, broʒir,   brother
       [. . .] ʒer Y ga,
       Þin lofe chaungyt my hwe,
       It dose me michil wa.[42]

The introductory words, *unum cantum quem audivi aliquando cantari*, make it clear that the quatrain is not of this preacher's making but an independent song, although *unum cantum* does not necessarily point to a *secular* song. The same can be said of what seems to be a couplet,

22   Wo is me, wo is me,
       For loue Y go ibunden,

which is introduced as *illud canticum Anglicum* that Christ could have said when he was bound in fetters.[43] The image of love-bonds is used elsewhere for the bondage caused by sins; here the introduction leaves no doubt that the quotation speaks of worldly love:

    Unde cantat lecator:
23   Luue bendes me bindet.[44]

The formula *cantus ille Anglicus* again introduces another quotation from a seemingly secular song, which is here used to illustrate the truth that God will not refuse to listen to insistent prayer:

    De eo enim dici potest cantus ille Anglicus:
24   That mi lef askes wit sare weping,
       Ne mai Ic it werne for nane kinnes thing.[45]

---

[42] *IMEV* 1123. Lambeth Palace MS. 352, fol. 218; see Wenzel, "A New Occurrence of an English Poem from the Red Book of Ossory," *N&Q* 228 (1983), 105-8.

[43] Cambridge University Library, MS. Ff.1.17, fol. 265. Previously printed in "Unrecorded," No. 95.

[44] "Item acerbius eum ligat diabolus post recidivacionem. Exemplum de incarcerato evaso et iterum deprehenso: durius et asperius ligatur funibus peccatorum suorum, etc. Unde cantat lecator . . ." Durham, MS. Cosin V.III.2, fol. 127ra.

[45] "Nemo ad eum aliquando cum lacrimis accessit qui non quod postulavit ab eo acceperit, sicut dicit Leo papa. De eo enim dici potest cantus ille Anglicus . . ." Durham, MS. Cosin V.II.8, fol. 58ra. These two manuscripts were brought to my attention by Dr. Ian Doyle.

Finally, the introductory marker is in some instances even further reduced to a bare reference to "that English" or "some English" [add "saying" or "song"]. Thus, a sermon on *Ostendam tibi sponsam uxorem Agni* ("I will show you the bride, the wife of the Lamb," Revelation 21.9) asks what the "knot of the bride" is and answers:

> The knot is the infallible certainty of true love, for as love is the measure of all human acts, so it is the knot of minds. Therefore it is said in some English [saying] of old:
> 25   Loue is knotte of mannes hertes,
>   Loue is mette of mannes werkes.   measure
>   Loue is helpere in euerech nude [*sic*],
>   Loue is ȝeuere of heȝlich mede.[46]

Similarly, the spring song put into the mouth of the Cistercian abbot who escaped eternal damnation by a hair's breadth is simply called *illud Anglicum*:

> 26   Þe dew of Aueril
>   Hauetȝ y-maked the grene lef to sprynge.
>   My sorow is gon,
>   Mi ioye is comen,
>   Ich herde a foul synge.[47]

Several of the items I have included in the preceding two paragraphs, introduced as "a song" or "that English [saying]," may of course not have had an independent existence and origin outside sermons. Even such labels as "love song" (15) and "song of lament" (19) do not guarantee their extra-homiletic provenance. In the absence of further unequivocal testimony, reasonable certainty may be gained only when the preacher states that he had heard the respective song at some time (16, 21). Consequently, there remains some doubt about the provenance of verses 15, 19, 20 (of which perhaps only the first couplet is an original posy verse), and 22-26. In the case of 26, however, the likelihood of secular origin is increased by the poem's peculiar metrical shape, so differ-

---

[46] "Respondeo quod nodus est amoris fidelis certitudo infallibilis. Sicud enim amor est mensura omnium actuum humanorum, ita est nodus animorum. Ideo dicitur in Anglico quodam antiquitus: . . ." British Library, MS. Harley 505, fol. 13. These lines do not function as a subdivision or distinction.

[47] Worcester Cathedral MS. F.126, fol. 248. For a summary of the story and the moralization, see ch. 2, pp. 57-58.

ent from the usual couplets or triplets found in preaching verses. In addition, the five lines are immediately moralized, and the preacher introduces them not as the abbot's actual words but as something he *might* have said: "Therefore that abbot could have spoken, as it were in the person of mankind, that English [saying]." I shall argue later that these two features, moralization and attribution to a possible speaker (*poterat dicere*), further increase the likelihood that the quoted verses come from outside the preacher's religious discourse.

Even less direct information is provided in the case of other English verses that are introduced with a mere *Anglice* ("in English") or with no transitional phrase at all. But even here I believe that their subject matter, which stands in sharp contrast to the language and tone of the sermon, suggests that these snatches are indeed fragments of popular songs. Moreover, it can be reasonably shown how the thought or theme developed in the sermon brought such a song to the preacher's or scribe's mind, who then jotted it down for possible use as an illustrative prooftext or message verse. In one instance of this kind, the preacher develops Pliny's lore of the "unicorn"[48] who sharpens his horn and with it kills the mighty elephant despite its precious tusks. This is applied to the spiritual life: man must not fear the devil,

> but show up his falsehood in all things and thus kill him with the horn of truth. Nowadays it is not necessary to go very far, because one can find falsehood everywhere.

> 27   A gurdul of gile,
> Ich wolde gon a mile
> To see þe mordaunt.[49]

If I understand the English lines correctly, the triplet stands in opposition to the preceding sentence: nowadays one does *not* have to go as far as the quoted lines say in order to find guile. Another sermon in the same manuscript, on *Apparuit precedens eos eques in veste candida armis aureis hastam vibrans* ("There appeared a horseman going before them in white clothing, with golden armor, shaking a spear," 2 Maccabees

---

[48] Really the Indian rhinoceros; Pliny, *Historia naturalis*, VIII.xxix.71.

[49] "Set certe unicornis, fidelis homo, constanter debet ipsum invadere, falsitatem suam reprimere, nec eius potestatem formidare, set eius falsitatem denudare in omnibus, et sic ipsum quasi interficere cornu veritatis. Non oportet modo quod tantum vadat, quia in omni loco falsitatem potest invenire. A gurdul . . ." Oxford, Merton College MS. 248, fol. 146v.

11.8), concludes its first principal, that Saint George went before us as a strong knight girt with the sword of charity, with the following exhortation:

> Lastly, our love must be persevering. "Be faithful," he says, "until death, and I will give you the crown of life" [Revelation 2.10], for it does not please him that you love him for a short while and then abandon him for the remainder of the year, as many do who make peace with him in Lent and promise him faithful love, but when summer comes and the mild season, they abandon him.

28   Janekyn of Londone,
      Is loue is al myn, etc.[50]

The same abrupt style of quotation—which is quite typical of sermon notes and even fuller sermons—characterizes another snatch found in a manuscript of sermons and sermon notes from the second half of the thirteenth century. Here again a word or image of the Latin context seems to have reminded the preacher of words from a different source, for the exhortation to "bind your mouth that it may not overflow, your hands that they may neither give nor receive, and your feet that they may not wander about" leads at once to the lines:

29   Ne sal it wite no man, wite no man,
      Hu Ich go ibunde for mi lemmon.[51]

Another thirteenth-century collection contains an even more interesting and mysterious snatch. Its context is a sermon outline providing a number of prooftexts. With reference to the Blessed Virgin's suffering, we find the following:

> Luke 3 [i.e., 2.35]: "Your own soul a sword shall pierce." Bernard: "Was not [Christ's word from the cross to her] more than a sword?" Job [*blank*; i.e., 30.12]: "At the right hand of my rising [or: the East] my calamities arose." The English [saying]:

[50] "Et ultimo debet esse amor perseverans. 'Esto,' inquid, 'fidelis usque ad mortem et dabo tibi coronam vite' [Rev. 2.10], quia non placet sibi quod diligas eum modico tempore in anno et deseras eum toto anni residuo, sicud faciunt multi qui faciunt pacem cum eo in quadragesima et promittunt sibi fidelem amorem set adveniente estate et tempore ameno ipsum dimittunt. Janekyn . . ." Oxford, Merton College MS. 248, fol. 148v.

[51] "Et liga in eis os, ne nimis affluat; manus, ne dent vel accipiant; pedes, ne discurrant. Ne sal it . . ." Oxford, New College MS. 88, fol. 402v.

30   Maiden stod at welle and wep: "Weilawei,
      Late comet [MS. cemet] þe lith of dai."[52]

A final example of such abrupt quotation concerns an item which may be proverbial in origin but which, in a variant form, reappears as the burden of a later carol.[53] In a thirteenth-century *summa* on the vices, it is one in a string of authoritative texts which prove that lechery makes man lose his taste for divine sweetness. Its immediate context reads as follows:

Augustine: "You have commanded, Lord, and so it is a reality, that every inordinate person is a pain to himself." In English:

31   Were þat his don for to done,
      Ne solde it neuer ben i-done,
      For none mannes bone.

Demosthenes said, "he loses [*or* it ruins] his appetite." The Psalm: "Their soul abhorred all manner of meat."[54]

The quotations so far surveyed, therefore, constitute a small but not inconsiderable corpus of fragments and verses from otherwise lost native English songs and sayings. In contrast to *Me þingkit* and *He lesus is myth*, most of them bear reasonably clear indications, in one form or another, of their secular, non-homiletic origins. Most are women's songs (2, 5, 9-11, 18, 21?, 24, 27, 28, 30, 31, 32?, 37-38)[55] and lovers' complaints (7, 15, 19, 22?, 23, 29, 34, 35 but spoken by a woman, 39-40). Two of them are *reverdies*.[56] Three others are designated as dance songs (5, 8 14), to which may be added 33 (below) because it seems to mark

---

[52] Bodleian Library, MS. Laud Misc. 511, fol. 110v. The Bernard quotation is from his *Sermo in Dominica infra Octavam Assumptionis Beatae Virginis Mariae*, 15, in *Opera*, ed. Jean Leclercq, C. H. Talbot, and H. M. Rochais (Rome, 1957-74), 5:273. This manuscript was brought to my attention by Sister Maura O'Carroll, S.N.D.

[53] *EEC* 455; *IMEV* 1330.

[54] "Augustinus: 'Iussisti, Domine, et sic est, ut pena sibi sit omnis inordinatus.' Anglice: 'Were . . .' Demostenes dixit: 'Amittit appetitum.' Psalmus: 'Omnem escam abhominata est anima eorum.' " Durham Cathedral MS. B.I.18, fol. 117; previously printed in "Unrecorded," No. 80. For a variant see *IMEV* 3897.5. The quoted authorities are: Augustine, *Confessions*, I.xii.19; "Demosthenes" unidentified; and Psalm 106.18.

[55] To these may be added *Alas, how shold Y synge* from the Red Book of Ossory (*IMEV* 1265). See also the discussion by John F. Plummer, "The Woman's Song in Middle English and Its European Background," in John F. Plummer (ed.), *Vox feminae: Studies in Medieval Woman's Song*, SMC 15 (Kalamazoo, Mich., 1981), pp. 135-54.

[56] 24 and *Myrie a tyme I telle in May* (*IMEV* 2162). In these lyrical types should further be included two *chansons d'aventure*: *Nou sprinkes the sprai* (*IMEV* 360) and *Vnder a law as I me lay* (see above, n. 6).

226

spatial separation and movement. They therefore represent several types of songs in which historians have sought the beginnings of the medieval vernacular love lyric. In tone they range from romantic lovesickness to low-class mating, coarse self-assertion, and the laments of maidens left pregnant (see below), and thereby reflect the differentiation between courtly and popular registers that is also found in later verse. It is perhaps not surprising that several images and themes which were widespread in medieval (and earlier) love song should occur here more than once. Thus, the image of being "bound by love" appears in 1, 22, 23, and 29; and the motif of "woman in the woods," which we encountered in 2 and 14, reappears in some all too brief sermon notes on Luke 7.44-47, "And turning to the woman, he said . . . 'Many sins are forgiven her, because she has loved much'," where the following is evidently said of Mary Magdalene:

> Fire in wet wood makes it drop tears; thus love does the same to her [Mary Magdalene]. Further, love shows itself openly, just as she makes a public confession. Further, heat causes one to throw off one's clothes, as can be seen in people sick with a fever. Thus does she flee the world for the desert:
>
> 32   Nu te wude, Marie, al sa ro.   deer
>   Ne sal hit wite noman wuder hith go.
>
> For my shirt [I have] thorns, as the nightingale sings among thorns.[57]

The purpose for which these verses were quoted in sermons need not detain us long. Most of them serve as what I have called prooftexts and message verses. Thus, a line from *Maiden in the mor lay* (14) is quoted to substantiate the simpler way of life in mankind's Golden Age where people could survive on "the cold water of the well-spring"; and the couplet

> Weylawey þat iche ne span
> Whan Y to þe ringe ran (see below, 38)

effectively formulates (or at least was intended to do so) the message of lost chastity. But several snatches seem to have been quoted more relaxedly in order to add color and realistic detail to the surrounding moral

---

[57] "Ignis in humido ligno facit stillare, sic ipsam amor. Item amor revelat, ut ipsa publice confitetur. Item calor proicit vestimenta; patet in febricitantibus; sic ipsa mundum fugit in desertum: 'Nu te wude . . .' Pro camisia mea spinas, sicut philomena cantat in spinis." Oxford, New College MS. 88, fol. 403v.

discourse. Such I think is the case with the proud youth's song *Jolyfte* (6) or the married woman's *Lete þe cukewald syte at hom* (10). Rather than prove a point or formulate the preacher's message, these round out a picture or add color to a story. Undoubtedly they kept the audience awake and created an atmosphere of common experience shared by the preacher and his congregation, much as some preachers today strive for popularity by quoting snippets from *Reader's Digest* or *Godspell*. We must be grateful to the former for preserving these bits and pieces from a ''folk-literature'' of which only too few traces have survived.

There is, however, an aspect of these poems' use that requires further attention. A number of them are not merely quoted but further subjected to moralization, in which the poems' lines and images are, step by step, given an allegorical meaning. A good example occurs in a sermon on *Ingredere civitatem* (''Go into the city,'' Acts 9.6), which was preached on the occasion of the enclosure of Alice Huntyngfeld, whose name and surname are quoted and moralized in the sermon's second principal part. In his third principal the preacher deals with the ''city of heavenly joy.'' He declares that any good and strong city has four qualities:

> It must be well walled and surrounded by water, in order to withstand external enemies; secondly, it must be at peace within; thirdly, it must be well stored with provisions; and fourthly, it must be well situated to receive fresh air so that it may better escape pestilence.

These four conditions are then applied to the heavenly city. As to the first:

> This city is, first, well surrounded by walls and water so that it cannot be taken by any enemy. For it once used to be said in a popular song:

33   We schun makyn a ioly castel
    On a bank bysyden a brymme;
    Schal no man comyn theryn
    But ȝyf he kun swymme,
    Or buth he [*MS.* be] haue a both of loue
    For to seylyn [*MS.* seykyn] ynne.

These lines are then allegorized as follows:

> This castle on the bank is the castle of the heavenly city, of which Ezekiel 40 [.2] says, ''On a very high mountain was the building of a city.'' But lest you think that what stands on high is unsafe, you can

observe that a square object stands most firmly. For on whichever side you turn a square stone, it will always stand firm. Thus, the heavenly city "lies in a foursquare," Revelation 21 [.16] so that it may stand firm. The water surrounding this city is the water of penance. Every human being is either just or a sinner. If a sinner, he cannot enter the city unless he swims through the water of penance. If he is just and without sin, he sails across this water in the boat of love.[58]

The homiletic procedure exemplified here is exactly the same as that which meets us on every page of *Gesta Romanorum* and other moralized *exempla* collections as well as in medieval bestiaries, lapidaries, and encyclopedias for preachers, where the properties of natural objects are one by one allegorized. What sets the quoted passage somewhat apart is that the object of its moralization is a vernacular poem, and one clearly marked as a popular song heard some time in the past. *We schun makyn*, therefore, is definitely non-homiletic in origin, and its images were obviously not felt to carry a spiritual meaning that was automatically understood by the audience. Rather, the preacher who quotes the song supplies or imposes a spiritual meaning upon the literal sense of the verse. This tells us nothing new about the moralizing tendency in medieval preaching. But it does tell us something about how secular songs were perceived by men whose profession it was to discern a sermon in every stone: the songs thus quoted as "popular" or "love songs" were manifestly felt to speak of a different kind of love from the love of God. This awareness of a distinction between a profane and a sacred world of discourse can also be seen in *Ich aue a loue vntrewe*, which was quoted ear-

[58] "Quod sit bene murata et aquis circumdata, ad resistendum inimicis exterioribus: secundo quod sit pacifica interius; tercio quod sit bene staurata victualibus; et quarto quod sit bene situata ad bonam suscepcionem aeris ut vitetur melius pestilencia . . . Ista civitas primo sit ita bene murata et aquata quod non potest ab aliquo inimico lucrari. Dicebatur enim aliquando in cantico wlgari: 'We shun makyn . . . .' Istud castellum supra illum bank est castellum civitatis celestis, de qua Ezechielis 40: 'Super montem excelsum nimie erat edificium civitatis.' Set ne putares quia alte stat quod staret insecure, ideo vides quod res quadrata firmissime stat. Quadratum namque lapidem in quamcumque partem verteris, firmus stabit, et ideo ut firmiter stet civitas celestis in quadro posita est, Apocalipsis 21. Aqua circumdans istam civitatem est aqua penitencie. Quilibet enim homo vel est iustus vel peccator. Si peccator est, non potest intrare civitatem nisi natet in aqua penitencie. Si iustus est et sine peccato, tunc navigat ultra istam aquam per navem amoris." Cambridge, Jesus College MS. 13, art. vi, fol. 83. The English verse was previously published (with error) in "Unrecorded," No. 79. For the motif of a lover crossing a body of water, see also the snatch *He may cum to mi lef bute by þe watere* (*IMEV* 1142), preserved without context.

lier (15). Here several conventional signs of romantic lovesickness, such as complaint, paleness, loss of sleep, and regret, receive a moral interpretation; furthermore, the stanza is labeled *amorosa cantilena*,[59] and it is explicitly transferred from the mouth of a cuckold left by his wife, to God. The transfer is effected by means of the phrase *[Christus] iam uti poterit illa amorosa cantilena* ("Christ could now use that love song"). Similar phrases, such as *Christus potuit dicere* ("Christ could say") or *tamquam diceret* ("as if he were saying"), occur elsewhere with the same function; they represent a standard device for embedding secular love utterances into a religious discourse (see verses 20-22).

Such point-by-point moralization occurs likewise in *Atte wrastlinge* (5), *Þe dew of Aueril* (26), *Wanne þo lokest* (28), and *Loue, þou art of mikel mit* (34, below). It is further applied to the poem with which this chapter has set out, *At a sprynge-wel*, though here the relation of the English lines to their context is more complex. The poem appears in a moralized *exemplum* in one of the notebooks made by John Dygoun.[60] Under "Confession" Dygoun records the tale of a noble knight living in a country whose king had issued a statute that any nobleman in his land who might fall into poverty should come to his court to receive aid. This nobleman finds himself in need but for a long time is too ashamed to beg for help. At last his need drives him to go to court. On the way he is prevented by three enemies:

What could he then do to gain help at court? He must send a secret messenger to court with a letter, to find a remedy there. But where is that? At a bubbling fountain under the hawthorn, where a little time earlier there was a remedy for grief. Near there stood a maiden fully bound by love. Whoever seeks for true love, it will be found in her. In English:

At a sprynge-wel vnder a þorn . . .

---

[59] The adjective *amorosa* may of course designate a spiritual song, as it does in Richard Rolle (*canticum amorosum*): *The Incendium Amoris of Richard Rolle of Hampole*, ed. Margaret Deanesly (Manchester, 1915), pp. 222, 241, 245, 246. But coming from a cuckolded husband, the song surely is not religious in nature. For *cantilena* as a secular song, see ch. 2, p. 57, above.

[60] Parish priest and canon lawyer in the first third of the fifteenth century, he became a recluse in Sheen Priory, Surrey, in 1435. At least seven of his books are now at Magdalen College, Oxford. See A. B. Emden, *A Biographical Register of the University of Oxford to A. D. 1500* (Oxford, 1958), pp. 615-16.

The entire *exemplum* is then allegorized, in a rather predictable way. Of special interest here is the exegesis of the poem:

> We must therefore send a secret messenger to God, namely a devout mind with holy prayer. The bubbling fountain beneath the hawthorn is Christ's open side whence blood and water issued forth: blood for the forgiveness of sins and water to show that through the water of regeneration we are healed and cleansed from Original Sin. The maiden standing there is the Blessed Virgin Mary. Whoever will love her perfectly will find perfect love, for she is always ready to receive the prayers of sinners, so that through her mediation they become healed of their sins. May Jesus, the blessed fruit of her womb, grant us to have her as our helper![61]

Since *At a sprynge-wel* is not explicitly marked as either secular or a song, one may reasonably query whether it ever had a non-homiletic existence at all or, rather, was made up by the preacher for his particular purpose. The way in which the English lines are embedded, which is quite different from any other cases discussed earlier, suggests that the English poem is primary and the Latin sentences before it a paraphrase. The Latin reply to the question where the noble knight may find a messenger reads exactly like a literal translation of the English, line by line; furthermore, whereas the English consists of two couplets, I detect no metric pattern in the Latin except for an incomplete attempt at end-rhyme; and lastly, the wording *ubi . . . ibi iuxta* is rather poor Latin, whereas *þer . . . þer bysyde* has a genuine English ring to it. Moreover, the poem's content does not fit the *exemplum* very neatly, since the maiden standing at a fountain is not, literally, a secret messenger who

---

[61] "Quid potuit ille tunc impeditus facere ad hoc quod sibi succurreretur in curia? Oportebat quod mitteret ad curiam secretum nuncium cum littera ubi remedium invenire posset. Set ubi est illud? Ad fontem scaturientem sub spina, ubi modicum antea doloris erat medicina. Ibi iuxta stat puella plena amore ligata. Qui querit veram dileccionem, in ipsa erit inventa. Anglice: 'At a . . .' . . . Secretum ergo nuncium mittere debemus, scilicet mentem devotam cum oracione sancta ad Deum. Fons scaturiens sub spina est latus Christi apertum, unde exivit sanguis et aqua, sanguis in remissionem peccatorum, aqua ad ostendendum quod per aquam regeneracionis salvamur et mundamur ab originali peccato. Puella / astans est Beata Virgo Maria. Quicumque voluerit eam perfecte diligere, perfectum amorem inveniet, quia illa semper est parata admittere preces peccatorum ut ipsa mediante salvi fiant a peccatis eorum. Quam adiutricem habere nobis concedat benedictus fructus ventris eius Iesus!" Oxford, Magdalen College MS. 60, fol. 214r-v.

can carry a letter to court. On the literal level, then, the coherence between the (Latin) tale and the (English) poem breaks down. It therefore looks very much as if this is not a tale of which an integral part is rendered in English verse (as happens in the case of so many other *exemplum* or message verses), but rather a tale into which an originally independent English poem has been inserted.

But does the song speak of *secular* love? So the various images the poem shares with other love songs would suggest. That the love-bound maiden is interpreted by the preacher as the Blessed Virgin does not argue against its secular origin since the same exegetical process was applied to poems that are clearly marked as "popular." It is therefore erroneous to label this poem "The B[lessed] V[irgin] by the fountain of love,"[62] because this confuses the poem with its subsequent moralization. Though the case of *At a sprynge-wel* is admittedly not as clear-cut as that of *We schun makyn a ioly castel* and others, in light of its context, especially of its subjection to moralization and of the peculiar way in which it has been inserted into the *exemplum*, the poem has a strong claim of being considered a non-homiletic, secular song.

Such adaptive quotation of secular poems does, however, not preclude the possibility that on occasion preachers might have created similar verses themselves. Preachers did certainly not hesitate to draw on the language and imagery of profane love for their homiletic prose. In this respect they merely followed the example of the Song of Songs and its commentators in the mystic tradition reaching from the Fathers to Bernard of Clairvaux and his successors. A fine example occurs in *Fasciculus morum*. In dealing with the topic of meditating on Christ's Passion as a primary means to foster in us the love of God, which is the best remedy for envy, its author addresses the question "at what hour, in what season, and at what time" Christ suffered. The verse from Canticles 1.6, "Show me where you feed, where you lie at midday," leads to the following reflection:

> At midday there is the greatest heat of the day, and thus the shepherd is glad if at this time he can find a pleasant place to rest. Such a place is called "pleasant" if it is lush with leaves and flowers, and especially if on one side there is running water or a bubbling fountain, and on the other tall trees spreading wide their branches with lush foliage. Such a place is very delightful in summer, as can be seen from Elijah's

[62] R. H. Robbins, *IMEV* 420.

juniper tree, Kings 19, and Jonah's ivy, Jonah 3. Tell these stories if you like. And especially in summer it seems to be very delightful to lie in the shade of the hawthorn, on account of the sweet smell from its blossoms and its shade.[63]

The details of this peaceful scene are then applied to Christ's suffering. The heat of noon was Good Friday, because:

Heat seems to be greatest when a man cannot stand the clothes he wears but throws them off. Thus did Christ suffer the greatest degree of the heat of love and charity on that day, that he threw off his clothes and wanted to lie naked on the cross and rest there for our salvation.[64]

The lush *locus amoenus* was the cross, the running brook the wound in Christ's side, and the shade of the hawthorn his crown of thorns. This image of the shepherd in a *locus amoenus*, despite its parallels in very early Christian art, does not seem to occur frequently in late medieval preaching. Nonetheless, the quoted passage must have been a set piece since it reappears verbatim in a later chapter of *Fasciculus morum*[65] as well as in the sermons ascribed to Holcot.[66]

The use of such "romantic" imagery with its overtones of noble love is better known from the homiletic commonplace that likens Christ to a courtly lover who champions the cause of a lady, is wounded or dies for her in battle, and is then either remembered forever or ungratefully forgotten.[67] Most familiar from its use in *Ancrene Wisse*, the allegory ac-

---

[63] "In meridie est estus et totus fervor diei, et ideo pastor animalium tunc temporis gaudet si possit locum amenum invenire ad cubandum. Qui quidem locus tunc amenus dicitur si sit virens frondibus et floribus, et precipue si sit aqua ex uno latere decurrens vel fons scaturiens, et ex alio arbores prominentes late ramos pretendentes cum foliis virentibus. Talis enim locus valde delicatus est in estu, sicut patet de iunipero et Helia, Regum 19, et de Iona et edere, Ione 3. Nota historias si placet. Et precipue in estate deliciosum valde videtur sub umbra albe spine cubare, nam ipsa ex floribus redolet et ex foliis umbram habet." *Fasciculus morum*, III.12; Oxford, Bodleian Library, MS. Rawlinson C.670, fol. 46.

[64] "Videtur homini maximus esse estus quando non potest sustinere vestes suas super se sed illas a se proicit. Sic revera Christus illa die tantum estum sustinuit amoris et caritatis quod pannis a se proiectis nudus pro salute nostra voluit in cruce cubare et quiescere." Ibidem.

[65] *Fasciculus morum*, V.8; MS. Rawlinson C.670, fol. 95v.

[66] Holcot, *Sermon 96* ; Cambridge, Peterhouse MS. 210, fol. 153v.

[67] The commonplace has been treated by Rosemary Woolf, "The Theme of Christ the Lover-Knight in Medieval English Literature," *RES*, n.s., 13 (1962), 1-16; and Woolf, pp. 44-66. See also J.A.W. Bennett, "Christus Miles," in *Poetry of the Passion. Studies in Twelve Centuries of English Verse* (Oxford, 1982), pp. 62-84. A number of Latin and

tually combines a number of motifs which recur in various combinations. Basic to them are the twin notions that Christ so loved man's soul that he would suffer death for it, and that he came into the world to do battle against man's archenemy. By themselves, these two motifs are of course ubiquitous in medieval literature and often lead to very elaborate allegories or narratives. The second, for example, may yield a moralized description of Christ's armor, or his appearance at a joust or "round table,"[68] or Langland's vision of—

This Iesus of his gentries wol Iuste in Piers armes.[69]

In combination, they create the figure of Christ as Lover-Knight, which again can be found in narrative *exempla* under a variety of different forms. In *Ancrene Wisse*, he woos and fights for a poor and ungrateful lady besieged by her enemies.[70] A closely related version focuses on the mortally wounded knight's coming to his hard-hearted lady's door after battle and imploring her to let him in, quoting a distich from Ovid's *Amores*.[71] Elsewhere, the focus lies on the knight's lady, here his faithful wife, who mourns for him in loving remembrance.[72] The motifs are also used in the *exemplum* "Elopement of Princess," discussed in chapter 5,

---

French analogues were printed or summarized by Wilbur Gaffney, "The Allegory of the Christ-Knight in *Piers Plowman*," *PMLA* 46 (1931), 155-69.

[68] Knights who come to a tournament or "round table" (*tabula rotunda*) hang their shields outside their tents. Their opponent comes and touches one shield, whose owner then must fight with him. The three persons of the Holy Trinity can be called "knights of the Round Table" because they are equals in virtue and power. The devil came and touched the shield of the Son, so that Christ had to fight with him for his lady, the soul. This *exemplum* and its moralization occur often, normally in sermons on Christ's Passion or the Last Supper: Cambridge, Jesus College MS. 13, art. vi, fol. 84; Oxford, Merton College MS. 248, fol. 166 (reference only); Magdalen College MS. 93, fol. 144; Worcester Cathedral MS. F.126, fol. 118; Brinton, *Sermon 39*, ed. Mary Aquinas Devlin, Camden Third Series LXXXV (London, 1954), p. 170. The *exemplum* is *GR* 113; No. LIV in Sidney J. H. Herrtage (ed.), *The Early English Versions of the Gesta Romanorum*, EETS, es, 33 (London, 1879), pp. 235-37; and again *GR* 221, which is the same as Holcot, *Moralitates* (ed. Basel, 1586), No. IX. *GR* and Holcot do not refer to the tourney as "round table."

[69] *Piers Plowman*, B.XVIII.22; ed. George Kane and E. Talbot Donaldson (London, 1975), p. 608.

[70] *The English Text of the Ancrene Riwle*, ed. Mabel Day, EETS 225 (London, 1952), pp. 177-79. This form of the *exemplum* also appears in British Library MS. Harley 7322, fol. 26r-v. Tubach No. 2913.

[71] In *Fasciculus morum*; see *Verses*, pp. 161-63, where other occurrences are noted.

[72] Lambeth Palace Library, MS. 352, fol. 217, an unusual application of the *exemplum* to Noemi and Elimelech of Ruth 1.3.

where the various male figures—her champion, the *mediator*, and her brother—all stand for Christ, who has saved man's soul through his Passion.[73] A very similar story of an adulterous wife who repents and sends her husband a letter and a golden ''trew-love'' with inscriptions identifies the husband as Christ, whose fierceness in combat and armor are then described in the moralization.[74] Finally, in yet another version the champion is a pilgrim who makes a pact with the lady that in case of his death she should hang up his pilgrim's staff and wallet in her chamber for her lasting remembrance:

A certain noble lady was so much oppressed by a tyrant that she was to lose all her lands unless she found a champion to fight against him. As the lady was grieving and sorrowing, an unknown pilgrim arrived and asked to fight for her. He set the date of combat, and for his reward he asked for nothing else than that after his death she would hang his staff and wallet before her in her hall to keep the pilgrim's memory alive. This she granted. Then the pilgrim killed the tyrant and afterwards died himself of the wounds he had received in battle. As he was dying, he said: ''Beloved sister, I close my life for your sake, rescuing you from danger. If you want to give me thanks, always remember me, now and forever.'' But soon thereafter she was wooed by a knight. At his command she removed the pilgrim's memorial first from the hall, next from her chamber, then from the chapel; and in the end, when she was joined to the knight, she forgot the pilgrim her savior altogether.[75]

---

[73] See above, pp. 168-69.

[74] In the *introductio thematis* of the sermon *Amore langueo*: Cambridge University Library MS. Kk.4.24, fols. 144v-145r. Tubach No. 3866, called ''Posy-Rings Sent by Wife.'' The story also appears in *GR* 225 and Holcot's *Moralitates* No. XXIV.

[75] ''Domina quedam nobilis in tantum a tiranno premebatur quod nisi pugilem / ad pugnandum cum eo produceret, terras eius omnes perderet. Et lugenti domine et merenti advenit peregrinus quidam ignotus et pugnam cupit. Et diem pugne statuit et pro premio nichil aliud peciit nisi quod post mortem suam baculum et peram coram ea in aula suspendat ad memoriam peregrini continuandam, et concessit. Et peregrinus tirannum occidit et postea de receptis in bello vulneribus obiit. Et moriens dixit: Soror mea preamata, /Pro te reliqui vite fata, /Te salvans a periculo. /Si mihi velis esse grata, /[Sis mei semper memorata,] / Nunc et sequenti seculo. Et cito post adamata a quodam milite, ad eius preceptum memoriam peregrini primo deposuit de aula, secundo de camera, tercio de capella, et finaliter coniuncta militi oblita est peregrini liberatoris sui.'' In the sermons of John Waldeby, Bodleian Library, MS. Laud Misc. 77, fol. 150r-v. The fifth line of the poem reads *mei semper memorata sis*. The story also appears in *GR* 25, but without the verses; and further in man-

Chapter 7

This is very much the stuff of medieval romance. At the same time, these and similar *exempla* all deal with one and the same central theme of Christian devotion, Christ's Passion, as did the *locus amoenus* passage. In an earlier chapter we had noticed the strong lyrical impulses emanating from this theme, so remarkable in Grimestone's work, and we now find the same again, for quite often narratives of Christ the Lover-Knight are rhetorically heightened by a lyrical poem. This may be strictly religious in language and theme, as is the following widespread meditative poem quoted in a thirteenth-century sermon:

> If a knight were to enter a fierce tournament for the love of some maiden, in which he received many wounds, and if he could choose whether he wanted to be healed either so that no sign of his wounds appeared or else so that the signs of all his wounds remained but without making him in any way ugly or weak, I judge he would choose the latter. For he would gain the advantage that every time that maiden saw him thus wounded for her sake, she would love him the more and give him thanks. Bernard: "Above all, it renders you loveable," etc. And thus in English:
> > Whan Ics on rode se
> > Iesu, mi lemon, etc.[76]

Or it may rather blandly reflect the message and language of the *exemplum* itself, as do the Latin triplets quoted a few lines above:

> Soror mea preamata,
> Pro te reliqui vite fata,
> > Te salvans a periculo . . .

---

uscripts of the revised version of *Fasciculus morum* (e.g., Oxford, Lincoln College MS. Lat. 52, fols. 131v-132). An analogue is the version in which a dispossessed queen is freed from the tyrant by a knight, but she remains faithful to the pact made with him and renews her promise by looking at his bloody armor or shirt: *GR* 66. To the same version belongs the story in *Ancrene Wisse*. Tubach 4020 lumps different types of this *exemplum* together.

[76] "Si miles pro amore alicuius puelle grave torneamentum subisset, in quo vulnera multa pertulisset, et posset eligere utrum vellet sanari, ita quod nullum appareret signum vulnerum, an ita quod apparerunt signa omnium sed quod per hoc in nullo fuerit deformior, in nullo debilior, estimo quod eligeret secundum, quippe hoc adderetur boni quod quantum enim videret eum illa puella sic vulneratum pro ea, eum magis amaret et gracias ageret. Bernardus: 'Super omnia amabilem te reddit,' etc. Et ideo Anglice: 'Wan . . .' " Bodleian Library, MS. Laud Misc. 511, fol. 123v. I owe the reference to this quotation to Sister Maura O'Carroll, S.N.D. The English verse is *IMEV* 3964, with variants 3961, 3965-66, 4107, 4141. The Bernard quotation is from *Super Cantica*, XX.2 (*Opera* 1:115).

Other cases, however, may quote a vernacular stanza which is definitely secular in language and imagery. An example occurs in the "Elopement of Princess" story:

Therefore Christ could then say:
34 Loue, þou art of mikel mit—
  Mi day þou tornis into nit
  And dos me sike sore.
  And al for on so swete a wit
  Þat onis þorw loue me trouþe plit
  To ben myn euere-more.

These standard images of a courtly love song are then moralized in precisely the fashion we have discussed earlier:

The first word is obvious because by his strength he [i.e., Christ] triumphed over the Three Enemies. The second, because all his life was full of suffering; similarly, "from the sixth to the ninth hour there was darkness over the whole earth" [Matthew 27.45]. The third, because he called out loud with tears, as in [the raising of] Lazarus, when he began to quake and tremble, be weary and weep bitterly [cf. John 11.33, 35]; likewise he gave up his spirit with a loud cry and his last tears. . . . The last word is evident because all we Christians offered him our faith in baptism for ever.[77]

The six-line stanza applied to the suffering Christ and moralized thus represents another case much like *At a sprynge-wel*, though here the reasons for considering it to be of secular provenance are perhaps less compelling. The provenance of such verses is less ambiguous in a quatrain that occurs within the *exemplum* "Posy-Rings Sent by Wife" used in the sermon on *Amore langueo*:

35 For loue Y morne,
  Y persche al for þy sake.

[77] "Primum verbum patet quia ex potestate sua de tribus hostibus triumphavit. Secundum patet quia tota vita dolore plena fuit. Similiter 'ab hora sexta ad horam nonam facte sunt tenebre super universam terram.' Tercium patet quia cum lacrimis alte clamavit, ut patet de Lazaro, cum cepit pavere et fremere et tedere et amare flere; eciam cum clamore valido et lacrimis ultimatis emisit spiritum . . . Ultimum verbum patet quia nos omnes Christiani in baptismo fidem perpetuo sibi optulimus." British Library, MS. Harley 7322, fol. 154. The verse is *IMEV* 2014.

Y hope al yn þy grace,
My lyf ys on þy face.[78]

Read by itself, this simple stanza might impress us as another lover's complaint of secular origins. But the context makes it clear that the four lines translate the Latin inscriptions on the golden "trewlove": *Amore langueo, Languendo pereo, Pereundo spero*, and *Sperando revivisco*. The translation is free, but definitely inspired by the inscriptions and therefore undoubtedly made by the preacher.

This freedom of preachers to draw on the imagery of secular love in producing verses of their own is similarly found in the rhymed division of the sermon just quoted, *He lesus is myth* (4), with its seven signs of love-longing. The same practice seems to have produced the following poem in Grimestone's collection (No. 208):

36   Mi loue is falle vp-on a may,
For loue of hire I defende þis day.
Loue aunterus no man for-saket,
It woundet3 sore wan it him taket.
Loue anterus may hauen no reste,
Quere thouth is newe þer loue is faste.
Loue anterus with wo is bouth,
Per loue is trewe it flittet3 nouth.[79]

Though we lack the context to be absolutely certain, these lines fit best into a sermon on Christ's Passion where the lover-knight "could have said" them.

There is at least one other area in which one may suspect preachers to have made up their own verses that speak of worldly love. A fourteenth-century sermon on the seven deadly sins, *Surge et ambula* ("Arise and walk," Matthew 9.5), in discussing *defloratio*, likens virgins in spring—both male and female—to the "wanton heifer" of Hosea 4.16 as well as to the nightingale, who sings most sweetly before building its nest but after mating changes its song to sighing:

[78] Cambridge University Library, MS. Kk.4.24, fol. 144v; *IMEV* 830. The *exemplum* is Tubach No. 3866 (see above, n. 74).

[79] *IMEV* 2260, printed in *RL XIV* 73. The structure of this poem, a series of statements about *loue aunterous* which at least in couplets 2-4 are syntactically parallel, is very similar to that of distinctions and inscriptions, such as Grimestone Nos. 167, 107, or 232, discussed in ch. 4, pp. 121-23.

Thus it goes with virgins. Before they are corrupted, they run about and sing and give themselves to every lustful pleasure. But when they have acquired new little bones and feel the pains of childbirth, they lay aside all joyfulness and burst into weeping and sighing. And then our virgins who have been corrupted in illegitimate wedlock have instead of their former song this on their lips:

37 Waylaway wy dude Ich so,
Vor nou Ic am in alle wo.[80]

Another verse of the same kind appears elsewhere:

While young maidens are chaste, they sing; but when their belly begins to swell, they change their song to lamentation:

38 Weylawey þat Iche ne span
Whan Y to þe ringe ran.[81]

The two couplets may of course be actual songs. But since they are introduced as former love songs turned into laments, could it be that they represent (serious) parodies created by the preachers? "Wailing" verses of this kind are plentiful in medieval sermons, placed especially into the mouths of sinners who repent too late; and their rhetorical and emotional effectiveness was recognized by at least one preacher who explicitly recommended their use at the end of sermon tales to "strike terror into your audience."[82] This suggests a common practice of which the two couplets could possibly show the literary results.

But even if we could be certain that the sermon-makers themselves were responsible for such verses, their production of poems that are secular in theme and language is at best meager. The real contribution of preachers to the history of secular love poetry, therefore, lies in preserving for us a wide variety of snatches whose contexts point to their secular provenance. Some of them proved to have great vitality and a life span of several centuries, in which the sermon quotations form a definite bridge between the lost originals and later adaptations. For instance, a

[80] "Recte sic est de virginibus que antequam corrumpantur discurrunt, cantant, et omni lascivie vacant. Set cum nova et juvenilia ossa collegerint et partus dolores senserint, omnem leticiam removendo ploratus emittent et gemitus, et tunc habebunt nostre virgines toro illicito corrupte pro priori cantu in ore: 'Waylaway . . .' " British Library, MS. Harley 505, fol. 83v. *IMEV* 3902.5.
[81] *IMEV* 3900.5, printed with context in "Unrecorded," No. 81. A variant is No. 2 quoted above.
[82] See *Verses*, p. 72.

Chapter 7

thirteenth-century treatise on the vices, in dealing with the signs of God's love for men, records the following snatch:

Notice that one sometimes refuses to let in a person who is knocking, and says: "You won't come in here because it isn't raining, and you stand in a dry place." Or else, because the person who knocks does not use pleasing words as he is knocking. The Lord rejects both these reasons in Canticles 5 [.2] when he says: "Open to me, my love"— for I love you fervently—"my sister"—I love you wisely—"my spouse"—I love you personally—"my dove"—I love you with sighing—"because . . . my head is full of dew"—that is, my blood— "and my locks of the drops of the nights"—that is, the spittle of the Jews. Notice the English [song or saying]:

39   So lange Ik aue, lefman,
         Stonden at þe yathe,
         Þat my fote is hi-frosen
         Fast to þe stake.

And as people say, he freezes who has lost his friends. But among his friends none was equal to his mother. Thus, when Christ had in a way lost his mother, his foot was frozen to the stake of the cross.[83]

The quatrain has also been preserved in a sermon collection of around 1300, and it is very probably the same song that is referred to in the description of a young gallant (7). The popular song and its images continued to appeal to religious poets writing about Christ's love for the soul. The great collection of English devotional poetry from the last decades of the fourteenth century contained in the Vernon MS. includes a long "Mournyng Song of the Loue of God," an expandable lyric. Its general theme, not surprisingly, is that "Mi loue al for to wynne / Ihesu bi-com my kniht" (lines 7-8); and its fifth stanza nicely incorporates the lover's song at the door:

[83] "Set nota quod aliquando negatur pulsanti introitus et dicitur: 'Non intrabis ita prope quia non pluit, set stas in loco sicco'; vel quia pulsans non pulcre loquitur cum pulsat. Utrumque excludit Dominus in Canticorum 5.e: 'Aperi mihi, amica mea'—quam amo ardenter—'soror'—sapienter—'sponsa'—individualiter—'columba mea'—gemebundo; quia ut alibi, 5.c: 'Capud meum plenum est rore,' idest sanguine, 'et cincinni mei guttis noctuum,' idest sputo Iudeorum. Nota Anglicum: 'So lange . . .'/ Et ut dicitur, congelatur qui amicis privatur. Set inter amicas nulla equipollens matri. Quando ergo Christus fuit quodammodo matre privatus, tunc fuit pes eius stipiti crucis congelatus." Durham Cathedral, MS. B.I.18, fol. 56v; in the chapter on envy of the *summa* on the vices, *Quoniam ut ait sapiens*. The English verse is *IMEV* 3176.3.

Þeroute al-þauh he stonde
　Callynge at my ȝate,
Til him frese fot and honde,
　Faste vn-to a stake,
He ne takeþ staf ne wonde
　Wiþ wraþþe me for to wake;
Mi loue him byndeþ as bonde,
　ȝif I him murþes make.[84]

It was once said that in the Latin love songs of the "wandering scholars" may be heard "the double flute of Ovid and the Song of Songs."[85] In the work of later preachers, especially in their allegories of Christ the Lover-Knight, this double flute was happily joined by the reed of vernacular English love songs.

This mediating role of medieval preachers extended far beyond the age of Chaucer into the world of the Tudors and of Shakespeare. A late fifteenth-century collection of poetry and prose, including material often used in preaching, records a poem here entitled "Come ouer the borne, Besse." It has twelve stanzas, each ending with the refrain "Come ouer." Later manuscripts that record the same song indicate that the full form of the opening lines is:

40　　Come over the burne, Besse,
　　　Thou lytyll, prety Besse,
　　　Come over the burne, Besse, to me.[86]

Of the twelve stanzas in the earlier manuscript, eleven form an address by Christ on the cross to mankind. The opening stanza sets the scene, as it were, and links Christ's appeal to the burden in precisely the process of point-by-point moralization that we have seen used by preachers in their quotations of secular love songs:

　　　The borne is this wor[l]d blynde,
　　　And Besse ys mankynde,

[84] St. 5 of *IMEV* 3760, of 32 stanzas. Edited by F. J. Furnivall, *The Minor Poems of the Vernon Manuscript*, part II, EETS 117 (London, 1901), p. 470.

[85] Attributed to Sir Stephen Gaselee by Helen Waddell, *Medieval Latin Lyrics*, fourth edition (1933; Harmondsworth, 1952), p. 334. But notice that in *The Transition from the Late Latin Lyric to the Medieval Love Poem* (Cambridge, 1931) Gaselee spoke of "the double inspiration, of the Song of Songs and the vernacular poems describing nature, . . . with a third influence, that of Ovid" (p. 33).

[86] See John Stevens, *Music and Poetry in the Early Tudor Court* (London, 1961), p. 348.

So praty can noon fynde
As she.
She dauncyth, she lepyth,
And Crist stondyth and clepith:
Come ouer [the borne, Besse, to me!][87]

This song was extremely popular in Tudor England.[88] Its opening triplet and stanza are found with music in a songbook (the Ritson MS) and two other sixteenth-century books.[89] They are further alluded to in Skelton's *Speke, Parrot*.[90] Later in the century, the triplet was quoted and incorporated in political poems. Eventually, it appeared in the idle babble of Moros, the fool, in a comedy by William Wager.[91] And at last it ended up in the topsy-turvy world of King Lear, Edgar, and the Fool:

EDGAR. Come o'er the bourn, Bessy, to me.
FOOL. Her boat hath a leak
And she must not speak
Why she dares not come over to thee. (III.vi.25-28)

Could it be that Shakespeare's audience was still sufficiently familiar with the song and its medieval moralization to catch the dark echo that the suffering Lear may be appealing for love—and threatening judgment—just like Christ from the cross, but that the *navis amoris* of his two older daughters will not float across the water, as the Fool in his wisdom seems to realize?[92]

[87] Cambridge, Trinity College MS. 1157, fol. 55; the last line is completed from the version printed by Stevens.

[88] In this respect *Come over the burne, Besse* is not alone. Parallel cases are: *This day day dawes* (*IMEV* 1450; see comments by Stevens, *Music and Poetry*, pp. 381-82; and *EEC*, p. 479); and *My loue she morns for me* (*IMEV* 2261.2; comments by Stevens, p. 53. The couplet appears as a random note in Cambridge, Trinity College MS. 1157, fol. 45v; the *IMEV* entry needs correction).

[89] See *IMEV* 3318.4; Stevens, *Music and Poetry*, p. 348; and Peter J. Seng, *The Vocal Songs in the Plays of Shakespeare* (Cambridge, Mass., 1967), pp. 208-10.

[90] Lines 235-37; John Skelton, *The Poems*, ed. Robert S. Kinsman (Oxford, 1969), p. 84.

[91] William Wager, *A very mery and Pythic Commedie, called The longer thou liuest, the more foole thou art* ([1569]), A.3; STC 24935-D.

[92] I have suggested a sermon background for Lear's Fool in "The Wisdom of the Fool," in *The Wisdom of Poetry. Essays in Early English Literature in Honor of Morton W. Bloomfield*, ed. Larry D. Benson and Siegfried Wenzel (Kalamazoo, Mich., 1982), pp. 225-40, 307-14.

8

Preachers

or

Poets

The preceding two chapters have already carried us briefly into the poetic world of *King Lear*. In concluding our explorations, it would be appropriate to ask what, if any, influence preachers' verses had on the major poets in their own period, such as Chaucer, Langland, or Lydgate.[1] As stated, the question is hard, perhaps even impossible to answer. That the great poets writing in the period during which sermon verses flourished owed a deep and manifold debt to the homiletic tradition in general and to specific aspects of sermon-making in particular is beyond question. Chaucer, Langland, and Gower can certainly be shown to have been deeply influenced by the language and imagery of preachers, to have drawn on their favorite topics and subject matter, and perhaps even to have shared some of their formal and structural concerns.[2] But their reaction or susceptibility to the use and form of sermon *verses* is harder to gauge. The main reason may be that they (and the same of course holds true of the Pearl-Poet) were fundamentally *narrative* poets. Instead of musing on what possible influence preachers' verses may have had on the poets, I therefore propose to ask how they differ from the work of poets who were not writing for sermons.

This question could be answered quite swiftly by taking the major stylistic characteristics we have found in preaching verses and claiming their opposites for the work of genuine poets. Thus, Grimestone's verse had been characterized by its "simple language, native diction, straightforward syntax, scarcity of images, and relative lack of wordplay and poetic wit."[3] The opposite of these qualities, to varying extents, would fur-

---

[1] By "poets" I refer, in this chapter, to the authors of verse that was not ostensibly written for, and does not occur in, sermons. My differentiation here does of course not imply a demotion of preachers or the best of their work, as I hope this book makes clear.

[2] For Chaucer, see my essay "Chaucer and the Language of Contemporary Preaching," *SP* 73 (1976), 138-61. For Langland, see my contribution to John A. Alford (ed.), *A Companion to Piers Plowman*, forthcoming (University of California Press).

[3] See above, ch. 5, p. 173.

nish an acceptable description of much fifteenth-century lyric verse. But close analysis can reveal more specific qualities. To do so I select two poems which, as it were, stand at the fork in the road where preachers' verses and non-preaching lyric poetry parted company. Both deal with topics or themes that were common to both preachers and poets but were treated with linguistic and poetic means that are markedly different.

The first, entitled "Medicines to Cure the Deadly Sins," comprises eleven stanzas and has been preserved in three manuscripts which seem to have no connection with preaching.[4] Its two opening stanzas run as follows:

> As I walkyd vppone a day
> To take þe aere off feld and flowre,
> In a mery morenynge off May
> When fflowrys were ffull off swete flauowre,   4
> I hurd one say, "O God verray,
> How longe shall I dure yn my dolour!"
> And one his kneys he began to pray:
> "Now, good God, send me thy succour,   8
> Maryes sone, most off honour,
> Thatt ryche and poore may ponyche and plese.
> Now geve me lyfe yn my langour,
> And yeve vs lycence to lyfe yn ese.   12
>
> To lyfe yn ese and his lawys to kepe,
> Grawnt me, God, yn blysse so bryght;
> And withyn þat cabone lett vs neuer crepe
> Ther as Lucifer lyeth, i-lok withowt eny lyght.   16
> My dedly wowndis ere derne and depe,
> I haue no place to represse þem aryght,
> And smertyng wyll nott suffer me to slepe
> Tyll a leche with dewte haue them dyght.   20
> Hitt most be a curate, a crownyd wyght,
> Þatt knew the querely off bene and pese;
> And els thes medicynys haue no myght
> To geve vs lycense to lyve yn ese.[5]   24

---

[4] The two manuscripts from which the poem has been printed may be classified as "miscellany" (Henry E. Huntington Library, MS. HM 183) and "poetic anthology" (Cambridge University Library, MS. Ff.1.6).

[5] *IMEV* 373; taken from *RL XV* 178.

244

The following stanza specifies that the speaker's "dedly wowndis" have been inflicted by "this wykkid wordyll" ("world," line 27), and that the "leche" who can heal him, beyond his curate, is he who relieved Lazarus, David, and Daniel of their disease (lines 33-34). Then comes a catalogue of the wounds, the seven deadly sins, each briefly described in one stanza and opposed by its appropriate remedy (sts. 4-10). The final stanza speaks of three further sanative herbs: contrition, confession, and satisfaction; and without explicitly marking a return from the spiritually sick complainant to the poem's persona who had heard his lament, the stanza changes from first-person singular to plural pronouns and ends with a prayer:

> Now, Lord, as thow madyst hevyn, erth and hell,   129
> Geve vs grace hym to serue and plese,
> And with-yn his gloryus blysse thatt we all may dwell,
> And geve vs there licence to lyve yn ese.

The poem is, thus, essentially didactic: it teaches the seven deadly sins and their opposite remedial virtues, much as Chaucer's Parson does in the major portion of his tale. Such listing of the chief vices and their remedies can be found in preaching verses as well. A very modest poem in eight couplets, for instance, presents "the vii vertwys agyn the vii dedley synys" in a most unpretentious fashion:

> Be meke and meylde yn hert and towng
> Ayens pryd boyt olde and yong.[6]

Grimestone similarly versified the sins in seven quatrains and opposed them, though not to the remedial virtues but to Christ's sufferings (No. 218). In contrast to those simple lines, *As I walkyd vppone a day* impresses us at once by its solid and substantial twelve-line stanzas built on the pattern of *ababababbcbc*. Its greater formal sophistication is further enhanced by its *chanson-d'aventure* opening (lines 1-4), the use of a refrain, and the concatenation between stanzas 1 and 2. In addition, the poem makes heavy use of alliteration in various patterns. As happens so often in the great alliterative poetry of the fourteenth century, the metrical requirements here, too, occasionally force the poet to use a vocabulary that is uncommon, semantically daring, and at times obscure.[7] Thus

---

[6] *IMEV* 469; printed in Henry A. Person (ed.), *Cambridge Middle English Lyrics*, revised edition (Seattle, 1962), No. 20.

[7] Compare the works of the Pearl-Poet, or such poems as *Middelerd for mon wes mad* or *Lord þat lenest vs lyf* ("On the Follies of Fashion") of MS. Harley 2253.

we find such strange—though not necessarily ineffective—lines as, "He ramagith sore both raw and rede" and "Nothir no corsiff will qwinch his quede," on Ira, or "A gritter gnawer þan ffelone or gowte," on Invidia.

It is precisely the use of these devices that sets what I would call a genuinely poetic treatment of the same theme sharply apart from that found in preaching verses. In their combination such devices are quite characteristic of much religious poetry written near the end of the fourteenth and throughout the fifteenth centuries. Refined stanzas with refrain, occasional stanza linking, alliteration, and a *chanson-d'aventure* opening occur repeatedly in the long lyrics of the Vernon Manuscript.[8] The same characteristics can be found again in several poems included in Carleton Brown's collection of fifteenth-century religious lyrics, as for instance a fourteen-stanza appeal of Christ from the cross, a twelve-stanza lament of the Sorrowful Mother, a ten-stanza lament at old age, and many others.[9] The topics treated here, even aspects of the language used including proverbial material, are very much like what we have found in preaching verses; yet their manner of treatment differs profoundly. Gone is the simplicity of preaching verses. It would be hard to imagine these poems being quoted in sermons; in fact, I know of no evidence, from their manuscript context or actual sermons, that such poems were used in preaching.

The differences reach even deeper into the language and texture of the poem considered. One stanza in *As I walkyd vppone a day*, for example, develops the sin of sloth and its traditional remedy, spiritual activity, in the following terms:

> Accidia is a sowkyng blayne,
> He bollith and bladderith with-yn my bowre;
> And makith me ffaynt both flessh and vayne,
> And kepith me yn cowch like a cowchour.　　　　88
> I hurde off an herbe þatt shold lyse þatt payne,
> Men seith hitt berith a dowbyll flour:
> Vigilate et orate. Vse well tho twayne,
> And hitt shall be-nyme the thi dolour,　　　　92
> As siker as bred is made off flowre.
> Smyll ham yn seson with þi nese,

---

[8] F. J. Furnivall (ed.), *The Minor Poems of the Vernon MS.*, Part II, EETS 117 (London, 1901), pp. 658-76.

[9] *RL XV* 105, 6, and 147.

And the swetnes off thatt swete savoure
Shall geve the lycense to lyve yn ese.   96

The metaphoric depiction of sloth as a wound and of its remedial virtue as a herb is demanded by, and entirely in line with, the general conceit on which this poem is based, namely that "this wicked world" has given the complainant a "wicked wound" that "nourishes" all the other seven. The two notions: that the chief vices are wounds in human nature,[10] and that they have been caused by wrong contact with the World,[11] were both conventions of long standing. What is odd in this poem is that *accidia* should be likened to "a sucking(?)[12] blain that swells and blisters in my chamber." This particular image, and the very use of such specific medical details in the description of the sin, are to my knowledge unique, certainly in Middle English literature. *Accidia* is normally compared to paralysis and occasionally to lethargy or podagra, but not to a blister or swelling.[13] Since other sins are here similarly envisioned as skin diseases (avarice, lechery, and apparently also wrath and envy), it is possible that the poem develops the notion that sin is spiritual leprosy, with particular sins or vices being various symptoms thereof, a notion often developed in sermons on the healing of the leper, from the pericope for the Third Sunday after the Octave of Epiphany.[14] This possibility derives support from the curious image of line 22 where the penitent's curate is described as one "Patt knew the querely off bene and pese." Brown suggested that "querely" was "an illiterate or colloquial spelling of O[ld] F[rench] *querele*" and that " 'bene and pese' is

[10] This notion is developed notably in the treatises on the vices and the remedial virtues used by Chaucer in his Parson's Tale. See Wenzel (ed.), *Summa virtutum de remediis anime* (Athens, Ga., 1984), pp. 9-10.

[11] For the view of "the world" as a force that is particularly hostile and dangerous to man's spiritual existence, see Wenzel, "The Wisdom of the Fool," in *The Wisdom of Poetry. Essays in Early English Literature in honor of Morton W. Bloomfield*, ed. Larry D. Benson and Siegfried Wenzel (Kalamazoo, Mich., 1982), pp. 237-40 and references in the notes on p. 313.

[12] The selection of this adjective is probably due to alliterative requirements: *accidia* was pronounced *assídia*.

[13] See Wenzel, *The Sin of Sloth. Acedia in Medieval Thought and Literature* (Chapel Hill, N.C., 1967), pp. 108-9.

[14] For example: Albertus Magnus, *Sermo XVII*, in *Opera omnia*, ed. A. Borgnet, vol. 13 (Paris, 1891), pp. 87-91; Bonaventure, *Opera omnia*, ed. Patres Collegii a S. Bonaventura (Quaracchi, 1882-1902), 9:183-86; William Peraldus, in *Guilelmus Alvernus, Opera omnia* (Orléans and Paris, 1674), 2:191-93; John Felton, *Sermo 11*, in University of Pennsylvania, MS. Lat. 35, fols. 30-33v.

evidently a pun on 'bene' and 'pax,' so that the line taken as a whole means, one who is familiar with his service book.''[15] In contrast to this rather desperate suggestion, I would read ''bene and pese'' literally and interpret the line as: ''who might know the suit *or* distinction between bean and pea.'' Now, to distinguish between one sin and another, and between sin and no-sin, and to find, recommend, or apply the appropriate remedy, had been considered the proper office of priests from patristic times on; and this office was described, with a biblical phrase, as the *iudicium . . . inter . . . lepram et lepram* (Deuteronomy 17.8).[16] It is therefore possible that the traditional concept of sin as spiritual leprosy informs the entire poem and is visualized to greater or lesser extent in the descriptions of the individual sins.[17]

If the clinical details of *accidia* in lines 85-86 need not carry a specific allegorical meaning, it is quite otherwise with the *effect* this disease has on the patient.[18] The faintness it produces, forcing him to stay in bed (87-88), agrees perfectly with a major aspect of the sin of sloth that was frequently singled out and depicted in literature as well as the visual arts. The same symbolic congruence can be found in the following depiction of *accidia*'s remedy. Instead of naming an abstract virtue, such as busyness or fortitude, the poet specifies the biblical injunction to ''wake and pray.'' Jesus' warning to the sleeping apostles in Gethsemane (Matthew 26.36ff.) was a standard authority cited in medieval discussions of this sin including poetic treatments,[19] just as waking and prayer were considered typical and specific practices to overcome the physical and spiritual torpor induced by sloth. That our poem should call the remedy a flower derives harmoniously from its general conceit likening spiritual remedies to medicinal herbs. That this remedy should be envisioned as a *double* flower reflects the twofold nature—physical (*vigilate*) and spiritual (*orate*)—which the concept of *accidia* had gained by the later Middle

---

[15] *RL XV*, p. 348.

[16] See F. Chatillon, ''*Inter lepram et lepram discernere* (Jacques de Vitry, *Lettres*, II, 1. 122),'' *Revue du moyen âge latin* 21 (1965), 21-30.

[17] Of specific relevance for the background of this poem may be the *exemplum* about a *senex* who wanders through the desert and searches for medicinal herbs for the king's daughter who had been given him for safekeeping. The latter is infected with leprosy. In the moralization, the princess is man's soul, who ''has as many blisters and boils in her face as she is subject to vices.'' *Fasciculus morum*, V.10 (fol. 99).

[18] For the practice of listing the effects of a sin as a major technique in discussing it, see *The Sin of Sloth*, pp. 84ff.

[19] Ibid., p. 102; *Piers Plowman*, B.V.450.

Ages.[20] Not so obvious is the reason why the victim of sloth should be asked to *smell* this flower. It is at this point that the poet's use of images becomes truly sophisticated, for another major aspect of *accidia*, on a deeper psychological level, was *indevotio*, the lack of devotion: by his negligence, the victim of *accidia* loses his taste for spiritual exercise, he does not feel the sweetness of prayer and its consolation, and he becomes altogether bored with the spiritual life. Such spiritual dis-gust or lack of taste can only be healed by savoring the sweetness (cf. line 95) that comes with proper devotion.[21] One may even find an extension of the poem's images of sweetness, savor, and smelling into line 93:

As siker as bred is made off flowre.

On the surface, the bread image may be no more than an expression of emphasis, similar to line 59. On the other hand, the line may well carry a reference to the Eucharist, the "bread of life," to whose reception the Church was constantly invited with the Psalm verse, "Taste and see how sweet the Lord is" (Psalm 33.9). That devotion to and reception of this sacrament was considered to be a primary spiritual remedy against sloth can be seen from *Fasciculus morum*, whose long discussion of *accidia* includes a chapter on the Mass and on the consecrated host, one of whose properties is *in gustu dulcedo*, "swete in þe smacking."[22]

Whatever one may think of line 93, it is evident that the major images of this stanza and their symbolic meaning, together with the poem's basic metaphor, are solidly anchored in the background of medieval theological teaching including sermons. It is not astonishing, therefore, that poems like this have been called "little homilies with proverbial refrain,"[23] and it is entirely possible that an actual sermon may still be found that uses precisely the same oppositions and images. However, it should be equally evident that the poem *As I walkyd vppone a day* differs

[20] Cf. *The Sin of Sloth*, passim and especially pp. 174-81.

[21] For *indevotio*, see ibid., pp. 60-63. To writers who conceived of this aspect of the vice as more central, the remedy was spiritual joy; see ibid., pp. 49, 55-56, and passim. For representative definitions of *accidia* as *taedium*, see ibid., Index, and p. 218, n. 17, items d-i.

[22] *Fasciculus morum*, V.1. In the schemata which related the sins to the petitions of the Lord's Prayer, *accidia* was most often related to that for "our daily bread." See *The Sin of Sloth*, pp. 56-57 and 74.

[23] The expression was used by Henry Noble MacCracken with reference to short didactic poems by Lydgate, but it obviously fits our poem as well; *The Minor Poems of John Lydgate*, Part II, EETS 192 (London, 1934), p. vii (Table of Contents).

significantly from the sermon verses studied in earlier chapters with respect to major stylistic features. Especially its imagery, as we have seen, is considerably more rich, varied, original, and coherent than anything found in sermon verses, even the most lyrical ones by Grimestone. Moreover, the imagery in the poem is self-explanatory, in the sense that the poem offers the basic symbolic references of its images explicitly and firmly integrated in its structure. Both the metaphorical diseases and their medicines are called by their technical, non-metaphoric names: *Accidia* and *Vigilate et orate*. This technique contrasts sharply with the secular lyrics of chapter 7, which were quoted and then subjected to a separate moralization of their images. If our poem were a *preacher's verse* of secular origin, it might have appeared in the following form with moralization:

> A sowkyng blayne bladdrith my flesh,
> It makith me cowch as cowchour.
> A dowbyll flour held to nese
> Shall soþly benyme me mi dolour.

Notice that according to the natural philosophers the second kind of leprosy is called elephantiasis; it springs from melancholy and signifies *accidia*. This sin makes people slow and lazy in God's service; hence Proverbs 19: "Slothfulness casts into a deep sleep." It must be overcome by waking and prayer, as the Lord taught us when he gave his apostles the twofold command, in Matthew 26: "Wake and pray." And lastly, Bernard teaches this remedy in his sermon *On Canticles* with these words: "When anyone feels himself lazy or full of *accidia*, he must resort to prayer before God, so that in praying he may receive the grace which expels *accidia* from him."[24]

As I walkyd vppone a day is therefore profoundly different from sermon verses, in its use of imagery, its language, its stylistic features. It is, in other words, the work of a genuine poet.

The much more sophisticated use of imagery can be further illustrated by a poem which has, with some hesitation, been included among the lyric poems by John Lydgate:

---

[24] The four lines are of course my selection. Sentence 1 of the hypothetical commentary is adapted from Albertus Magnus, as quoted above, n. 14, p. 89. Sentence 2 is conflated from Albertus and Peraldus, *Summa de vitiis*, V.ii.3 (on somnolence). Sentence 3 reflects Peraldus, *Summa*, V.iii, the fifth remedy. And sentence 4 is Peraldus' eighth remedy, the Bernard reference being to *In Cantica*, XXI.5.

My fader above, beholdyng thy mekenesse,
As dewe on rosis doth his bawme sprede,
Sent his gost, most souerayne of clennes,
Into thy brest, a, rose of wommanhede!
Whan I for man was borne in my manhede;   5
For whiche with rosis of heuenly influence
I me reioyse to pley in thy presence.

Benyng moder! who first dide inclose
The blessed budde that sprang out of Iesse,
Thow of Iuda the verray perfite rose,   10
Chose of my fader for thyn humylite
Without fadyng most clennest to bere me;
For whiche with roses of chast innocence
I me reioyse to pley in thi presence.

O moder, moder, of mercy most habounde,   15
Fayrest moder that euer was alyve!
Though I for man have many a bloody wounde,
Among theym alle there be rosis fyve,
Agayne whos mercy fiendis may nat stryve;
Mankynde to save, best rosis of defence,   20
Whan they me pray for helpe in thy presence.[25]

The lyric represents an address of the Infant Jesus to his mother, similar to Grimestone's verse 5 though it is not a dialogue. Jesus speaks about his incarnation, his mother's virginity, and her future intercession for mankind warranted by his Passion. The poem very cleverly utilizes the traditional symbolic multivalence of the rose image. The first two stanzas are built on the contrast between likening Mary to a rose (lines 2, 4, and 10) and the roses with which Jesus is playing—evidently envisioning a scene in which the Infant on his mother's lap plays with a bunch or wreath of roses or perhaps a rosary[26]—real roses which become sym-

[25] *IMEV* 2238, ed. MacCracken, *The Minor Poems*, I; EETS, es, 107 (London, 1911), p. 235. I reproduce the text with some changes in capitalization, punctuation, and line indentation.

[26] The artistic representation of such a scene which would fit the poem best, as far as I know, is a votive painting of the Fraternity of the Rosary of Cologne, in which the Infant plays with a rosary that hangs around his mother's neck. See Paul Perdrizet, *La Vierge de Miséricorde* (Paris, 1908), p. 99 and plate XIII.1. But this form of the rosary and such a confraternity are rather late for Lydgate. The whole relation of Lydgate's poem with pictorial art demands further investigation.

bols of Christ's divine nature or incarnation (line 6) and of Mary's pure maidenhood (line 13). The third stanza, however, presents a change. In its first section the rose image is no longer applied to Mary but to Christ's five wounds.[27] Likewise, the refrain drops the image of Jesus playing with roses and instead continues the symbolic use of "roses" for Christ's wounds,[28] thus closing, as it were, the gap between the two different referents of the image that had been developed and utilized structurally in the first two stanzas. This progression in the use of the symbolic meanings of the poem's central image neatly parallels the progression in its themes, from Annunciation (3) and Nativity (5) through Mary's continuing virginity (12) to Christ's Passion (17) and Mary's everlasting intercession (20-21). To this can be added another, parallel progression through several forms or levels of figurative speech. In the first occurrence of the rose image, a real flower is referred to in a simile (line 2). Next, in "rose of wommanhede" (4) and "of Iuda the verray perfite rose" (10), the flower functions as a metaphor signaling perfection or the highest degree of worth. In the first two refrains (6 and 13), *rosis* again refers to real flowers but is made to carry a symbolic meaning by means of the prepositional phrases. Finally, the *rosis* of line 18, while subsuming the metaphoric meanings of highest degree, preciousness, and blood-like color, becomes fully a symbol of Christ's suffering. It is as if by playing with *roses* the poet were celebrating Christ's raising nature into a higher reality.

Such poetic "wit" in the use of imagery is reminiscent of earlier medieval hymns but totally unparalleled in preaching verses. In addition, the poem contains other formal and stylistic features that set it unmistakably apart from the verses of Grimestone and his fellow preachers. "The Child Jesus to Mary, the Rose" contains a refrain, much like *As I walkyd vppone a day* and many similar poems already mentioned. But in con-

---

[27] This symbolism, too was traditional and apparently a favorite topic with Lydgate. See especially the poem entitled "As a Mydsomer Rose," in John Lydgate, *Poems*, ed. John Norton-Smith (Oxford, 1966), No. 7. To the reference given by Norton-Smith on p. 142 may be added the moralization, in *Fasciculus morum* VII.20, of a shield with a lion rampant who wears a golden crown and a red rose on his chest: "The rose on his chest is that wound in the side by which this shield [i.e., Christ's body] was pierced."

[28] For the notion that Christ's wounds afford protection by being a place of refuge, see Douglas Gray, "The Five Wounds of Our Lord," *N&Q* 208 (1963), 85-86 and 129. "Rosis of defence" also evokes the image of protecting a castle by showering roses on the attackers, as in courtly-love images as well as in *The Castle of Perseverance*, lines 2145 and 2208-25; ed. Mark Eccles, *The Macro Plays*, EETS 262 (London, 1969), pp. 66 and 68-69.

trast to those, its stanzas are in rhyme royal, the stanza form introduced to England and made immensely popular by Chaucer. The most significant difference between Lydgate's poem and *As I walkyd vppone a day* is not so much its rhyme-pattern as its use of the five-stress line, which was to supersede the four-stress line that had been fairly much the preferred metrical vehicle in English rhyming poetry before Chaucer and certainly predominated in sermon verses. The poetic limitations of the popular and traditional four-stress line, and conversely the greater possibilities for structuring expression in poetry gained with the innovation, have been analyzed in a perceptive and illuminating essay by Robert D. Stevick, who pointed out that "the verse norm of traditional Middle-English lyrics was conducive to assertions and questions confined to small multiples of major syntactic unit lines organized by rhyme," but that in contrast to such limitations the five-stress line has "more 'weight' " and "greater variability."[29] This poetic and expressive superiority can be demonstrated *ad oculos auresque* with some examples from Chaucer. The second hexameter of the popular Latin saying,

> Dampna fleo rerum, sed plus fleo dampna dierum.
> Quis poterit rebus succurrere, nemo diebus,

had been translated by Grimestone as follows:

> Þou godes ben lorn, I may han more.
> Tim lorn aȝen comen ne may.[30]

The two lines, part of a quatrain, are not without poetic and rhetorical effect; but they illustrate well the typical progression by separate, disconnected units, each filling and limited to one line. In contrast, Chaucer's adaptation reads as follows:

> For "los of catel may recovered be,
> But los of tyme shendeth us," quod he. [i.e., "Senec"]
> (MLIntro, II.27-28)[31]

Here the two lines are linked by a coordinating *but* and thus form a single syntactic unit. Furthermore, the epigrammatic compression of which

[29] Robert D. Stevick, "The Criticism of Middle English Lyrics," *MP* 64 (1966-67), 103-17; quotations from pp. 115 and 114.
[30] Grimestone No. 235; see above, ch. 4, p. 133.
[31] Chaucer quotations are from *The Works of Geoffrey Chaucer*, ed. F. N. Robinson, second edition (Boston, 1957).

Chaucer was elsewhere capable when he wished (as in the related line "For tyme ylost may nought recovered be," *Troilus* 4:1283) is here loosened up by the parenthetic *quod he*. Such loosening is found very frequently when Chaucer makes use of items that form the arsenal of preachers' verses, such as biblical and other authoritative quotations, proverbs, or message verses. Suffice it to quote two borrowings from *The Distichs of Cato*:

> For Catoun seith that he that gilty is
> Demeth alle thyng be spoke of hym, *ywis*.
>
> (CYProl, VIII.688-89)

Here the rhyming couplet, which renders *Conscius ipse sibi de se putat omnia dici*, is loosened up with an introductory clause and the final *ywis*. Elsewhere Chaucer similarly lightens his source, *Virtutem primam esse puta compescere linguam*, with an interjected address and clause:

> The firste vertu, *sone, if thou wolt leere*,
> Is to restreyne and kepe wel thy tonge.   (MancT, IX.332-33)

This last quotation shows another tendency in Chaucer's use of material that was standard in preachers' verses: he more often than not avoids rhyming couplets and instead, where the quoted authority extends to the end of the second line, prefers to distribute it over two different rhyme-words. Witness the Pardoner's quoting Jeremiah 4.2:

> "Thou shalt swere sooth thyne othes, and not lye,
> And swere in doom, and eek in rightwisnesse";
>
> (PardT, VI.636-37)

or his presenting a typical memory verse, which may well be of Chaucer's own invention:

> This fruyt cometh of the bicched bones two:
> Forsweryng, ire, falsnesse, homycide;   (PardT, VI.656-57)

or the final message verses of the *exemplum*:

> Allas! mankynde, how may it bitide
> That to thy creatour, which that the wroughte,
> And with his precious herte-blood thee boghte,
> Thou art so fals and so unkynde, allas?   (PardT, VI.900-903)

In these and many other instances, material characteristic of sermon verses has become syntactically and rhythmically integrated into the surrounding narrative context, and this with the greatest of apparent ease, naturalness, and fluency. In this achievement, the five-stress line is a prime and indispensable factor.

The greater "weight" and "variability" that the five-stress line afforded English poets can likewise be seen in Lydgate's "The Child Jesus to Mary, the Rose." There is, however, an aspect to this gain other than flexibility and fluency, in fact almost their opposite. Lydgate's first stanza, in which the flow of the main sentence is repeatedly interrupted with apostrophes and modifying clauses and with phrases whose structural relationships require several readings before they are grasped, strikes us as tortuous, artificial, or "rhetorical." Chaucer, too, was capable of producing such passages, especially in rhyme royal,[32] and his fifteenth-century successors followed his example with eagerness.[33] But this kind of rhetorical stance or pompousness should be seen less as poetic incompetence than as a deliberate attempt to disrupt natural and everyday speech rhythms. Together with aureate diction and the use of classical images and mythology it forms part of the poets' attempt—an attempt that seems essential to the poetic enterprise in any age—to counter, to break away from common speech and find new verbal and stylistic ways of expressing thought and emotions. Unquestionably, much of this rhetorical posturing and aureate diction is hideous—poets are not always successful. But the point here is that in Lydgate and his contemporaries we see an experimentation with new verbal and metrical forms on the part of genuine poets. Such experimentations were diametrically opposed to the versifying work of preachers, who instead strove to remain simple and on the level of the popular and familiar.

Let it be said, though, that true poets of the period could indeed achieve lyric stanzas of great power without those devices that their successors eventually rejected as aberrations, as the following example from Lydgate's *Testament* illustrates:

> Tarye no lenger toward thyn herytage,
> Hast on thy weye and be of ryght good chere,
> Go eche day onward on thy pylgrymage,
> Thynke howe short tyme thou hast abyden here;
> Thy place is bygged aboue the sterres clere,
> Noon erthly palys wrought in so statly wyse,

---

[32] For example: *Troilus* I.1-7; II.1-7.
[33] For Chaucer's influence on Lydgate, see Derek Pearsall, *John Lydgate* (London, 1970), pp. 49-63.

Chapter 8

Kome on, my frend, my brother most entere!
For the I offered my blood in sacryfice.[34]

This stanza differs significantly from the sermon verses surveyed in this book by its metrical form, its diction ("brother most entere"), and its imagery ("aboue the sterres clere"). Lydgate clearly has learned much from "my mayster Chaucer." Yet in its quiet and earnest appeal it shares and thus continues some of the simplicity and power—or perhaps we should say, power through simplicity—of the lyrics written nearly a century earlier by popular preachers.

[34] *The Minor Poems of John Lydgate*, I, 362, reproduced with slight changes as above (n. 25).

Index of

Manuscripts

Cited

Manuscripts frequently quoted are briefly characterized according to the categories described in chapter 1.

ABERDEEN
University Library, MS. 154: 163

AREZZO
MS. 325: 73

CAMBRIDGE
Corpus Christi College, MS. 392: 161
Corpus Christi College, MS. 423: 168
Gonville and Caius College, MS. 221: 86
Jesus College, MS. 13. A collection of several manuscripts of the late fourteenth and fifteenth centuries. Probably from Durham. Sermon collections. Quoted pp. 87, 91, 119, 153-56, 158, 229, 234
Pembroke College, MS. 258: 191
Peterhouse, MS. 210. Fifteenth century. Sermon collections: sermons ascribed to Holcot. Quoted pp. 85, 92, 207, 233
St. John's College, MS. 111: 51
Trinity College, MS. 323: 8
Trinity College, MS. 1157: 242
University Library, MS. Add. 710: 21
University Library, MS. Ff.1.6: 244
University Library, MS. Ff.1.17: 222
University Library, MS. Ii.3.8. A collection of several manuscripts of the fourteenth century, including several treatises on the decalogue and an *Ars praedicandi*. Part 6: sermon collection. Quoted pp. 92, 123, 125-26, 188, 220
University Library, MS Kk.4.24. Fifteenth century. Two sermon collections:

Exhortaciones fratris Iohannis Brome-yard, fols. 1-116; *Sermones de tempore et de sanctis*, fols. 123-304. Quoted pp. 14, 68, 90-91, 94-95, 99, 117, 123-24, 147, 190, 213, 235, 238

DUBLIN
Trinity College, MS. 277: 147, 213
Trinity College, MS. 301: 51
Trinity College, MS. 347: 217

DURHAM
Cathedral, MS. B.I.18: 119, 226, 240
University Library, MS. Cosin V.II.8. Second half of thirteenth century. Quoted p. 222
University Library, MS. Cosin V.III.2. Second half of thirteenth century. Several sermon cycles. Sermon collection. Quoted p. 222

EDINBURGH
National Library of Scotland, Advocates' Library, MS. 18.7.21. Apparently written by John de Grimestone in 1372. Preaching tool. See discussion and bibliography in chapter 4. Quoted chapters 4-5 *passim*
National Library of Scotland, Advocates' Library, MS. 19.2.1 (Auchinleck MS.): 187

LINCOLN
Cathedral, MS. 44: 114, 120

LONDON
British Library, MS. Additional 6716: 180
British Library, MS. Additional 24361: 73
British Library, MS. Arundel 231: 219

257

Index of Manuscripts

Index of
First Lines

The index lists all medieval poems quoted in the preceding chapters, with their respective numbers in *IMEV* and in Grimestone's collection (Gr). Not included are Grimestone verses that have been only referred to, and rhymed translations of biblical authorities and divisions (chapter 3).

260

General

Index

Index

Index

Index

Index

Library of Congress Cataloging-in-Publication Data

Wenzel, Siegfried.
Preachers, poets, and the early English lyric.

Includes indexes.
1. English poetry—Middle English, 1100-1500—History and criticism.   2. Preaching—
England—History—Middle Ages, 600-1500.   3. Christian poetry, English—History
and criticism.   4. John, of Grimestone—Criticism and interpretation.   5. Sermons,
English—History and criticism. I. Title.

PR317.P73W46   1986   821'.04'09382   85-43322
ISBN 0-691-06670-1 (alk. paper)

ACW-4238